Recovering the self

This important book seeks to place questions of morality and justice at the heart of social theory. By exploring the works of Marx, Durkheim and Weber it shows the hidden complexities of a modernity too often identified with a unified vision of the rational self later to fragment within post-modernity. Reinstating the body and emotional life, Seidler sets new terms for respect and equality showing ways the self is undermined in its sense of self-worth and adequacy through the workings of relationships of power and subordination.

Drawing upon feminism and ecology, Seidler places the issues of morality right into the centre of the 'self problem'. Through reinstating connections between the self and the historical adventures of socialism, feminism, masculinity, ethnicity and – autobiographically – Jewish identity, he shows the intimate affinity between these different categories of experience.

Responding to a crisis in traditional forms of authority and suspicious of a modernity that sets reason against emotion, culture against nature and mind against body, Seidler shows that identities are not 'freely chosen' but involve a coming to terms with histories of gender, sexual orientation, class, race and ethnicity.

Critical of post-modern theories in which anything goes and in which fragmentation of the self is too easily celebrated, this book is concerned with the reassertion of value and recovering a viable tradition in which we can again explore issues of freedom, morality and social justice.

Victor J. Seidler is Reader in Social Theory, Goldsmiths' College, University of London.

For Tony, Teddy and Michael
and in memory of Johnny

Recovering the self

Morality and social theory

Victor J. Seidler

London and New York

First published 1994
by Routledge
11 New Fetter Lane, London EC4P 4EE

Simultaneously published in the USA and Canada
by Routledge
29 West 35th Street, New York, NY 10001

© 1994 Victor Jeleniewski Seidler

Phototypeset in Palatino by
Mews Photosetting, Beckenham, Kent
Printed and bound in Great Britain by
Biddles Ltd, Guildford and King's Lynn

British Library Cataloguing in Publication Data

A catalogue record for this book is available from the British Library

Library of Congress Cataloging in Publication Data

Seidler, Victor J., 1945–
     Recovering the self: morality and social theory / Victor
Jeleniewski Seidler.
          p. cm.
     Includes bibliographical references and index.
     1. Social sciences–Philosophy. 2. Ethics. I. Title.
H61.S454 1994
300'.1–dc20   93-4903(
                                                                                CIP

ISBN 0-415-11150-1 (hbk)
ISBN 0-415-11151-X (pbk)

Contents

It's futile . . . to become perfect in preparation for heaven. You are doomed to just striving, striving, striving to be something other than what you are. Just be who you are and try and improve here and there the things that are hurting you and other people . . .

Alice Walker *The Voice*, 10 November 1992

You may be certain that the world is heading for destruction, but it's a good thing, a moral thing, to behave as though there's still hope. Hope is as contagious as despair. Your hope or show of hope, is a gift you can give to your neighbour, and may even prevent or delay the destruction of his world.

Primo Levi in a 1985 interview

Preface and acknowledgements

The hopes that filled people's lives as they witnessed the diverse challenges to authoritarian rule in Eastern Europe and the former Soviet Union renewed a trust in freedom and democracy. It felt, for a moment at least, as if the old order had been shaken as people in different parts of Europe were taking control of their lives. It was a precious moment of revolutionary change as we saw established structure of power giving way to popular movements for change. People dared to talk about the truth and dignity and morality as they rejected the regime of lies they had been forced to live with.

For a time at least, there was a refusal of traditional forms of the political rhetoric which have so often betrayed peoples hopes and aspirations. But it proved difficult to sustain the moment for people had to overcome long years of distrust. For a long time people have been conscious of the material advances in the West and they yearned for the goods that the capitalist market promised. It was as if people could only put their faith in goods that they could touch and hold, for everything else had betrayed them.

The vision of a new more peaceful and democratic world order was soon dashed by the technological brutalities of the Gulf War and the brutal language of 'ethnic cleansing' that we heard with the disintegration of the former Yugoslavia. It seemed as if the old enmities had not gone away, but simply gone underground waiting for their time. When the dreams of the capitalist market turned sour, as people left without the material goods that the West had for so long promised as the reward for overturning old enemies, somebody had to be blamed.

Many people felt betrayed and bitter because they had been duped by the promises of a new life. Only later were they told of the human costs of mass unemployment as old industries faded. Distant echoes of racism and anti-Semitism were increasingly heard as people sought a target for their frustration and rage. It became pressing to think about the sources of racism, xenophobia and anti-Semitism again. It felt as if little had been learnt.

The dissident voices that inspired the movements in Eastern Europe recognised themselves for a while in Vaclav Havel's aspiration of 'living in truth', as bearing witness against the brutalities of the regime. Because of the subtle ways people were drawn into complicity with the regimes, speaking the truth assumed a new importance. As Havel wrote in his essay 'The Power of the Powerless': 'If the main pillar of the system is living a lie, then it is not surprising that the funda- mental threat to it is living the truth. This is why truth must be suppressed more severely than anything else' (Havel 1987: 57). So it becomes crucial to reflect upon how truth as a factor of power works. This draws Havel into a way of thinking that is strikingly at odds with the discourses of post-modernity that have become influential in the West. It reminds us of how uncomfortable we have become until quite recently with a moral language which, within a dominant structuralist and post-structuralist tradition, has too easily been denigrated as 'essentialist'. Have we not often had to learn about how the subject has been 'decentred' and was not the faith in the rational self a crucial weakness of modernity? But possibly, as Foucault seemed to realise towards the end of his life, we have to be prepared to think again and question some deeply embedded rationalist assumptions if we want to begin to heal the split between morality and social theory.

Havel talks in terms of a moral language that can still draw us, even if we have lost touch with the ways it can be validated. Possibly we have grown suspicious of morality in the West because it is hard to separate it from the moralism of the 1970s that disfigured so many of the crucial insights of sexual politics. Somehow it seemed as if feminism had fostered a unified conception of women as subjects, which legislated how women were supposed to be if they were 'liberated'.

It seemed to many as if differences between women could only be recognised if feminism was to be theorised within a post-structuralist framework. For post-structuralism had helpfully illuminated the ways women's identities were constructed through the available images presented by the media. It also seemed to help with questioning a liberal theory which suggested that women were free and autonomous, by giving ways of recognising the fragmentation of identities and the power of dominant discourses to order women's lives.

But while a post-structuralist framework seemed to provide a way of presenting central feminist insights theoretically, it unwittingly worked at the same time to subvert ways of linking women's exper- ience to diverse mechanisms of power and oppression. It fostered an idea that languages of experience and oppression were suspect because they had to depend upon an 'essentialist' conception of self. It worked to silence many women as they felt that their experience was no longer so recognisable within the academic discourses of feminism.

As women learnt to recognise the very real differences that separated them it helped, for instance, women of colour, lesbians and Jewish women to appreciate the particularities of their histories and cultures. Feminism that was centred around a unified conception of women as subjects, came to be replaced by feminist theories that gave voice to the very different experiences of women. Early feminism was increasingly challenged for its 'universalism', for its supposed attempts to talk for women in general when it talked of 'women's oppression'. So the ground was prepared within a post-structuralist tradition to argue that feminism, as it was originally conceived, was part of the project of modernity because it presented women as a unified historic subject which, in its struggles against patriarchy, would find liberation. Feminisms became yet another of the grand narratives of modernity, as Lyotard has it in *The Postmodern Condition: A Report on Knowledge* (1985). So as people began to talk about 'post-modernity' they increasingly began also to think about 'post-feminism'. But this was radically to misconstrue the nature of the feminist challenges to the subtly reinforced masculinist terms of modernity.

As consciousness-raising helped women to question the modernist separation of reason from emotion so they also challenged the distinction between the 'personal' and the 'political' and the assumption that had structured diverse traditions of social theory cast within the terms of an Enlightenment modernity. For Marx, Weber and Durkheim, despite crucial differences, shared a sense that oppression and injustice are only 'real' and 'objective' if they take place within the 'public realm'.

If social theory was to be conceived in scientific terms, it had to remain faithful to the distinction between science and morality so that questions of values were often excluded. Morality was often reduced to an individual concern to do with decisions individuals made for themselves within the private realm. Through the Kantian identification of morality with reason, morality could claim its own form of 'objectivity'. With the disenchantment of nature which was no longer a source of meaning and value the critical Enlightenment distinction between 'nature' and 'culture' held sway. It was because nature was given and historical that only through the terms of culture could we find freedom, equality and justice within the 'public realm'. Identities are supposedly prepared for us through the dominant cultural discourses, for if they are not to be 'given' by nature they are to be conceived of as 'socially and historically constructed' within the realm of culture.

Within the terms of a structural tradition 'experience' becomes suspect and denigrated as falling on the side of nature. It is supposedly only through the categories of the mind that our 'experience' becomes constituted within a rationalist tradition. In *Unreasonable Men: Masculinity and Social Theory* (1994) I have explored how, with a particular relationship between masculinity and modernity, the separation of reason from emotion leaves us with an 'unreasonable' form of reason. Weber, in *The Protestant Ethic and the Spirit of Capitalism*, also talks of the irrationality of an instrumental form of reason when, within a capitalist society, work becomes an end in itself. So it is that within Western traditions of philosophy and social theory the body and emotional life are devalued and made 'subjective' concerns of 'personal life', since emotions and feelings cannot be validated as sources of knowledge. Though Freud came to recognise in *Civilisation and its Discontents* the misery and unhappiness that is created through the repression of sexuality within Western culture, it has been difficult to appreciate the diverse challenges he makes to traditional rationalist forms of social theory. We still tend to think of emotions and feelings in personal terms alone.

Feminism was important in reinstating emotions and feelings as sources of knowledge through the connection it made between the 'personal' and the 'political'. Consciousness-raising provided a bridge between social theory and emotional life and relationships. It refused to accept that women should be identified with the 'emotional' and the 'unconscious' while men were able to make reason in their own image. Rather in insisting that women should be given the space and time within consciousness-raising to tell their own story, it sought to validate women's individual experience. But it did not conceive of experience as 'given' and waiting to be 'interpreted' through the external intervention of reason or the insights of an analyst. Too often in the past this had led women to blame themselves, as they internalised guilt and responsibilty. This is what they wanted to escape from, but they needed other women to recognise the 'reality' of their suffering.

A rationalist tradition finds it hard to appreciate the challenges of consciousness-raising for it is intolerant of the personal voice, always seeking what can be generalised in more formal terms. But as women learnt to share their experience they learnt to speak from the pain of their oppressions, from the ways their experience had been discounted and diminished as 'unreal' and 'personal' by partners who often assumed they 'knew best' because they had reason on their side.

Feminism helped to challenge the terms of an Enlightenment rationalism for it learnt the meanings of emotional life. It discovered how easily women had learnt to blame themselves and how difficult it was to accept that it was the workings of relationships of power and subordination that undermined their sense of self-worth and dignity.

In learning to recognise the integrity of emotional life, women learnt that it could be as important to respect and honour your emotions and feelings as your ideas and thoughts. It was wrong to diminish your personal and emotional lives because they did not conform to the external logic of reason. Women could learn to trust their emotions and feelings as sources of empowerment, as part of defining their individuality more clearly.

Women learnt to recognise their own voices, so they grew in self-confidence, making decisions and choices for themselves on the basis of what they wanted for themselves, rather than on what others expected of them. But as women explored aspects of a subordination that they shared with other women within patriarchy, this did not deny the very real differences of class, ethnicity and sexual orientation that existed between women. There was a recognition that as you learnt to appreciate what was shared with other women, you did not become less yourself or become submerged in some universal definition. Rather your individuality was strengthened as you learnt to define yourself more clearly and as you refused to see yourself through the eyes of men. This was part of a process of recovering the self, which had been forsaken or lost within the terms of a liberal humanism which assumed that differences between people were accidental and contingent, for what mattered about us was our equal existence as rational selves. Women began to identify ways in which they had been led to betray their own feelings and understanding through accepting this definition of themselves, which had defined women by what they lacked, namely reason and rationality, so legislating the terms of a dominant masculinity presented in universal terms.

Crucial feminist insights were drawn from the Black movement and its experience of learning to value those very qualities that had been negated within a white society. The idea that 'black is beautiful' still carries powerful resonances as people of African descent rethink their own history and culture. Gay men and lesbians have also struggled to write their own experiences and histories, rather than accept the ways they are derided and pathologised within the dominant scientific discourses of modernity.

Jews have also had to come to terms with the implications of seeing themselves through the eyes of a Christian culture. Within modernity Jews had learnt that they could only be 'acceptable' if they were prepared to treat their Jewishness as incidental to their experience, as a private matter of religious belief alone. They also had to accept being the objects of tolerance, as they were often trapped into proving themselves in terms not of their own making. In the context of these different social movements we have been forced to question the terms of a liberal humanism that refused to acknowledge the integrity of difference – of different cultures, sexualities and traditions.

But rather than helping us to engage critically with the tradition of liberal humanism in its complexity, recognising the significant values it has helped sustain, a structuralist tradition has argued for a break with a tradition organised around a centred self. In Althusser's still influential formulations in *For Marx* (1970) this involved a movement from a classical tradition of humanism that depended upon a unified conception of human nature, towards a science of history and politics that fully recognised the ways that identities were the 'effects' of dominant discourses.

Even if Althusser's scientism has fallen by the way, the framework that he prepares and its antagonism towards both 'humanism' and 'essentialism', which are rarely carefully defined, live on in much post-structuralist work and work influenced by Foucault. We are encouraged into a rationalism which is unable to recover the self, however fragmented, as an emotional, somatic and spiritual being. Rather we learn to disdain any notions of the self as necessarily marking a failure to appreciate the insights of deconstruction. We fail to recognise the force of quite different feminist and ecological challenges to the terms of an Enlightenment modernity. Assuming that the fragmentation of identities is an insight of post-structuralism alone we lose touch with how feminism has provided a critique of modernity. Preferring to assume that feminism defines 'women' as a unified subject we dull its questioning and become blind to its insights by categorising it back into the rationalist terms of modernity.

Feminism has insisted that the woman cannot be separated from what she says and that what remains crucial is the experience out of which she is speaking. The 'personal' is a source of truth that cannot be defined and this challenges the terms of a modernity which insists that the truth can only be conceived in 'impersonal' and 'universal' terms. The devaluation of the 'personal' and the 'emotional' is closely connected with the masculinist terms of modernity. We have to be careful to recognise that the Cartesian self, so often the target of deconstruction, rarely 'present' to itself, because it is cast in impersonal and masculinist terms.

At the same time the Cartesian self could not recognise its connections with its somatic and emotional experience because these were separated off as aspects of 'nature'. Somehow there is an important connection which I want to explore between the devaluation of nature – of bodily and emotional life – and the thin and attenuated conception of self we inherit within modernity. Learning to identify the self with reason and mind, we learn to discount our emotions and feelings as 'temptations' and 'distractions' that would lead us astray from the path of pure reason.

The single path that reason helps to discern is part of the arrogance of power that is inherited within modernity. It allowed the West to define the character of modernity in its own terms, thus leaving 'others' to define themselves as 'backward' and so as 'requiring development'. If theories of post-colonialism have helped us question the authority of this voice they often need to be connected to the insights of feminism and ecology if we are to question the disdain for both 'inner' and 'external' nature that has been so deeply inscribed within a structuralist tradition.

Feminism has been understandably hostile to arguments from nature which have often been used to legitimate women's subordination, with the result that a structuralist insistence that 'nature' and 'culture' can be so clearly demarcated proves appealing. But feminism theorised in these terms alone threatens to lose core insights into the integrity of the personal voice.

It was the early Foucault of *The Archaeology of Knowledge* who insisted that he was not interested in who it was that was speaking, only in what was said that set the terms for what could be investigated in the neutral terms of discourse analysis. Since identities were to be provided through subject positions within discourses, it was supposedly only through language that we could know our experience. So it was that the tension between language and experience was often lost within discourse theory and gradually languages of oppression and liberation seemed to lose credibility.

Feminism potentially provides a challenge to Foucault's conception of discourse theory with its insistence on the integrity of speech. The person who is speaking needs to know that she is being listened to attentively and it is all important that she – and no other – is talking now. The personal voice is irreducible because it reflects a particular level of experience, a qualitative connection to self. For what is being explored is the ongoing dialectic between what has been experienced and the relationships within which she is living. Here there *is* a space and time for acknowledging differences between women, even celebrating difference. It is only from the viewpoint of a later post-modern theoretical position that we hear disdainful talk of the homogenisation of women's experience as a unified subject.

But within early feminism there was also sometimes arrogance and misunderstanding as certainties about the nature of women's subordination and oppression meant feminism was sometimes construed as holding a truth which other women lacked, even though at some level this went against its spirit. But Black, Asian, Chinese, Jewish, Catholic women and many others had to find their own voice. They came with their own histories, traditions and cultures which needed to be explored in their complexities. As there has been more recognition of difference within post-modern theories, more space has been created for these explorations, though new dangers have emerged too as feminisms become sidelined as discourses trapped within the terms of gendered subjects.

Discourse theory has established the priority of text over speech and has argued that the text could be analysed in its own terms. This was part of the challenge to authority of the author being able to determine and so control the reading of the texts. But this has fostered its own relativism as people have defended a plurality of readings, insisting that meanings are always open for people to explore in their own ways. Though we might always discover new meanings in a text, there are issues of judgement and truthfulness to the text that cannot be ignored.

But of course if in post-structuralist work 'truth' is itself conceived of as the effect of a particular discourse, we have to be very careful about how we refer to it. I think feminism can still help us sustain a sense of the 'truthfulness' of someone's voice and experience so that we cannot so easily make the separation between speaker and text upon which discourse theory is premissed. This has to do with the relationship between 'truth' and 'morality' and the ways that feminisms, ecology and psychotherapy can help us think this relationship differently. At the end of his life I think Foucault came close to recognising this in *The Care of the Self* (1990), knowing that he needed a new beginning if he was to think about the relationship between morality, truth and the self.

As women learnt to listen to each other within the contexts of consciousness-raising groups there was an implicit reworking of inherited notions of 'truth' and 'morality'. As women sought to share the truth of their experience they also learnt how to make connections with prevailing relations of power and subordination. Affirming a person's experience did not mean you had to agree with the ways issues were presented.

Rather than presenting a unified conception of women, feminism was a practice in many ways alive to the issues of fragmentation long before they appeared within the language of post-modernism. Feminism was aware of the pain and hurt of fragmentation for consciousness-raising implicitly conceived of difference within a moral framework that sought to connect issues of identity, power and emotional life. Women struggled with how hard it was to make themselves understood when they felt so diminished in their experience and patronised by men who claimed reason as their own exclusive possession. But it proved difficult to explore the way different feminisms perceived the relation between morality and politics because the temptation to theorise feminism in structuralist terms alone tended to denigrate languages of experience and morality as necessarily invoking essentialist conceptions of human nature.

The grounding of thought in experience was a critical element in the social movements that emerged in the late 1960s. It reflected a distrust of language, which could so easily mislead and lead us astray. A non-empiricist understanding of 'experience' was a hidden connection between feminism and the philosophical work of the later Wittgenstein, in *Philosophical Investigations*. Along with a reading of Simon Weil these were independently feeding my thinking and politics through the 1970s. We had learnt as students to speak truth to power and to distrust the languages of power for they served interests of their own.

We lived through a period when the liberal establishment supported the Vietnam War while talking about freedom and democracy. So it was that political language was debased, as it has again become in the 1990s, and we felt that we had to test and weigh each word before we could allow ourselves to speak it. This was a generational experience that connected people in different parts of the world. Havel talks about something similar in *Living in Truth* (1987) in his struggles against authoritarian rule in Czechoslovakia when it was impossible to trust what you read and heard. You learnt to listen to what was *not* said as you learnt to read what was between the lines. Early seeds of deconstruction were sown, though hardly recognised as such.

Havel explains that the 'personal' should not be contrasted with the 'universal' for, as Freud knew, it is often when we are most personal and intimate that we can touch an experience which speaks more 'universally'. As Havel puts it

> It has always been my hope in my writing that, by bearing witness to certain specific experiences of the world, I will be able to disclose something *universally human*, specific experience only being a way and a means of saying something about being in general.
>
> (Havel 1987: xiii)

It is too easy to misunderstand such sentiments for we fail to appreciate the ways they challenge – as do feminism, ecology and sexual politics – the terms of an Enlightenment modernity, or at least show us a different aspect of it. This is equally true when Havel writes in his essay 'The Power of the Powerless' that

> Individuals can be alienated from themselves only because there is *something* in them to alienate. The terrain of this violation is their

authentic existence. Living the truth is thus woven directly into the texture of living a lie. It is the repressed alternative, the authentic aim to which living a lie is a response.

(Ibid.: 57)

If we resonate to these notions, they have become difficult to appreciate within a theoretical tradition that has been so firmly set within post-structuralist terms. But there is a voice here that harmonises with the struggles of many people of colour, women, gay men and lesbians to 'recover the self' through the difficult processes of consciousness-raising. It recognises an aspiration towards truth and honesty with yourself that restores a sense of self-worth and dignity.

People who have lived a lie for so long, feeling ashamed of aspects of their experience, know the sense of freedom that comes from refusing to live a lie both with yourself and with others. This is not to deny the many crucial insights into the workings of power, language and identity that a post-structuralist tradition has provided. But we have to be ready to engage critically with this tradition as with other forms of rationalism.

It is an aspect of modernity to distrust custom and tradition and to be prepared continually to discover new ground, different ways of doing things. In many ways this initiative and tradition-breaking is to be welcomed, but often, as Benjamin and Weil knew in their own ways, it can make it harder to appreciate what has been lost and to retrieve from the past values that can still be important for us. In looking towards post-modernity we have been too ready to dispense with a language of values and ethics, leaving the traditions of modernity behind before we have learnt how fully to evaluate them.

As the Frankfurt School appreciated, we have to be careful in our critical evaluations of modernity, learning how it has both trapped us through its visions of progress as involving the control and domination of nature and inspired us towards aspirations of freedom, equality and justice. In the movement towards post-modernity we have been too ready to put aside Marx's challenges to capitalist society before we have begun to appreciate the ways he remains trapped by the terms of an Enlightenment modernity.

It is too easy to dismiss diverse traditions of work as embodying grand narratives of modernity, as if there is little more to be said. I was interested in exploiting the resources of modernity because I was disturbed by the absence of a sustainable moral voice within both modernity and post-modernity and the continuities that remain unthought. It felt as if, for instance, the denigration of nature which was so much part of modernity in its categorical distinction between reason and nature was still linked to the devaluation of our inner emotional lives. Unless we could retrieve a different sense of morality than that offered by the dominant Kantian tradition within a liberal moral culture, we could find it hard to recover the self, not simply in personal terms but also in social and political relations.

Since 1970 I have been involved in a project to rethink the relations between respect, equality and difference within modernity. This project has included a study of Kant and liberal theory in *Kant, Respect and Injustice* (Seidler 1986). It has also explored the continuing resonances of Christian thought that have powerfully shaped our secularised visions of modernity to make us think we can abstract from social relations of power and subordination to treat others as equals in our personal relations with them. In *The Moral Limits of Modernity* (1991b) I investigated the difficulties of reinstating a moral language of dignity, love and oppression within the dominant terms of a secular rationalism. In *Recovering the Self* I am still concerned with exploring the difficulties of sustaining a full enough notion of the self to be able to acknowledge our emotional and somatic lives within western Marxism, as well as the related difficulty of sustaining a moral voice within different traditions of social theory. If aspirations towards equality are not to be forsaken and we are to be able to reimagine socialist traditions, then we have to find ways of rethinking the relationship between equality and difference, love and power.

Reinstating a moral vision does not mean defending the dream of universality that was so central to the aspiration towards modernity. We do not have to crave some ideal point which allows us to 'rise above' the empirical realm of difference so that we can communicate through the pure tones of reason. At one point it seemed possible to think not just about different traditions and aspects of humanity, but about the very essence of the human as such. As Terry Eagleton has expressed it 'It was the lingua franca of a divided social order, the common tongue that underlay our sublunary squabblings, the ideal point where we merged into unity' (*Guardian* 27 November 1992: 6). We cannot rise above differences of culture, tradition and class as if there is a noumenal realm in which we can relate to each other as human beings alone. This does not mean that we cannot learn from dreams of rational constructivism but we have to be very careful about dreams of returning to a golden past of a shared morality and about the status of the theories of equality and justice we might create. We have to be aware of the ways in which modernity has set the terms of 'humanity' as collections of individuals as 'rational selves', terms that have served to exclude and marginalise 'others' who have been treated as 'less that human'.

Eagleton is right to suggest that if we are still to make a sense of a project of a 'common humanity' it 'would have to work in and through the concrete differences of human groups, rather than – as with the abstract universality of traditional culture – bypass or suppress them' (1991: 6). He does not welcome a world of mutually uncommunicating cultural traditions but recognises that 'until ignored and excluded groups have reclaimed their heritage and submitted ours to some critical scrutiny, they just won't be in as equal partners on the cultural conversation' (1991: 6).

But we have to be careful to specify whose culture we mean and recognise how much work there is still to be done in rethinking and re-working the terms of modernity. This is something in which feminism, gay and lesbian scholarship, Black studies and ecology all have a part to play, for they encourage 'us' to ask different questions of 'modernity'. Post-structuralism and theories of deconstruction have raised new and important questions, but we should be wary of treating them as almost universal methods that can be uncritically and neutrally applied. If we are able to rethink the ethical relations of knowledge to power, questions of self, identity and emotional life have to be recovered.

This study has taken me many years to bring to completion and many concerns have found themselves reflected in its pages. I hope that it helps to create a bridge between morality and social theory, for these disciplinary concerns both influenced the direction the work has taken. Often it feels hard and isolating to be working across different disciplines, wanting to bring together ideas that seem to speak so directly to each other. Sometimes you find yourself seeking refuge in one to draw nourishment for the other.

But the distinctions have never felt real to me and some of the most significant thinking seems to have emerged out of feminism, ecology and psychotherapy, which in their different ways have helped to challenge the rationalism that prevailed in such an entrenched way within the academy. But there is nothing new in this, since much philosophical work has always found its sources far away from the universities and since academic philosophy as we have inherited it is relatively recent. When I was a student it was the teaching of Wittgenstein which refused to distinguish between the ways we think and how we live. This was also true for Simone Weil, who insists on linking morality, politics and social theory. These teachings seemed to have the deepest impact on me, but it took me years to find a voice which was not a mere imitation. As disciplinary boundaries begin to soften it is becoming easier to make some of these connections, so beginning a process of healing the splits between our thoughts and feelings, beliefs and actions. We learn to change ourselves as part of transforming the social world.

Many people have supported me in the long years of completion and have read and commented on the manuscript in its different incarnations. I started writing out some of these ideas in the late 1970s and my work still carries some of the hopes and aspirations of that very different time. As the times changed so did this manuscript as I was forced to rethink and reframe as new questions came into focus. Some will no doubt be surprised by the form this book has eventually taken. Bob Young was very encouraging at an early stage as was Richard Kuper, and each read an early draft. Dave Mussen was also helpful. Michael Apple gave detailed comments that proved very stimulating in reworking an early draft, as did Janet Ransom who has watched the manuscript grow through its different forms. More recently I have been helped in different ways by Isiah Berlin, Zygmunt Bauman, David Boadella, Terry Cooper, Larry Blum, Paul Gilroy, Anna Ickowitz, Lucy Goodison, Sally Inman, Dave Walsh, Sheila Ernst, Joanna Ryan, Jeraint Hazan, Caroline Ramazanoglu, Nikolas Rose, Tony Seidler, Sheila Rowbotham, Paul Morrison and Steve Nathan. Anna Cawdery is owed special thanks for retyping what became a very messy manuscript.

Anna Ickowitz has tolerated my split attention and has reminded me that other things matter in life through her love and understanding. We have shared many years of exploration and growth together and have had hard times as well as good times. Living with someone who writes so compulsively is no easy matter. I've had to learn to balance very different feelings and find ways of becoming more present, for as men we inherit few models that we can wholeheartedly trust.

Daniel and Lily have grown up with this work and have continually reminded me of the love and joy that is available if we dare to be truthful to ourselves. As children they share their emotions and feelings in a way that so often reminds me of the capacities I do not want to lose. The process of recovering the self has many aspects that inevitably also take us into some hard and painful places that we might prefer to avoid. But it can be a rich and empowering experience that needs to be appreciated within the terms of social theory, morality and politics if we are to be faithful to the different traditions we inherit.

Chapter 1

Introduction
Modernity, Morality and Politics

POLITICS AND THEORY

In the 1990s there has evolved a sense of moral crisis and unease about the breakdown of traditional forms of authority and it has become relevant again to listen to Antonio Gramsci's assertion that 'It is essential to destroy the widespread prejudice that philosophy is a strange and difficult thing just because it is the specific intellectual activity of a particular category of specialists' (1971: 323)[1] The influence of the writings of Louis Althusser on the Left has established a particular tone and expectation of the character of theoretical work which has continued long after the demise of Althusserian influence itself in the post-structuralisms of Michel Foucault and Jacques Derrida.

Despite crucial differences much theoretical work shares a critique of 'essentialism' and 'humanism', often without being clear about the different ways these terms are invoked. The disdain for ethics and values which until very recently characterised post-structuralist work marks a pervasive difficulty in being able to think about the relationship between morality, truth and politics. If many people have found these writings often unnecessarily difficult and abstract, it has only confirmed their expectation that theory has to be 'strange and difficult'.

It is important to challenge this 'widespread prejudice' if a more meaningful conception of theoretical work is to be developed. Althusser has helped many people challenge economistic traditions within Marxism and many people have learnt from his writings.[2] But at another level this tradition still sets the terms for thinking about the relationship of morality to social theory. It has made it much harder to develop a more fundamental questioning of reductionist traditions for post-structuralism has in large part remained loyal to certain oppositions initially developed by Althusser. Even if it does not remain trapped within a particular self-conception of scientific Marxism it often prevents us from learning from other important traditions of thought and feeling, too easily dismissed as 'humanist'.

How did this objectivist and scientistic conception of Marxist theory come, until quite recently, to have such a dominant position? At one level its emergence in Europe in the mid-1970s seemed to be related to the disappointments of many hopes raised by the politics of the late 1960s. There was a real feeling in the late 1960s that the world was going to change quickly and profoundly. There was an important and widespread experience on the Left of community and industrial politics, as well as of people changing the ways they lived their every-day lives. There is still relatively little theoretical work that shares this history with new generations and that has learnt from the experience, joys and frustrations of those now increasingly distant years. Rather, in the mid-1970s there developed a widespread tendency to dismiss much of this experience as 'naïve' and to look towards an independent realm of theoretical work for political clarity and understanding.

This coincided with the sharpening of the economic crisis in the West in the mid-1970s. For many people there was a withdrawal from active political engagement. The theoretical developments of Althusser, Levi-Strauss and Lacan dazzled a generation but did not offer much understanding of the changing conditions of life in late twentieth-century capitalist societies and the struggles against the new forms of dominance and control. But if this tradition of work has now exhausted itself, it has left marks upon our sense of theoretical writing and reading, even in the terms that have been set in the late 1980s for the widespread discussion about modernity and post-modernity. Theoretical credentials are still often set against a supposed 'essentialism' that was primarily a structuralist construction. E. P. Thompson's *The Poverty of Theory* (1979) was extremely important in combating an Althusserian dominance and getting people to think for themselves again. At the same time, it was written out of a particular generational experience that tended to minimise the importance of the politics and theory of the late 1960s.

At another level the women's movement and sexual politics more generally have been strongest when they have not been integrated into a structuralist tradition, which draws a sharp rationalist distinction between 'science' and 'ideology'. Post-structuralist work continues to discount experience, so making it difficult to recover a very different feminist relationship between 'theory' and 'experience'. Feminism has helped to resist the reductionism so often implied in Marxism and to reclaim the complexity of lived experience. Sexual politics has helped develop and validate a practice of consciousness-raising which has made people more aware of their subjective experience of sexual oppression and hurt. This has also helped foster a sense of shared experience as well as reinstate an active subject, which was too often reduced to an effect of ideology or discourse within structuralism.

Sexual politics has promised a much deeper and embodied understanding of our subjective experience of social relations of class, ethnicity, gender and sexual orientation while resisting a reductionism of the individuality of our lived experience. Consciousness-raising has sometimes helped to create its own atmosphere of trust and vulnerability, one that is far removed from the rationalistic forms of intellectualism which have so long dominated theoretical work, especially for men. I want to appeal to this vulnerability which does not automatically split thought from emotion and experience, while at the same time giving some account of what makes it so hard for us to develop this kind of understanding within a dominant moral culture. This is to rethink the rationalist terms of an Enlightenment vision of modernity which treats reason alone as a source of knowledge.

Identifying a relationship between modernity and a dominant form of masculinity involves coming to terms with a rationalist tradition of moral and political theory which, echoing Kant, would identify our 'humanity' with an independent faculty of reason. It fails to recognise the dignity of our emotional lives and so fails to reinstate the subject in her or his fullness as an embodied mental, emotional and spiritual being. This involves the systematic subordination of our emotions, feelings, desires and wants as genuine sources of knowledge. This is not to argue against reason, as I have made clear in *Kant, Respect and Injustice* (Seidler 1986), but only against its categorical opposition to nature and so its modernist separation from other aspects of our human experience. It means recognising that Kant and the rationalist tradition he has inspired have left us with a thin and attenuated masculinist conception of the person as a 'rational self'.

Recognising a break with traditions of Marxist work which have fallen into crisis in the West following the revolutions in Eastern Europe and the break-up of the Soviet Union we have to ask new questions, we have to acknowledge that we cannot any longer separate our investigations of what a socialist society would be like from our understanding of the needs, wants, desires and emotions of individuals. This involves reworking the historical relationship of Marxism to morality, otherwise socialism threatens to become, as it did for Althusser, simply a more 'advanced mode of production' to which we have to sacrifice and subordinate ourselves. Rethinking the relationship between socialism and democracy we cannot forgo the freedoms which a liberal culture seeks to protect. Languages of socialism have become discredited as socialism becomes a goal that involves subordinating individualities rather than enriching different aspects of ourselves.

I want to explore some of these tensions in Marx's own relationship with morality for this casts significant light upon the relationship between modernity and morality. It is not simply a question of offering a systematic reinterpretation of Marx, but of showing the enduring historical influence of some of these tensions. This calls for a different kind of critical engagement with Marx's writings.

In the process I have wanted to appeal to common insecurities, not simply refer to them abstractly, because it is in the working of emotional insecurities and inadequacy, and not just in the workings of surplus value and exploitation, that the individualistic and competitive institutions so central to capitalist relations work. This is to show how ideology as a material force works on our very sense of self and so to help us to a rethinking of the contradictory moral relations of capitalist societies.

I have drawn from examples of schooling experience because this is an experience most of us have shared, even though we rarely allow ourselves to reflect upon it as a crucial learning of fear and inadequacy. It is also because the kind of schooling that we have experienced reflects the social relations of the larger society, whether it be supposedly capitalist or socialist. It is also to show, in contrast to Althusser, that the recognition of ideology as a material force cannot be secured if we isolate ideological issues into an autonomous and independent realm of their own.[3] I have tried to show more concretely how ideas and values which have become almost invisible to us because we take them very much for granted have been embodied in the social relations of power and dominance in the everyday organisation of schooling.

I have also invoked examples to help clarify the meaning of some of the more theoretical concepts I refer to. This allows concepts to be meaningfully grasped rather than simply given formal definitions. This is something we can constantly learn from the later Wittgenstein.[4] I think his writing on grounding language in experience is central to developing a more qualitative research methodology. It stands in direct opposition to the prevailing Saussurian emphasis on semiology and a general theory of signs which still remains a source of the formalism we discover in so much post-structuralist work. This is not a form of 'conceptual softness' because it does not offer ostensive definitions; rather it relies upon the complex processes of concepts being gradually grasped as we discover what meaning they have in different contexts. This is fundamentally to question rationalistic forms of theory which assume that language alone is the source of our modes of classification and representation.

Wittgenstein's work in the *Philosophical Investigations* (1958) breaks with his earlier work to show the inadequacies of rationalist discourse conceptions, though this has rarely been appreciated within social and political theory. I am not simply appealing to authorities to think of language in terms of Wittgenstein rather than Saussure so we can sustain experience as a source of knowledge, but hope to show what I mean through sharing my own explorations. If this creates a different, more tentative and exploratory sense of theory, this is something I am only glad of. It is a time, with the collapse of Communism in the Soviet Union and Eastern Europe, for a more fundamental questioning about the very meaning of 'socialism' in our time. If it means repeating at certain moments, coming back to themes people feel I should already have settled with, then I hope this reveals a different connection that might not otherwise have come to light. Possibly it also shows the difficulty of gaining clarity when you are working against the grain of current intellectualist traditions in philosophy and social theory.

With the revolution in Eastern Europe and the changes in the former Soviet Union we are still trying to find our bearings within a post-Communist world. If we are to learn from history, I think the early questioning of Rudolf Bahro, a refugee from East German communist politics who wrote so significantly about the East German system in *The Alternative in Eastern Europe* (1978) before engaging with liberal capitalism in the West,[5] can still help connect a political generation with the historical experience of Eastern Europe.

E. P. Thompson has also reminded us of how much was lost when the New Left turned away from learning from the struggles in Eastern Europe after the 1956 uprising in Hungary. The earlier generation of the New Left was ready to learn more easily from the historical experience of socialism than the later generation, who had grown up to accept a divided Europe as given:

> Whether consciously or unconsciously, we were expectant of exactly what occurred in 1956. These 'revelations' represented less a rupture in our understanding than a fulfilment of our half-conscious hopes. From that preposterous military orthodoxy we had hoped for controversy, acknowledgement of human frailty, a moral vocabulary . . . We had seen, not the potential (for this was soon crushed) but the living, indomitable agents of that potential at work within these societies. Behind the posters, novels and films of Stakhanovites we saw (to our relief) workers who were absentees, pilferers, time-servers, as well as workers who were learning to defend themselves, organize, and take common cause with intellectuals.
>
> (Thompson, E. P. 1979: 94)

Thompson is recognising the importance of recovering a 'moral vocabulary' which the revolutionary events in Eastern Europe in 1989 and the example of Havel, Michnik and others have reawakened, as we are forced to think again what it might mean to live in truth. It is too easy to be continually, if unknowingly, compromising our inner truth and integrity.

This would also help us recognise the neglected notion that if we can still talk meaningfully about 'socialism' we are talking about freedom, equality and justice in the social lives and lived experience of people. Stalinism had produced in Eastern Europe its own objectivist language which treated the truth as if it were the exclusive property of the party. Truth was to be manipulated to serve its own interests since it saw people as functional to the larger structures.

MORALITY AND POLITICS

I have tried to reconsider traditions and assumptions we inherit about the meaning and significance of moral theory and understanding, particularly within Marxist writing, to help rethink the relationship of morality and politics. This involves questioning the totalistic ways in which Marxists often conceive of 'bourgeois morality', too often conceding important ground to prevailing liberal conceptions of freedom, rights, equality, justice and dignity.

Sometimes these notions have been too easily dismissed as simply the legitimation of class relations of power and dominance. This allowed the Libertarian Right to claim the moral ground in the 1980s. If moral and political theories are understood simply as the cover for underlying class, gender or ethnic interests there is limited space for moral concerns. It becomes difficult to *show* the inadequacies and limitations of prevailing moral and political conceptions of both Left and Right within a liberal moral culture.

Often socialist discussion disarms itself as it refuses to enter the arena, too secure in its conviction of the nature of morality and justice. With the Eastern European revolutions questions of freedom and democracy in relation to different forms of market capitalism have become vital in the restructuring of relations between state and civil society. Experience of authoritarian state regimes has proved the priority for freedom as a moral concern and the dangers of reducing morality to a form of politics. Nor can economics and material interests alone be recognised as the only things that matter, for this is to fail to engage with a diversity of meanings and values within civil societies and the West. Thus too often happens with the utilitarianism that underpins so much social democratic politics. It has been a significant strength of right-wing politics in the 1980s and 1990s in Europe and America that it has taken the initiative in moral and political discussion.

Politics has to be able to engage critically with the moral culture of liberalism, showing the ways it serves to legitimate a particular form of class rule. This is more complex, as is its relationship to structures of race, gender, ethnicity and sexual orientation. The 'freedom' and 'justice' which traditional politics of Left and Right promise have to be *shown* as existing, if at all, within the public realm alone. But the challenges of feminism and ecology must also involve a fundamental investigation of the meaning of socialism and its different Enlightenment sources. If we are to challenge the ways traditional forms of politics sustain a particular distinction between public and private spheres, we need to explore how they serve to marginalise and diminish concerns with identity and experiences of sexuality, emotional life and love.

Fulfilment and self-realisation supposedly take place only within the public realm of work and citizenship, whatever lip service we learn to pay towards relationships and children. It has often been this very framework which defines politics as a matter of the public realm alone which explains the lack of critical moral and political discussion. This has meant we have too often unwittingly reproduced some of the assumptions of a bourgeois society we wish to contest in our conception of the struggle for a more democratic socialist society.

This is something Walter Benjamin and the Frankfurt School warned about in their discussions of the ideology of work, when they argued that socialism reproduced central elements of a Protestant work ethic.[6] Individual achievement and self-denial within the Protestant ethic have been embedded within a taken-for-granted conception of work. Ideologies of work have become particularly relevant since the 1920s with the dominance of assembly-line production and changes in the labour process of capitalist production. Relationships to work have more recently taken on fundamentally new forms with the advent of computerisation and new technology.

We have to investigate people's changing experiences of work, whether work can be emancipatory in these changed conditions. But this also involves a basic, philosophical questioning of utilitarian conceptions of happiness and Marxist visions of self-realisation through labour. This becomes part of reworking the terms of a modernity which has cast work as a source of emancipation and identified progress with the control and subordination of nature to human ends and interests.

This involves an investigation of the contradictions – or at least uncertainties – in Marx's own writings. While showing the continuing importance of Hegel for Marx's thinking we need to go beyond identifying Marxism in its orthodox form as a grand narrative of modernity. This has led to an abandonment of Marx before we have begun to ask different questions. This helps not only in questioning the orthodox and Althusserian interpretations of Marx which identify Marxism as a scientistic practice following a single path towards modernity. Suggesting how modernity has been shaped in the guise of a dominant form of masculinity also opens up a theoretical space for sexual, post-colonial and ecological politics. This also allows me to introduce and question the assumed rationalism of the Frankfurt School. It is potentially important that sexual politics, along with ecological consciousness and post-colonial theory can offer a different, transformed sense of the relationship of theory to experience.

In their different ways, sexual, post-colonial and ecological politics help us understand the need for our intellectual understanding to be grounded in our experience, as they refuse the separation of reason from nature that has been a defining feature of modernity. Having suffered from being defined as 'closer to nature' and so being unable to take their 'humanity' for granted they question a Eurocentric vision of modernity that has been set largely within rationalistic terms. They offer a much more open and less formalistic grasp of the relationship of theory to race, class and sexual experience.

Recovering the self also means coming to terms with a relationship with an inner nature of emotions, feelings and desires so often despised within a secularised Protestantism able to recognise reason alone as the voice of conscience. In questioning the implicit rationalism of the Frankfurt School I am also questioning the way its members often tended to separate critical theory from a politics of experience. Nevertheless their work remains crucial because it provides a way of transcending the reductionism of so much of Marxism and recognises a politics of identity and emotional life as integral to capitalist relations.

But this is also to question the ways within a positivist culture that we often separate ourselves off from our own individual and personal experiences just because we assume these are 'subjective' and so bound to be limited and partial. This is a pervasive assumption of a moral culture which disempowers through splitting knowledge from experience. Not only is it connected, as Nietzsche realised, to a morality and politics of self-denial but it carries implications for our understanding of morality and politics.

I show the particular connection of these issues with the social formation of a dominant masculinity because, in large part, modernity has been shaped as a reflection of a masculinity identified with reason. Often rationalist forms of social theory and philosophy are underpinned by an ideology of self-denial that has produced a culture of masculinity that has proved peculiarly resistant to self-understanding.[7] This is because, as white, heterosexual men, we are often strangely invisible to ourselves, even if we have no difficulty taking space within the public realm. We are often brought up to treat emotions as a form of 'weakness' and to assume that there are always 'more important things to do' than to face our own individual and social experience as men. This is taken to be a form of self-indulgence that is also often too threatening to contemplate. Often the way we have been brought up as men to relate in the social world, to be constantly proving ourselves individually and testing ourselves against others, has moved us away from an awareness of our emotional and bodily experience.

Often, as heterosexual men, our bodies become estranged and we have only an externalised relationship to them as our identities are fixed around a rational self. It is as if our bodies are machines we unwittingly have to learn to manipulate and control. As men, our language often seems to have come to have a character of its own which has become depersonalised and instrumental. It becomes difficult to express ourselves more personally and directly. This involves a vulnerability that must supposedly be reserved for our most private and intimate relationships. But then we can discover, to our anger and frustration, that we do not know how to formulate and share our more intimate thoughts and feelings even if we want to. This is a painful realisation for it means we cannot control language through will alone.

I have tried to show some of the broader cultural and social conditions for the maintenance of what Nietzsche identified as a morality of self-denial, connecting it to issues of masculinity. I have also tried to show the significance of Weber's discussion of the Protestant ethic in revealing the historical construction of a dominant masculinity which has often been too easily assumed within socialist theory. I have also illuminated conceptions of individualism in Marx's writings, showing ways they can still potentially question forms of 'possessive individualism' which remain central to notions of self-identity within capitalist democracies. At the same time I work to subvert and transcend some formal and ahistorical oppositions that so often govern social theory, such as, for instance, the opposition between individualism and collectivism, self and society, essentialism and social constructionism. If issues of identity and individuality are to be rethought carefully it is often necessary to transgress traditional boundaries that have shaped modernity.

If this involves rethinking the terms in which the oppositon between modernity and post-modernism is traditionally set it also involves working for a more dialectical and historical form of theory which can also acknowledge the processes of emotional and spiritual growth and development. It also suggests a much deeper critique of the rationalist traditions that have provided the framework so often taken for granted within contemporary theoretical discussions of social and political theory. It has been a facet of the importance of sexual politics that it has helped us question the dominance of patriarchal traditions of thought which would set reason firmly against desires, feelings and emotions.

In this crucial regard feminism potentially remains an important challenge to the terms of a rationalist modernity. This is connected at some level with the conception of instrumental reason the Frankfurt School criticised, even if discovering few ways of breaking with it decisively. For sexual politics, when not set within a structuralist mode, can help to reinstate the body and emotional life as sources of knowledge. Reminding ourselves of an ethics of value and integrity challenges an instrumentalism that would treat women merely as sexual objects.

We need to reassert the potential of a sexual politics which, while learning from post-structuralist insights, is not limited in its vision of ethics and relationships. Rather it looks to the relationship between the workings of these different forms of power and subordination as part of a process of recovering the self. It is through sexual politics that the conceptions of 'instrumental reason' can be grounded in forms of mistreatment and oppression. Certain forms of feminism are significant because they have opened up a way of introducing issues of fragmentation, self-worth and self-blame into social theory, so transcending the boundaries of a sterile discussion about needs as brute and essential.

Feminisms have helped to recognise the importance of difference and diversity, though possibly only with the challenges of lesbian women and women of colour have the issues at stake been clarified. Feminism in its different forms has refused to reduce women's struggles against oppression, so challenging the notion of the single path towards progress central to Enlightenment modernity. Insisting that class divisions are only one form of social division and that the liberation of women cannot wait for the resolution of class struggles, also helps to open up a space to think seriously about issues of race, ethnic and sexual identities and relationships. Within modernity a dominant masculine form of reason has assumed that it could legislate what was good for others. This involved the marginalisation and discounting of a diversity of voices of particular kinds. So it is, especially as men, that if we learn to discount our emotional needs we expect 'others' to do the same, for we define the terms of 'humanity'.

It is one of the strengths of sexual politics, post-colonial theory and ecology that they help in their different ways reinstate other values and other needs, and at least insist on conceiving them more substantively in their own particular terms. They refuse to be subsumed by the dominant Eurocentric discourses that have worked for too long to marginalise, exclude and silence them, as they insist on discovering their own diverse voices.

Although Marxism often appears in polarisation with liberal think-ing, the fact that both traditions have their roots in an Enlightenment vision of modernity means that they have this problem of legislating what is good for others, although in different ways. The point is that needs and desires are not adequately grasped either as simply given, as they are often assumed to be within liberalism, or as 'social con-structions', as they have been described within structuralist Marxism.

A full enough grasp of somatic, emotional and spiritual needs is not possible in terms of any theory which dissolves the subject itself or which treats discussion of the diversity of human needs as 'essen-tialist' and so flawed. Similarly, since both market capitalism and socialism have traditionally identified progress with science, technology and the domination of nature, they unwittingly suppress any acknowledgement of needs for a particular relationship with nature or with our inner emotional selves. This has had important, largely unexplored, implications for an insensitivity to self in our inherited moral and political visions.

Chapter 2

Morality

MORALITY AND SCIENCE

Marx's writings are often set against the very conception and understanding of morality. Within the traditions of orthodox Marxism, moral understanding and moral argument are easily derided as 'idealistic', 'utopian' or 'ideological', in strict opposition to the 'scientific' and 'materialist' analysis of the capitalist mode of production. In the period of the Second International, which lasted from 1884 to the outbreak of the First World War, Marxists were anxious to prove the scientific status of Marx's writings. This meant generally accepting the terms of criticism and evaluation of positivistic science.[1]

This involved showing that the scientific analysis of the capitalist mode of production was completely independent of considerations of values. If there was a concern with questions of morality, Marxists thought that Marx's scientific writings needed to be supplemented by a separate theory of morality. Within Austro-Marxism in particular, this involved connecting an understanding of Kant's morality of the categorical imperative to Marx's scientific analysis. The fundamentally Kantian distinction between 'facts' and 'values', between empirical and scientific investigation on the one hand and moral understanding and political practice on the other, had reasserted itself.[2]

The pervasive, theoretical and methodological division between 'science' and 'morality' is firmly embedded in bourgeois culture and society, having its source in the Enlightenment and the Scientific Revolution of the seventeenth century. It has had a deep hold on the formation and history of the social sciences within modernity since at least the 1820s, particularly within the positivistic tradition in economics and sociology.[3] Historically it has been in periods when capitalist society has been most firmly established and least challenged by working-class movements that notions of science have been most firmly separated from questions of morality and politics. In these periods scientific investigation too easily becomes a description of the prevailing institutions and social relations, without questioning how social conflicts are maintained and reproduced within the prevailing relations of power and subordination.

In the structuralist Marxism of Althusser, which was influential in England in the 1970s, particularly with the closing of an intense period of working-class and community struggles in the early 1970s, we discover a critique of positivism, but this time in the name of a more rationalistic notion of 'science' and 'theory'. We can hear echoes of Kant's earlier critique of Hume and the limits of empiricism. But this need hardly be surprising since we discover somewhat paradoxically that the Althusserian notion of a Marxist science still operates *fundamentally* within the Englightenment polarities of empiricism and rationalism. Structuralist Marxism is established as a form of rationalism very much in contrast to the 'essentialism' and 'humanism' that were taken as characterising classical social theory. Lukács, if he is not read through Althusser's eyes had already critically illuminated this in his *History and Class Consciousness*, as the abiding polarities of bourgeois thought and experience.[4]

But this is to return to the very ground from which Hegel struggled to free himself. In some sense, rationalism has always provided the internal critique of bourgeois class relations, which would otherwise be frozen within the static categories of empiricism. If this has allowed for the internal transformation of capitalist social relations, it has meant, as Marx crucially realised, that the structure of class relations of power and subordination could be maintained largely unchanged.

What is shared by traditions of Marxism construed as a science, whether it be the orthodox Marxism of the Second International or more recent forms of structuralist Marxism, is a notion of historical materialism that insists upon a distinction between 'science' and 'ideology', and so also a generalised antipathy to Hegel's influence on Marx. This is not surprising if one recognises how critical Hegel is of any fundamental distinction between science, morality and politics. Hegel has worked hard to develop a critique of the very rationalism in Kant that Althusser seems to want to make his own.[5]

Morality and moral discussion are systematically undermined within the scientistic tradition of Marxism, whether it be genuinely positivist or not. This is to abandon a conception of the diversity of human needs and personal and social identities, for it is to treat race, gender and sexual identities as products of underlying class relations or else as social and historical constructions with no moral difference. Often this reproduces, within a Marxist tradition, familiar utilitarian notions of self-interest dressed up as 'realistic' politics. Historically, this has legitimated certain disastrous forms of instrumentalism towards others as we have become trapped into instrumental conceptions of morality. Within a Leninist tradition, whatever seems to promote the interests of a working-class revolution is automatically defined as 'moral', on the general assumption that the ends of socialism justify whatever means are available.[6]

We implicitly assume an instrumental conception of rational action as goal-directed, without questioning the historical and philosophical sources of this conception. This is one of the damaging assumptions of Leninism, which have had such disastrous historical and human consequences, as the revolutions in Eastern Europe have reminded us. But if the insights of Marx's work are not to be abandoned they need to be reframed. This makes it all the more urgent to reconsider the ambivalent place of morality within Marxism.

MORALITY AND CLASS

Within an orthodox Marxism which fundamentally defines Marxism as a form of economic determinism, it has been easy to identify morality with the ideology of a particular class. 'Morality' is identified with 'bourgeois morality' and dismissed, or else contrasted with some idea of 'proletarian morality'. This was also a weakness in Lukác's writings. Post-modern theory helps us question inherited traditions of thought and feeling which become so quickly totalistic, for instance as we learn to recognise morality as 'class morality', this encourages us to see 'bourgeois morality' as a homogeneous whole, so making it difficult to develop a critical relation to fragmentations of gender, race, ethnicity and sexual orientation. Rather, we assume a class morality has to be either accepted or rejected in its entirety. This is not to argue against identifying a distinct 'bourgeois morality', but against dominant conceptions of it, generally encouraged by particular visions of the relationship between ideology and material interests.

We can talk more specifically about the character of moral ideas and values that embody the power of the bourgeoisie as a class. We learn from Marx how a particular mode of production establishes a certain structure of power and domination within society. We also learn how a certain morality can work to legitimate this structure of social relations, and thereby the power of the bourgeoisie within capitalist society. I am talking about such notions as 'individual competitiveness', 'acquisitiveness', 'possessiveness' and 'success', but not simply, in Max Weber's terms, as 'values' held by individuals either as preferences or as conceptions they favour. Rather these values are embodied in social practices and lived out in the social relations of power and subordination people experience in their everyday lives.

Edward Thompson has worked most profoundly with these issues in terms of class, trying to bring them back into the heart of Marxist discussion. I was initially encouraged by his formulation of the issues in his 'An Open Letter to Leszek Kolakowski':

> The mode of production and productive relationships determine cultural processes in an *epochal* sense; that when we speak of the capitalist mode of production for profit we are indicating at the same time a 'kernel' of characteristic human relationships – of exploitation, domination, and acquisitiveness – which are inseparable from this mode ... within the limits of the epoch there are characteristic tensions and contradictions, which cannot be transcended unless we transcend the epoch itself: there is an economic logic and a *moral* logic and it is futile to argue as to which we give priority since they are different expressions of the same 'kernel of human relationships'. We may then rehabilitate the notion of a capitalist or bourgeois culture ... [with] its characteristic patterns of acquisitiveness, competitiveness, and individualism.[7]
>
> (Thompson, E.P. 1979: 14)

Thompson helps us focus on the critically important issues of class which have too often fallen by the way in post-modern discussions of the fragmentation of identities. But, if we agree that class relations of power need to be rethought too much attention has been given in Marxist discussions to issue of priority. I wonder whether Thompson helps in his talk about 'an economic logic and a moral logic'?

How are we to understand them as 'different expressions of the same "kernel of human relationships"'? Is there not always a constant temptation for them to fall apart into two separate and independent 'logics'? Do we not also need to grasp as critical to Marx's understanding that 'economic' relations are not autonomous but always exist *as* social relations of power, and, thereby, also as involving moral relations? Is this not why Marx insists on talking about the social relations of production? As Thompson realises, these questions are important because they bear directly upon our understanding of historical materialism. This is not simply a matter of taking issue with Thompson, but rather of being encouraged by his writing to take some of his questioning further. It will also involve us looking back at the historical source of certain tensions and contradictions within Marx's own writings, setting them within the context of an Enlightenment vision of modernity rather than simply joining the argument about different interpretations of Marx's writings.

IDEOLOGY AND MORALITY

Different traditions of Marxism encourage us to see capitalist morality as a total complex of 'values' which have to be 'uprooted' or 'replaced' through a social revolution, with an alternative 'proletarian' set of values. This conception has deep roots in orthodox Marxism, but also lives on in certain New Left ideas. Within an orthodox conception which operates within a simple 'base' and 'superstructure' framework, 'morality' is seen as part of 'ideology', and generally as an aspect of 'false consciousness'.

Within this conception, crudely, it becomes 'naïve' to think you can really change or transform 'morality', without transforming the objective structure of social relations which maintain and support this morality. This realisation has been all too blinding. The truth this insight still contains has been distorted beyond all recognition, so much so that it has badly misled us about how ideology and morality enter our lives and are lived in our everyday social relations. It also limits our sense of history and the ways we can understand our lives.

Again we find an important challenge to this orthodox position in Thompson's writings, where he is talking of his

> sympathy and intellectual respect for Christian forms, movements and ideas, which as you insist (and as Christopher Hill in this country has long insisted) must be studied in their own reality and autonomy, and not as figments of 'false consciousness' in which other more real and material interests were masked.
>
> (Thompson, E.P. 1979: 14)

Even if we agree, it is not easy to learn how to do this without slipping back into sustaining ideas of the autonomy of morality. It is partly a matter also of appreciating the ways morality can be a real material force in people's history, culture and lives.

For some time it has been easier to learn this sympathy and understanding from the practice of socialist historians in England, such as Christopher Hill and Eric Hobsbawm, than from social theorists and philosophers.[8] But this is partly because of the privileged place of philosophy within English culture and the difficulties of discovering historical precedents for developing a genuinely oppositional philosophical culture.[9]

More recently, especially with the influence of feminism, sexual politics and post-colonial theory, it has been easier to challenge the identification of morality with 'naïveté' and the equation of politics with 'material struggles'. This embedded Marxist orthodoxy has been challenged with a renewed interest in the politics of identity. For a generation politicised through the experiences of 1968, morality was inseparable from politics and an impatience with an education that seemed incapable of illuminating the moral and political realities of Vietnam. But if a connection between morality and politics was briefly rediscovered, this quickly became a matter of individual moral commitment, because it could not be sustained theoretically. Rather it was generally forsaken within the turn towards structuralism.

For a period there was at least the hope that theory would be brought into relation with practice. This hope was sustained by the recognition of how much could be learnt from experience, and how our intellectual understandings had to be *grounded* in our experience. This was sustained in different ways through feminism and intellectually through Marx and Wittgenstein. They promised a very different sense of the relationship of theory to experience, and thereby a much less formalistic grasp of the relationship of theory to practice.

Looking back through the darker days of mass unemployment and recession in the 1970s, as well as over a decade of Thatcherism, possibly it was as mistaken for a generation of political activists to think theory would follow inevitably from practice as it was for intellectuals around the New Left Review, who championed an Althusserian Marxism, to think politics was a matter of introducing theory into some kind of cultural vacuum.

By the closing years of the 1970s, as the recession took its hold, it was difficult in Europe and America to develop a practice that could relate closely to ongoing working-class struggles. Socialist politics, in Britain at least, had become rhetorical and were identified with taking on a state apparatus that was increasingly experienced as remote and oppressive. Libertarian Left politics declined and traditional far Left politics lacked any shared understanding of the meaning of a socialist transformation, obsessed as it was with issues of power. Left politics lost touch with the moral and political concerns of working people, who increasingly found their only voice in the individualism and moralism of the Right.

The 1980s were a difficult decade in which people generally lost any confidence in the possibilities of political change. Sexual politics and a politics of experience, as it was developed within feminism and gay and lesbian politics attempted to heal the split between the personal and the political. The new social movements were exploring ways of connecting to people's lived experience and so of preparing grounds for reconsidering the place of moral theory within Marxism.

A politics of identity helps to appreciate the potential significance of Gramsci's ideas in *The Prison Notebooks* as a crucial starting point for the reworking of a socialist tradition:

It is a matter therefore of starting with a philosophy which already enjoys, or could enjoy, a certain diffusion, because it is connected to and implicit in practical life, and elaborating it so that it becomes a renewed common sense possessing the coherence and the sinew of individual philosophies. But this can only happen if the demands of cultural contact with the 'simple' are continually felt. . . . Critical understanding of self takes place therefore through a struggle of political 'hegemonies' and of opposing directions, first in the ethical field and then in that of politics proper, in order to arrive at the working out at a higher level of one's own conception of reality. Consciousness of being part of a particular hegemonic force (that is to say, political consciousness) is the first stage towards a further progressive self-consciousness in which theory and practice will finally be one.

(Gramsci 1971: 333)

Gramsci understood the real force of Catholic ideas in 'first the ethical field and then in that of politics' in Italy. He was forced to confront the very real power that religious ideas continue to have over people's lives rather than simply dismissing them as 'irrational'. He crucially recognised that it was not enough to offer people 'correct' analyses of their exploitation without also helping them to a deeper understanding of themselves and their situation. He felt that it was partly through this self-awareness and understanding that people would understand a connection between genuine freedom and the need to have greater control over their lives.

This was an essential aspect of any meaningful process of political education. Part of Gramsci's crucial significance in helping build connections with feminism and sexual politics as well as with race and ethnicity was through restoring the moral insight and integrity of Marxism. So Gramsci helps us understand that morality is not simply a reflection of bourgeois material interests, as if we have to 'see through' the morality to uncover the 'material interests', which are supposedly the only 'real forces' or 'determinants' in the situation.

But this does not mean that a certain scepticism we can learn within Marxism about morality is not well founded. We can learn from history how often the bourgeoisie have presented their own interests as 'universal' and hidden their own class interests through talk of care, concern, generosity and helping others. This often served the legitimation of class, race and gender exploitation. We also learn about the nature of class power when we realise that poor relief was only finally given because of the threats of the poor to the middle class and its 'civilised order of society'.

Marx taught us to be suspicious, if not contemptuous, of the self-conceptions of the bourgeois class, knowing how much it gained from the ways capitalist society is organised, but Marx also underestimated capitalism's capacity to reform itself and provide people with civil rights and material security. He was also too inclined to marginalise the sufferings of racism and sexism. We still have to be aware of the broadly conceived material interests of different classes, genders, races and ethnic groups, in preserving the present order of social relations and in presenting the relations of power as if they are somehow in the interests of the whole community.

This is tied to the universalism we find embedded in the Kantian moral tradition we inherit which helped shape visions of modernity. It has been partly because of a need to legitimate a particular class rule as somehow in the best interests of the whole community within capitalist democracies, that ideological questions have become so crucial to traditions of Western Marxism.[10]

Because of the need to present social democracy as the only possible form of democracy, liberal theory is centrally concerned with presenting capitalist structures of power and inequality, making them appear somehow 'equal', 'fair' and 'just'. Marxism has often disarmed itself in these discussions through too easily regarding moral and political questions as secondary. Throughout the 1970s and much of the 1980s there was more discussion about the theoretical status of ideology than there was concrete questioning of central conceptions of Thatcherism until the intervention of Stuart Hall and *Marxism Today*.

The social and political language of socialism has largely been discredited by the revolutionary events in Eastern Europe; it has been slow to confront the moral and political concerns of liberalism and to learn to contest the inherited traditions upon which it tacitly draws. If anything, democratic socialist theory often sought to realise itself in the image of such influential liberal writing as John Rawls' *A Theory of Justice* (1972).

The structuralist Marxism of Althusser has left a binding legacy, even if it is no longer supported. It recognises the reality of ideology as a material force at the very moment that it paralyses meaningful ideological investigation, by portraying socialism not as a more human and equal society but simply as a more advanced mode of production. It fragments Marxist theory into what Gramsci had already warned against in his discussion of orthodoxy in the *Prison Notebooks* – a distinct philosophy and a theory of history and politics. This separates ideological questions into a sphere of their own and so unwittingly sustains the very autonomy of morality upon which liberal moral theory depends. It reproduces the old orthodox prejudices against ethical concerns, but in a more sophisticated form.[11]

Marx warns us against taking liberal, moral and political theory at face value, so we can learn to identify the concealed class interests in universalist claims. But we must be careful not to generalise this insight too hastily to say something about the character or place of morality. We must also face Marx's blindness to issues of gender, race and ethnicity, resisting the priority that is still too easily given to issues of class. Nor can we assume that these issues can automatically be treated in similar terms as so often still happens.

If Althusser has helped many see that it is quite wrong to see ideology simply as a 'veil' or 'cover' for 'underlying material interests', he has not helped understand the specific character of ideology, or the ways it is lived out in our emotional lives and relationships. If we no longer discount ideology as a veil for underlying material interests, we discount it in Althusserian theory through isolating it into a realm of its own.

So, for instance, just to give an example, we are left powerless to grasp the ways ideological questions enter into ongoing struggles in a factory about who should control the speed of the line, or whether management should have the right to move workers between jobs, or whether workers can insist that 'this is my job, so you don't have any right to move me'. Again, the 'economic logic' cannot be so neatly separated from the 'ideological' or the 'moral'. We have to return, for a time, to investigating the historical and theoretical sources of some of these distinctions.

MATERIALISM AND MORALITY

When we are introduced to the emergence of the concept of ideology, we are often introduced to the writings of De Tracy, Helvetius and Holbach in the period before the French Revolution. But we rarely contextualise those writings as part of the preparation and struggle of an emerging class to legitimate its rule.[12] Their early writings were directed against the 'spiritualism' of the Church so often used to legitimate the power of the aristocracy. This was part of the assertion of the 'reality' of 'material life', as against the 'unreality' of 'spiritual life'. Historically, this was an essential part of undermining the power and legitimacy of the Church and the aristocracy.

But these writings already contained the dangers of a reductionism, from the 'unreality' of religious ideas to the 'unreality' of all ideas. This was often grounded in an implicit empiricist conception that in many ways is democratic, namely that one can only rely upon one's own sense experience as a source of knowledge. This is part of the complicated history of the relationship of epistemology to relations of power. The educational implications of a crude empiricism allied to authoritarian teaching were to be sharply criticised years later by Dickens in *Hard Times*.

Marx was much more anxious to differentiate his understanding of materialism from the 'defect of all previous materialism' than is acknowledged by traditions of orthodox Marxism, which have simply focused on a crude distinction between 'materialism' and 'idealism'. This has historically been significant in discouraging us from exploring the diverse forms of materialism we grow up taking for granted. It also helps explain why Marx's formulations are so often presented in an abstract and lifeless form.

The anxiety of traditions of orthodox Marxism to hold tight to their materialism and radically to separate themselves from any traces of idealism has often served as some kind of badge of honour. It has treated an engagement with idealist traditions as a form of pollution that needs to be eradicated. It has also made Marx's writings appear to be a series of abstract positions with little connection to the everyday experience of injustice, subordination and oppression in capitalist society.

Rather than a revealing theory which helps working-class people understand and analyse their experience within capitalist society, which was supposedly Marx's intention, all too often Marxism comes to be presented as a remote scientific theory analysing a mode of production.[13] Neither the orthodox Marxism of the Second International nor Althusserian Marxism will then be open to the philosophical and political challenge of Gramsci:

> The philosophy of praxis has been a 'moment' of modern culture. To a certain extent it has determined or enriched certain cultural currents. Study of this fact, which is very important and full of significance, has been neglected or quite simply ignored by the so-called orthodoxy, and for this reason: the most important philosophical combination that has taken place has been between the philosophy of praxis and the various idealistic tendencies, a fact which, to the so-called orthodoxy, essentially bound to a particular cultural current of the last quarter of a century (positivism, scientism), has seemed an absurdity if not actually a piece of chicanery.
> (Gramsci 1971: 388)

We have to be aware of the cultural and historical assumptions with which we read Marx. Unless we develop a critical consciousness, as Gramsci calls it, of the 'common-sense' ways of thinking and feeling which we grow up assuming, we will often reproduce these assumptions unwittingly in our reading of Marx. It becomes difficult, especially in the 1990s when people have turned away so sharply from Marx, to learn about the character of Marx's historical materialism, because we are rarely aware of the forms of materialism we take for granted.

Utilitarianism is a form of materialism which has deeply affected our cultural formation in North America and in Britain. It becomes 'common sense' to assume that self-interest is the only 'real' motivation for people's behaviour even if people would like to think otherwise. We readily assume that people are acting out of material self-interest in almost everything they do. This is generally accepted as part of the 'realism' of bourgeois society. We become suspicious if people do things for others, thinking there must be some kind of ulterior motive or self-interest, though they may not be conscious of this themselves.

This defines central questions of our inherited liberal moral theory, set as it is with individualistic and egoistic assumptions. We become concerned with discovering 'reasons' for why people should do things for others. Much of our moral sensibility and moral theory becomes trapped within a framework of arguing for altruism, while believing that people are fundamentally egoistic.

Rather than helping us become aware of the tendencies towards idealism in liberal moral culture, Marxism can often simply feed the 'materialism' already dominant in the taken-for-granted utilitarian morality.[14] Often it simply helps confirm the idea of 'material self-interest' as dominant, without helping us discover ways of identifying and escaping the limitations of a utilitarian morality. This has made it extremely difficult to develop meaningful critiques of liberal morality, or fully to appreciate the ways periods of working-class, Black, feminist and gay agitation and cultures have practically challenged central conceptions of capitalist relations and morality.

Sometimes this means socialist morality is simply presented as the reverse of bourgeois morality, so that, if bourgeois morality enshrines the idea of 'self-interest' then socialist morality must involve 'selflessness'.[15] Often this simply involves reproducing the dichotomies of liberal moral theory, which at some level, as I argue, within modernity have a strong connection with an identification of masculinity with reason. It allows men in particular to engage with, or legislate, what is best for others rather than produce any sustained critique of the diverse moral relations of bourgeois society.

This is particularly clear in the way notions of duty have traditionally played such a central role in communist societies. We discover this in the discussions of 'motivation' and 'moral incentives' in China.[16] Sometimes we find stark alternatives where, for instance, capitalist society supposedly puts individual self-interest first, while socialist society puts the 'society' or the 'state' above individual interests. This can involve the need for individuals systematically to subordinate themselves, out of a sense of duty, to the 'goals' set by society.

In its own way this simply reproduces the structure of a Kantian Protestant morality, even if this is directed towards a different vision. Though we seem to be reversing and opposing the individualism of possessive self-interest, we are to be caught within a structure of morality which remains fundamentally the same. This can help define one way of thinking about the limits of the moral inheritance of Marxism in its aspiration towards greater equality and justice.

Somewhat paradoxically, Marxism can be taken as posing an 'alternative morality', only because morality is very much conceptualised in terms of an alternative ideal. It is partly because, within liberal morality, we are not given a way of grasping the significance of our moral and cultural history and experience that could help us discern both material and ideal features within our moral inheritance, that we so easily reproduce the 'idealism' of liberal morality. This particular aspect of modernity is bound up with a Kantian influence which encourages us to see morality as a matter of setting up 'ideals' we have to live up to.

Within a liberal moral culture influenced by Kant we inherit a strong sense of moral duty and a willingness to prove ourselves morally worthy by being ready to subordinate our inclinations and desires.[17] This produces an insidious, if often unacknowledged, self-righteousness. A sense of individual self worth is secure through the knowledge of the sacrifice of wants, desires, feelings and emotions, which in turn helps develop a particular form of 'moral character'.

As Max Weber investigates, in *The Protestant Ethic and the Spirit of Capitalism* there is a particular identification of masculinity with a conception of instrumental rational action. This presupposes that, especially as men, we set certain 'goals' or 'ideals' for ourselves, as we do for our work, that become an end in themselves. These are set by reason alone and in theory include the subordination of our emotion and feeling, which could supposedly only interfere in this process of rational decision-making. We come to need certain 'goals' to organise our activities and identities around, especially as men who have learnt to identify our very sense of self with such an inherited conception of male identity. We are brought up, especially as middle-class men, to believe that without these goals life would be 'pointless' or 'meaningless'.[18]

Competitive male identity is structured into the social relations of schooling for boys where we can usefully begin to experience the contradiction set up in our experience of learning. I remember that by the time I was twelve, what mattered to me was not the content of the subjects but the marks I got at school. I often felt I enjoyed the subjects I did well in, unable to discern any other means of inner judgement. Like many others I found I was working for marks, rather than for understanding.

This often meant learning, as John Holt so usefully explored in *How Children Fail* (1969), what the teacher wanted me to know rather than developing my own understanding. My learning suffered and I developed little sense of what I was interested in myself. This shows up contradictions in the official language of liberal schooling. Though such a language talks readily about individual learning, the power relations of schooling, organised around hierarchy and individual competition, often work to undermine this very process of individual discernment, growth and learning.

MORALITY AND MASCULINITY

Marx's *Critique of the Gotha Programme* (1875) shows that Marx had to confront, in his own lifetime, pervasive misinterpretations of his writing. But did Marx's writings somehow encourage many of these interpretations by failing to appreciate the significance of moral conceptions in shaping our expectations of self?

Certainly the history of socialism shows the ease with which socialism became identified with greater production more equally distributed. Somehow this becomes the 'goal' people have to be ready to make sacrifices for rather than the individual success and achievement we find people aspiring to within a capitalist society. This notion of socialism as a more equal distribution of goods embodies a conception of justice that can somehow be separated from the quality of human relations and experience.

Socialism as equal distribution maintains a vital connection with distributive conceptions of justice, in particular with the ways utilitarianism is ready to define happiness and human satisfaction as a 'good' people could accumulate like any other commodity. The logic of bourgeois morality readily transforms human social relations into relations of possession and appropriation. This has roots in the relation between property and notions of personal identity to be found in Locke.[19]

Without a developed theory of the relationship of morality to masculinity it was easy for Marxism constantly to slip back into voicing what Marx identifies as 'crude materialism'. Utilitarianism cannot simply be dismissed as an aspect of 'bourgeois ideology'. Rather we first need ways of investigating how it continues to order our relations and affect the ways we implicitly think and feel.

This can also help us explain the ways 'production' became an overriding goal and end in itself in so many socialist societies, to which people had to learn to subordinate themselves. This echoed the capitalist identification of progress with the control and domination of nature. There were no ethical limits placed on the uses of nature once it had been reduced to matter bereft of intrinsic meaning. Increasing production may well be essential within developing societies operating within a capitalist world economy. But this is a different matter from socialism itself being identified with increasing production and so with reproducing the same, if not worse, relationships to nature.

There is a crucial difference between people recognising the need to make certain limited sacrifices for the well-being of the larger society, and these sacrifices themselves becoming a way of life, the latter being closely identified with socialism. In this way material production becomes identified with a socialism for which sacrifices have to be made. Nature is exploited for it is assumed to have no intrinsic value or meaning of its own, for as matter it is simply the background against which people supposedly order their relationships with each other. There remains a fundamental identification between work, individual achievement and masculinity.

Weber clearly understands some of this when he explains in *The Protestant Ethic and the Spirit of Capitalism* (1930) how central Protestant morality was for preparing people to accept the subordinations and disciplines of capitalist production. Now we have to learn how a Protestant work ethic also implicitly informs and organises conceptions of socialism. When production has to be maximised, as an end in itself, issues of distributive justice can be easily forgotten. The moral structure remains the same even if reversed. In place of God, we have to prove ourselves in production. We inherit the same antagonism to nature, the body and emotional life which must supposedly all be remade within the image of a dominant masculinity.

Though we live in a secularised culture, Christianity continues to influence the structures of the inherited moral cultures of modernity. Within Christianity people had to learn to subordinate themselves to God's will. They could not expect to understand his ways. This was a matter of faith. In the Catholic Church it meant accepting the mediations of the clergy. People did not have, nor did they deserve, direct access to God. But also within a Protestant tradition, if people trusted their nature they would simply be led astray. They would be led towards an animal life, but this could not be a human life.

Rather, within different traditions of Christianity, people had to be saved from their animal selves, so that they could learn to identify with their spiritual selves. The antagonism to our 'animal natures' was culturally prescribed as our humanity was identified with our existence as rational selves and so as an inner relationship of superiority to nature. As we learnt to despise animals so we also learnt to silence our emotions, feelings and desires.

Because of our assumed radical ignorance morality is not something we could get to know through our intelligence, but only through faith. In early Christian Europe work and production were not then ends in themselves.[20] People had to dedicate themselves to the ends of salvation. The medieval world view helps us question how we have come to take material self-interest for granted in modern capitalist democracies as somehow 'natural' to people. Tawney helps us clarify this:

> That economic interests are subordinate to the real business of life, which is salvation, and that economic conduct is one aspect of personal conduct, upon which, as on other parts of it, the rules of morality are binding . . . But economic motives are suspect. Because they are powerful appetites, men fear them, but they are not mean enough to applaud them . . . There is no place in medieval theory for economic activity which is not related to a moral end, and to found a science of society upon the assumption that the appetite for economic gain is a constant and measurable force, to be accepted like other natural forces, as an inevitable and self-evident datum, would have appeared to the medieval thinker . . . as irrational.
>
> (Tawney 1926: 31)

For Weber, it was the development of Calvinism that was crucial to the development of capitalism. Protestantism had managed to perpetuate the subordination of people's inclinations, wants and desires, while they served God. This was part of establishing a historical identification of morality and masculinity with reason and made a deep impact upon the different ways both men and women were to think and feel about themselves. But Protestantism also helped people to a sense of their own individuality and an individual search for salvation built around individual conscience. Paradoxically, this was established through setting the moral will against nature, and was not to help people trust in themselves, in the sense of their wants, feelings and desires.

AUTHORITY AND MORALITY

The source of moral authority was to be essentially external, even if we were free to develop our own individual relationship with it. If anything, Protestantism seems to have brought a more pervasive psychological control of individuals, who had to be ready to humiliate themselves before God. Luther was clear about this in his comments on Paul's letter to the Romans:

For God wants to save us not by our own but by extraneous [*fremde*] justice and wisdom, by a justice that does not come from ourselves and does not originate in ourselves but comes to us from somewhere else . . . That is, a justice must be taught that comes exclusively from the outside and is entirely alien to ourselves.

(Martin Luther, *Vorlesung über den Romerbrief*, Chapter 1,1, quoted in Fromm 1991)

If Protestantism was to help us recognise and value our rationality, this was only so that we would know the sources of external authority. The sources of knowledge have an authority which is fundamentally external. Kant was to secularise this notion for liberal morality, articulating a central tension between the dignity of the individual as a rational agent and the need to subordinate ourselves to an external authority.

It is because we are rational that we can come to know the dictates of the moral law. It is a test of our moral worth whether we can act out of a sense of duty doing what the moral law dictates, thereby subordinating our inclinations and desires. Freedom lies in a recognition of the necessity of the moral law, even if it also carries an ambiguous notion that the moral law has to be individually affirmed. So it is that we can learn to identify our individual happiness with the subordination of our wants, desires, emotions and feelings. This morality of self-denial is deeply embedded in liberal moral culture to the extent that we hardly recognise its workings.

We learn to subordinate ourselves to the moral law and to feel a sense of achievement in our subordination. Similarly we can also learn to subordinate ourselves to the market. We can use our reason, even if this is also limited, to discerning the laws of the market better. The laws of the market like the moral law themselves cannot be changed and, if the ideology of liberal capitalism is to be believed, our 'freedom' lies in submitting ourselves to these laws. In this way liberal morality manages to work a fudamental fragmentation of our experience.

We are encouraged to identify 'happiness' with individual achievement and with realising our goals, though this may now have little connection with the satisfaction of our individual needs, wants and desires. Rather we learn to subordinate these feelings and desires, recognising them as having no part in defining our individualities, as we learn to identify them as part of our 'irrational' animal natures.

Within the middle class this takes on a particular form as we become threatened, especially as heterosexual men, by our emotions and feelings, often having very little ongoing relationship with them. Our sense of masculine identity and virtuousness comes from knowing that we have successfully controlled and subordinated them. We pride ourselves in our independence and self-sufficiency, knowing that we are reliable and dependable in regard to others while needing nothing ourselves.

In a very real sense, we are brought up as heterosexual men to identify our masculinity with our goals and achievements so that, unknowingly, we become virtual strangers to ourselves and to our experience as men. So much in Protestant culture makes us think and feel it is 'selfish' and 'self-indulgent' to think about the nourishment and satisfaction of our individual wants and desires. It becomes difficult even to conceive of a society organised around individual and collective development and growth in a way that allows us to satisfy our individual needs and desires in our relationships with others.

It is important to recognise that capitalist morality is tightly geared and institutionalised to setting up external goals of individual achievement and success with little connection to the *quality* and *meaning* of individual lives. Time is not to be wasted and work becomes a goal in itself. Within a capitalist society, heterosexual men are brought up, through a dominant ideology of work to subordinate themselves to maximising production and thus personal relationships become secondary as male identities are established in the public realm of work. We become more sensitive to the needs of work than the quality of our lives and our work relations with people.

But this was no less true in many, former socialist societies, in which production too easily became a 'goal' outside and beyond the lives of individuals and where people were systematically denied human rights. This issue, of how we come to value different aspects of our lives, whatever exchange value they may claim on the market, leaves us with the need for basic theoretical and practical questioning about the relationship of ethics in a post-modern world when many of the aspirations towards universal emancipation no longer carry conviction.

A rationalistic structure of thought has provided, within modernity, for the taken-for-grantedness of goals external to the quality of people's experiences, since we learn that these are to be identified through reason alone. Marx did not entirely break free of this structure but shared some of its universalist aspirations: therefore it is necessary to look for a while at Marx's own ambivalent relationship with this rationalism.

Chapter 3
Modernity

MODERNITY AND REASON

I think it is important to investigate some of the tensions in Marx's early writings if we are to grasp how Marxism has inherited an Enlightenment identification of masculinity with reason, and give ourselves a fuller sense of the different traditions influencing Marx. This can help ground some of the interpretations given to Marx's writings, showing the basis they have in the tensions Marx himself experienced. This is not simply an exploration in the history of ideas, since these temptations are still very alive for us, deeply rooted as they are within a liberal moral culture. In particular, I want to explore some of the Englightenment sources of Marx's critique of religion since they seem to sustain the identification of masculinity with reason.

Within the Englightenment conception of reason, it was easy to think of religion as a matter of false belief. Religion was quite generally conceived of as 'superstition', which would be dissolved through the light of reason. An important source of bourgeois materialism, especially in France, was the critique of the spirituality of religion. The ontological foundation for the domination of science in the seventeenth century was laid in the conception of 'matter' as separated from 'spirit' or 'energy' and in the suspicion of all forms of metaphysics. The new sovereignty of a reason separated from nature was part of a new masculinist philosophy which would firmly identify progress with the domination of nature both within ourselves and also externally.[1]

In declaring the spiritual to be an 'illusion', materialism has been a doctrine which in different forms since the eighteenth century, confronted the power of orthodox religion. In Britain this took a fundamentally empiricist form, which took all knowledge to be derived from 'sense experience'. This challenged the authority of faith. But Marx was more deeply influenced by French traditions, where the power of Cartesianism reflected the strengths of rationalism.[2]

Somehow the sovereignty of 'reason' and the intellect involved less of a coming to terms with the deep structures of Catholicism than the familiar denigration of the body and emotional life being set in scientific terms. The hierarchy of Catholicism was replaced by a hierarchy of knowledge with 'reason' at the summit. In France a focus on people, usually men, as 'rational creatures', goes along with an emphasis on logic as somehow providing independent and autonomous 'rules of rationality'.

Through reason and logic we can independently establish certain strict notions of 'right' and 'wrong'. In many ways Kant was to give moral expression to the dualistic conceptions of Descartes.[3] In Kant this involves a conception of individual moral worth and human dignity closely identified with a masculinity assumed to be essentially rational and so with the subordination of our emotions, feelings and desires, which can only interfere with the workings of our reason. So it was that women, who were assumed to be closer to nature, had to learn to accept the control and guidance of men, the rational sex.[4]

The Enlightenment was important in undermining the ideological legitimation of aristocratic power as it brutally reorganised sexual relations between men and women through the witch trials and witch burnings.[5] It developed a sense of equality, as equal rights, that was to be crucial in legitimating the developing rule of the bourgeoisie, but also of men in relation to women.

It is part of the political heritage of the Enlightenment that, because we are rational creatures, we share certain rights. Our rights were to be derived fundamentally from our power of reason, almost as a direct consequence. This was to ground a liberal conception of equality in a notion of citizenship and the possession of equal rights, while making it harder to detect the workings of relationships of power and subordination. Equality becomes a matter of the individual possession of rights.[6]

But, somewhat paradoxically, this can also mean equality has little to do with the quality of human relationships and the character of social life, since it only concerns those who can traditionally be thought of as independent and self-sufficient. This was Hegel's central criticism in *The Philosophy of Right*. He was also aware of how the contractual relations of bourgeois society undermine a sense of human community. He helps us, as he helped Marx, to think about the ambiguities in the liberal notion of equality as citizenship.[7]

If we are 'equal' as rational beings, we also have different powers of reasoning. Our thinking about liberal equality becomes more concerned with the opportunities people have to compete for unequal positions of power and influence. As Marx was to comment much later in his *Critique of the Gotha Programme* (1875), this was a matter of an equal opportunity to become unequal. But unfortunately he never says enough to help us understand how the contradiction and tensions of liberal equality can be superceded within a socialist society in which there remains a centralisation of state power and resources.

Some of the sources of bourgeois confidence are to be found in the Enlightenment. There can be little doubt of the importance for liberal conceptions of equality of the definition of people as 'rational creatures'. Even if we want to question the form of rationality this assumes in relation to other aspects of our being, there is no doubt how fundamental this is in sustaining liberal ideas of individual dignity and self-respect. Kant's ethics were crucial for legitimating the moral confidence of the aspiring bourgeoisie. He provided the foundations for the moral calculus which was to establish the independent authority of the moral law, as well as the independence and autonomy of law, morality and politics within a liberal society.[8]

The workings of the categorical imperative enables us to discover what is 'right' and 'wrong' without our having to appeal to our emotions and desires. Access is given to a realm of moral truths which exist fundamentally independently of our natures. We have to be ready to do our duty and learn to silence our inclinations so that gradually they have less and less hold over our behaviour. Kant gives an independent authority to the moral law. Within modernity this helped give enormous self-confidence to the bourgeoisie, who could feel they were not acting out of their narrow class interests, but somehow in the name of a universal rationality. Kantian ethics was also implicitly connected to a redefinition of a dominant masculinity which, being identified with reason, could appropriate to itself the right to speak in the name of all. It became the universal voice of reason.

RATIONALISM AND RELIGION

Marx learns from Feuerbach's critique of religion that, in a fundamental sense, religion is other than it seems.[9] Very crudely, in religion we 'project' our earthly ideals that cannot be realised in our everyday lives, and we create a conception of God which reflects our conception of ideal qualities we would want for ourselves. In this way religion reflects needs which cannot be fulfilled in an exploitative and oppressive society, projected into another realm. Within modernity this remained fundamentally an Enlightenment notion even if it breaks with aspects of an Enlightenment rationalism. At some level a rationalist critique of religion as 'superstition' continues a belief that with a transformation of society that allows people to realise themselves within their own earthly lives they would not need to invent religion, and so religion would disappear.

An Enlightenment rationalism often assumes that religion does not meet any genuine human needs, but develops in its totality as a way of enabling people to endure the hardships of their everyday lives. This is consonant with the much quoted conception of religion as an 'opiate', used by the ruling classes to distract people from the real sources of their misery. If there is truth in this realisation, it has encouraged a very damaging interpretation of Marx's writings. I think this was also a conception Marx was partly trapped by, perhaps because it espoused a rationalism that enabled him to deal with his ambivalence concerning his own Jewishness.[10]

This understanding of religious ideas at least subverts the rationalism of the Enlightenment in allowing us to recognise that if human needs are not met in an exploitative and oppressive society they will find some kind of expression, even if in another sphere. It challenges the influential idea of human wants and needs as socially and historically determined, as if people can simply be 'moulded' to fit dominant expectations and aspirations.

Even if within dominant discourses of modernity it remains difficult to characterise these spiritual needs, it shows that despite what Althusser wanted to think in *For Marx* (1970), Marx is not 'historicist' even in his early writings, in the sense that he does not assume people's needs and values are 'shaped' by society. This also challenges the conception of functionalist sociology, that needs are simply functional for social order.

Marx recognises the powerful critique religion contains of the injustices of the existing social order, even if these are unconsciously expressed in another realm. This remains in continuous tension with a rationalism which tends to see religion simply as false belief, and so makes it difficult to understand the reality and importance of religious understandings and practices within people's lives. It is Marx's continuing commitment to an Enlightenment rationalism that tempts him to assume that these 'needs' would simply dissolve in a society without exploitative relations.[11]

There is something in the rationalist structure of this argument which illuminates difficulties in Marx's conception of human needs. It can help explain the instrumentalism which has characterised so much orthodox Marxism. Put briefly, it is too simple and too swift in its analysis and understanding of the very different needs people meet through religion. It is its continuing Enlightenment heritage which explains how this argument focuses upon the 'structure of society'.

Even if it is true that our religious and spiritual needs express unrealised earthly needs, we cannot thereby assume that all our spiritual needs will disappear once we live in a more just society.

It is also important to recognise this because aspects of a rationalist tradition are carried through in the positivist and functionalist traditions within sociology. A failure to break with this tradition or to identify it clearly means that we can talk about the transformation of society without having to consider possibilities of self-transformation and tensions and contradictions between individual and social needs and desires.

A tendency to subsume the self also reflects upon a central weakness within both the structuralist Marxist tradition and the holistic traditions within functionalist sociology. In each of these we inherit a thin and attenuated conception of personal identity and a marginalisation, or discounting, of human needs of particular kinds. Both traditions, though set against each other as contrasting discourses within modernity, want to develop a language which allows a theorisation of the social totality as an independent and discrete discourse which can be sustained independently of concern with individual needs and desires.

It was this definition of the 'social' which was to be in Durkheim's formulations the defining characterisation of sociology as a science.[12] This legitimates a form of social engineering which at some level echoes a rationalism which goes back to Plato's *Republic* in its desire to subsume individual experience and the quality of human life into the goals of the larger society. These ways of thinking and relating have come to dominate both positivist and structuralist Marxist traditions.

This calls for a reconsideration of the relationship of Marxism to liberalism and democracy and an investigation into different aspects of liberal individualism, which cannot simply be dismissed as 'bourgeois ideology'. We need to recognise the importance of certain individual liberties, not simply as the mystifications of class rule, but as rights that have been bitterly fought for.[13] If the common sense of a liberal moral culture does split individual from society, it also preserves within liberalism a way, however misleading, of thinking about and respecting individual wants, needs, hopes and aspirations, even if these are firmly secluded within the private sphere and often isolated from class, gender and ethnic relations of power and subordination.

The Eastern European revolutions have forced us to face the historical experience of socialism and this teaches us how easily and often brutally individual rights and well-being have been sacrificed. This does not simply involve a defence of liberal market values as the only realisable alternative to a state socialist society, but it does make understandable calls for a critical relationship to ideas of freedom, equality and individual rights. Rather than rejecting Marxism as yet another grand narrative within modernity we can still learn from Marx's criticisms of bourgeois conceptions of freedom and justice in terms of individual rights. At the same time we can also understand the sources within the Marxist tradition, and within Marx's own writings, that have worked to legitimate the often cruel subordination of individual and collective needs, wants and desires.

NEEDS AND INSTRUMENTALITY

Marx recognised an insight in Feuerbach about the ways we respond to the frustration of our needs. We do not simply adapt to what is allowed to us, but we find a way of realising our frustrated needs 'in another realm'. This is an insight developed in a very different way in Freud's understanding of the mechanisms of repression and displacement. It is easy to miss the full force of this critique in conventional and post-modern forms of sociological relativism. These have become the common sense of so much recent anthropology and sociology which simply assumes that in different societies people develop different needs. Similarly they often assume that individuality is itself socially and historically constituted, or else an effect of prevailing discourses.

Post-modernism can help us appreciate how this loses a crucial edge of the argument as it can easily lead to a false totalism, where the emphasis is on the organisation of the larger society. But it finds it harder to illuminate ways in which we *lose touch* with the reality and tensions of people's everyday lives. It is very easy to miss Feuerbach's initial insight and to understand Marx's materialisation of his argument as a simple reversal. This crude dismissal of Marx has characterised much post-modern writing. We slip into a simple reduction, namely that if you can change society the need for religion will disappear.

As we focus on this level of transformation we unknowingly learn not to take people's expressed needs and experience too seriously, since they grow out of the current conditions of exploitation and oppression. We implicitly learn to *discount* people's needs, simply 'explaining them' as growing out of the society people live in. This lays the ground for an instrumentalism towards people, because of the superior knowledge which a positivist vision of science gives us of social processes. This is a crucial Enlightenment source for later positivistic sociology.

Rather than learning to discern different forms of religious expression and the kinds of needs expressed through them, we tend to discount the reality of spiritual needs. We assume within post-modernism too that they will take on a different form once the larger society has been transformed or when articulated through secular discourses. This helps us establish a ground for an instrumental conception of reason and science that Adorno and Horkheimer found in the Enlightenment.[14] It shows how an important recognition of the social totality can at the same time so easily legitimate the subordination of people's wants and needs. This is part of the contradictory inheritance for contemporary social theory of the Enlightenment.

Little of this helps us investigate the needs that religion might be serving, the importance of rituals of birth and death, of loss and suffering, of celebration and emotional expression. This would involve relating to these practices, trying to appreciate how these needs fail to be recognised in everyday life, rather than assuming they have little basis in reality. Freud has given us a way of appreciating these processes of transformation, though he is also trapped within a rationalism which assumes that spirituality is a form of false belief and requires explanation in terms of other areas of people's experience.[15]

The narrow materialism that came to dominate Russia after the Russian Revolution had a rhetoric of human needs but did not, for instance, begin to recognise the quality of human relationships and the depth of human needs. An instrumental conception of reason drawn from an Enlightenment vision of modernity is bound to underestimate the needs people have for each other and the suffering and pain we endure through loss or separation. So, for instance, there were striking similarities in the ways people were encouraged to deal with bereavement and loss, between Russia and Western capitalist societies.

Both were inclined to voice a utilitarian ethic that 'you shouldn't waste time mourning', 'you can't bring people back to life', 'there are more important things that you should be putting your mind to doing'. So it is that we learn to separate from our experience – an estrangement that Marx could recognise in our relationship to work, but not in more personal areas of life where he was equally trapped by a vision of a dominant masculinity as rational, independent and self-sufficient.

It is almost as if within the rationalism that ties so much postmodernism to a modernity it disdains people are still to learn from Feuerbach that they create God in their own human image, so that God is really a human invention. This kind of 'material grounding' which is given a linguistic form within post-modernism shows that our belief in God is 'irrational' and that, therefore, people should turn their attention towards recreating identities or within the terms of modernity the transformation of society.

Within an orthodox Marxism people are encouraged to understand that the source of their particular misery and oppression, whether it be the oppression of women, gay men, lesbians or of Blacks and

Asians, lies in the structure of capitalist society, so they can do nothing else but fight for the total transformation of capitalist society. At one level this might be true, but it tends to be too reductionist, leaving little room for an understanding of how struggling against particular forms of oppression can itself be a source of empowerment and an integral aspect of a social transformation.

Rather it makes 'social transformation' something qualitatively different, somehow separating it off from the struggles of oppressed groups for a more human life. An orthodox vision has helped blind Marxism to issues of sexual and racial oppression, thinking that social transformation can only be the outcome of class struggle. There is a connection here with the ways we are not helped to recognise the importance of genuine spiritual needs that might be expressed through religion, for instance, the opportunities it gives us for remembering and honouring the dead. Our feelings of mourning should *not* be invalidated because they fall within a general critique of religion. This is crucial because it can help us understand what made it so difficult for Marx to develop a language of needs even though this was central to his critique of capitalism.

Socialism will require these rituals, even if they are to take on a different form, since it can only be strengthened and nourished through an appreciation of the importance of human needs, desires and relations, which a capitalist society is always going to negate in its pursuit of profit. If socialism is to express a fundamental belief in people and a trust in human nature, we will also want to recognise difference and diversity and the possibility that some religious beliefs are sustained, not because people are 'stupid' or suffer from 'false consciousness', but because they also serve genuine needs. In the end this is something people have to decide for themselves.

For Marx the discussion of a dialectic of needs gets caught within his dialectics of labour as the exclusive form of self-realisation and his analysis of capitalism in terms of the production of commodities. Even this, as he makes clear, has its source in his early reflections on religion, which is why it is so important to identify the rationalism at work in this discussion. We have tended to interpret the notion of 'false consciousness' in too intellectualist a way. This is partly because it allows us to voice the cultural inheritance of the Enlightenment which would dismiss religious belief and practice as a form of ignorance and stupidity.

We need to acknowledge that religion is not simply sustained through deception or within post-modernity through discourse alone. It is through recognising diverse emotional and spiritual needs as part of developing a language of human experience, capacities and needs and showing how people can live more human lives, that modernity can break with the instrumentalism it has so clearly inherited. If a language of socialism is not to be discredited completely because of the experience of Eastern Europe, or forsaken with the temptations of a post-modernism that promises a freedom to continually remake our identities in the present, we will have to rework its meaning as we heal the wounds with both our inner natures and the natural world with which we have lost relationships.

HISTORY AND HUMAN NATURE

The history of the positivist social sciences has often been the history of legitimating an instrumentalism towards people and nature. This has affected both traditional bourgeois and socialist thought and practice. We discover sources in the social theory of Montesquieu, but also in the social practice of Owen.[16] This has developed into the broadly accepted cultural assumption that people are the 'products of the society they live in'. This can sustain a particular form of radicalism, though we rarely notice the capitalist language of commodities in which we express the idea that people are the products' of the society they grow up in. Along with this goes the familiar idea that human nature is 'malleable' and takes different forms in different societies.

Althusser made a lot of this in his idea that classical liberal theory depended upon a unity in its conception of human nature as some kind of unchanging essence which 'is the attribute of "each single individual" who is its real subject'. This is how he characterises it in his essay 'Marxism and Humanism' in the collection *For Marx*:

> The earlier idealist ('bourgeois') philosophy depended in all its domains and arguments (its 'theory of knowledge', its conception of history, its political economy, its aesthetics, etc.) on a problematic of *human nature* (or the essence of man). For centuries, this problematic had been transparency itself, and no one had thought of questioning it even in its internal modifications.
>
> (Althusser 1970: 227–8)

Althusser wants to characterise 'bourgeois philosophy' in this way, though he is referring to an earlier period in which the bourgeoisie had not yet achieved their full power as a class.

Such characterisations draw upon a sharp duality that misleads us about the complexities of social and political thought that played such a crucial role in the nineteenth and twentieth centuries, even if it allows Althusser to introduce Marx's thought in the starkest terms. In doing so he prevents us thinking clearly, both about the character of historical materialism and about the developments of social theory. If anything,

he claims as Marx's achievement some of the damaging consequences
of nineteenth-century positivism:

> By rejecting the essence of man as his theoretical basis, Marx
> rejected the whole of this organic system of postulates. He drove
> the philosophical categories of the *subject*, of *empiricism*, of the *idea*,
> *essence*, etc., from all the domains in which they had been supreme.
> Not only from political economy (rejection of the myth of *homo*
> *oeconomicus*, that is, of the individual with definite faculties and
> needs as the *subject* of the classical economy); . . . when Marx
> replaced the old couple individuals/human essence in the theory
> of history by new concepts (forces of production, relations of
> production, etc.), he was, in fact, simultaneously proposing a new
> conception of 'philosophy' . . . by a *practice* (economic practice,
> political practice, ideological practice, scientific practice) in their
> characteristic articulations, based on the specific articulations of the
> unity of human society.
>
> (Ibid.: 229)

Althusser confuses Marx's critique of *homo oeconomicus* 'as the *subject*
of the classical economy', with *any* conception of the human subject.
If Marx recognised how misleading it was to construe political economy
as developing out of the fixed needs and faculties of individuals, this
did not mean that people's needs and qualities were to be replaced
by a discourse that does not refer to them at all. The fact that the
capitalist economy did not produce for people's needs, recognising
the ways these change, but for profit through the medium of exchange
values, was at the heart of Marx's critique.

In a similar way the inherited rationalism of Althusser's thought
poses a false dichotomy between a fixed human essence conception of
human nature, which he takes as characterising bourgeois theory in
general, and the reducibility of human needs and wants completely
since they are produced within a particular social formation. This very
reduction of human needs and wants, and the legitimation of the ways
they are to be subordinated to the needs of the 'larger society', is a
central feature of both positivist and functionalist traditions within
sociology.

We are left bereft of an adequate conception of self-identity
and personhood and so of any language of alienation, estrangement or oppression. This was something Marx recognised in his
Critique of Political Economy. He knew that bourgeois theory would
always attempt to eternalise the structures of power and dominance
of capitalist society, presenting them as the only possible form
and legitimating them as somehow in the interests of all. It would
blind us to the ways in which individual lives are damaged and

exploited through the workings of these relationships of power and subordination.

Althusser confuses the idea that human nature is fixed and unchanging so that any plans for social reform are bound to fail, since they are built on illusions about the 'true character of human nature', with bourgeois theory in general. Rather than identifying with a fundamental insight of Marxism, a reductionist theory which sees individuals simply as 'products' or 'functions' of particular societies or 'social formations', we need to locate this reductionist vision of human nature within the modernist traditions of the Enlightenment. In this task the historical sensibility of the Frankfurt School, despite its own rationalism, opens up more questions than Althusser's structuralist Marxism.

Adorno and Horkheimer appreciated the significance of an Enlightenment vision of modernity for grasping the culture and common sense we grow up to take so much for granted within a capitalist society. Modernity was the source of the identification of science with progress and of the aspiration to reconstruct society according to the dictates of 'reason'. This is how Herbert Marcuse understands this enormous development in *Reason and Revolution*:

> Man's position in the world, the mode of his labour and enjoyment, was no longer to depend on some external authority, but on his own free rational activity. Man had passed the long period of immaturity during which he had been victimised by overwhelming natural and social forces, and had become the autonomous subject of his own development. From now on, the struggle with nature and with social organisation was to be guided by his own progress in knowledge. The world was to be an order of reason . . . Man is a thinking being. His reason enables him to recognise his own potentialities and those of his world. He is thus not at the mercy of the facts that surround him, but is capable of subjecting them to a higher standard, that of reason.
>
> (Marcuse 1967: 3,6)

There was an important recognition that society had to be reorganised on a rational basis for people to be able to realise themselves in their everyday lives. If only society were governed by reason, instead of superstition and privilege, people would be able to live happy and fulfilled lives. The Enlightenment challenged the prevailing aristocratic structures of power and dominance, knowing that they had to be transformed if people were to live rational and fully human lives.

Hegel's conception of reason was in constant tension with the later positive idea of reason that did not involves a negation of the existing order to make it 'rational'. Positivism held to the idea that there was already a 'social order' which could be discovered implicit in the existing order. It was this notion which was to dominate positivistic interpretations of Enlightenment thought from Comte onwards. Positivism would endeavour to create social theory in its own image. It assumed a rationality implicit in the existing social order and so endorsed what Marcuse identifies as a 'positive' conception of reason, rather than Hegel's negative reason that was critical of the prevailing order, because it did not allow human fulfilment through the satisfaction of human needs.[17] But there is an unsettling problem in the rationalist form of this latter conception.

As I have mentioned, Kant assumed a strong opposition between reason and nature. His identification of morality with reason meant following the dictates of reason, which gave access to a moral law set in an independent realm. The link was broken between morality and any sense of satisfying our wants and needs. Rather we have to show our moral worth through subordinating our 'inclinations', our wants and needs, to be ready to do what the moral law dictates. Reason was to claim its own independent authority and logic, which were separated radically from any connection with human wants, desires and needs.

Kantian ethics was to maintain a continuity between Christian and bourgeois traditions, with the difference that, within a rationalist tradition, it was through the faculty of reason that a divine plan was to be uncovered. This prepares the epistemological basis for the identification within modernity of progress with the domination of reason and science as involving much less of a break with a Christian denigration of nature and the body than is commonly thought. Post-modern theories cast within rationalist terms have taken time to recognise the Christian assumption that underpinned secular forms of social theory and the ways the Enlightenment helped to present modernity as a secular form of Protestantism that could now clothe itself in a universal light. People learnt to *distrust* their own emotions, feelings and intuitions as partial and subjective, and to listen only to the clear and confident voice of reason and argument. It was an essential quality of reason that it be impersonal and impartial and this reflected a particular dominant form of masculinity which was able to cast modernity very much in its own image. It is partly because of this that feminism potentially provides a more sustained questioning of modernity than post-modern theories allow.

AUTHORITY AND MODERNITY

The radical focus of the Enlightenment did challenge the power of the traditional authority of church and aristocracy, in the name of reason. It set new terms for the relationship between authority and modernity. The 'divine plan' could be known through the progress of reason and science. But for Descartes and Newton this was not a matter of setting reason against faith even though the story is still told that way. There was no necessary contradiction between their science and their religion, even if their science involved a particular challenge to religious conceptions of the universe. This also helped produce the conditions for the essentially contradictory character of liberal conceptions of freedom and authority.

Within an Enlightenment vision of modernity there is a radical impulse that meant freedom could only be realised with a radical reconstruction of society. But this was in tension with the notion that freedom involved accommodating the laws which govern the social order. This was the repressive conception of freedom that also echoed in the positivist tradition of Comte and Durkheim. Since these laws were to exist above the conflicts of society and were to present individuals with a higher vision of the self they assumed that people would subordinate their individual needs and wants, so as to fulfil the 'higher' dictates of reason and science.

As people had been ignorant of the intentions of God and had to accept a higher wisdom as a matter of faith, they now had to accept their own ignorance in the face of reason and knowledge. In a very real sense the theorists of positivism were in different ways to re-establish the power of a scientific church. The negative freedom of Hegel and Marx which involved a challenge to existing relations that could not claim to be rational just because they were real, was soon to be undermined in the positivist tradition developing after the French Revolution out of Enlightenment thought.[18]

In a very real sense the freedom Kant was to legitimate philosophically was circumscribed very quickly, as people were educated at the same time to accept the authority of reason and the moral law. This was to involve a real fracturing of human experience, since learning to believe in oneself as a rational self could now only mean believing in the rational aspect of oneself, while denying any rationality to one's needs, wants, desires and hopes. It was a matter of accepting, almost as second nature, the new authority of reason and science.

This silencing of aspects of the self as bereft of dignity or integrity is often rendered invisible within rationalist visions of social theory, as it is generally accepted as 'reasonable'. It is rarely appreciated as the form of self-denial that it is, for men in particular. It is partly through learning to identify masculine identity with ideas of individua success and achievement that we render such self-denial invisible. The bodily experience of happiness becomes unfamiliar as we are ofter disconnected from somatic life having learnt to identify with our minds alone and as we are brought up to assume that 'happiness' comes with individual achievement and success. According to the Protes tant ethic 'happiness' is something that has to be worked for.

Since the deep structures of Catholicism maintained a deeper cultural hold in France despite the French Revolution, in the period of the Restoration it was easier to build upon the hierarchies of Catholicism. It was easier for a positivist science of society to presen itself as uncovering a male hierarchical 'rational order' people had to submit to, whatever their personal feelings and needs. So a positivis social theory could be in tension with the more democratic and egalitarian impulses of the Enlightenment.

Gouldner is clear about how Comte developed positivism in a way that was 'aimed primarily at blunting the criticisms that the philosophers had directed against almost all the institutions of the ancient regime'. He goes on to show how this was specifically aimed at limiting their conception of freedom:

> Insofar as the 'positive' implied an emphasis upon the importance of scientifically certified knowledge, it was using social science as a rhetoric, which might provide the basis for certainty of belief and which might assemble a consensus in society. It preached 'an end to ideology' under the formulation of 'an end to metaphysics'. In other words, positivism assumed that science could overcome ideological variety and diversity of beliefs. Comte had, in this vein polemicized against the Protestant conception of unlimited liberty of conscience, holding that this led men each to their own differing conclusions and thus to ideological confusion. This disunifying liberty of conscience was, in Comte's view, to be supplanted by a faith in the authority of science that would reestablish the los social consensus and thus make society whole again.
>
> (Gouldner 1970: 114

POSITIVISM AND AUTHORITY

Before we investigate some of these ideas, it is as well to be warned about a positivism that sees itself as independent of issues o metaphysics, morality and politics and yet so easily passes for a common-sense conception of social science. This is what E. A. Burt had had to say:

There is an exceedingly subtle and insidious danger in positivism. If you cannot avoid metaphysics, what kind of metaphysics are you likely to cherish when you sturdily suppose yourself to be free from the abomination? Of course, it goes without saying that in this case your metaphysics will be held uncritically, because it is unconscious. Moreover, it will be passed on to others far more readily than your other notions, inasmuch as it will be propagated by insinuation rather than by direct argument.

(Burtt 1932: 225)

Even if the human sciences have learnt since the 1960s to feel dissatisfaction with the limits of positivist formulations, our ability to go beyond the intellectualist critiques of Weberian interpretive sociology and phenomenology has been systematically undermined by these ideas themselves, in the same way our trust in our emotions and feelings has been undermined. For all the challenges to positivism, in a scientistic culture we are still more likely to blame ourselves for our own stupidity and ignorance if we have difficulties in accepting the truths of science. In a strange way we somehow learn to trust our knowledge and disbelieve ourselves. We even begin to doubt our own thoughts and feelings.

The authority of science calls upon deep cultural roots that need to be uncovered if we are to challenge a framework of social theory that up until the mid-1970s would present interpretive sociology as the only viable alternative to positivism. In itself this settles for an Enlightenment framework in which meanings are either given or else assigned by individuals themselves in what has become a disenchanted world bereft of meaning. People no longer provide meaning for their own experiences or for nature that has now supposedly died, having been reduced to matter with no value other than the classifications provided for it.

Self-doubt is much more ambiguous within an individualist Protestant culture which gives more open recognition to the importance of individuality of expression and freedom of conscience. Protestantism provides some of the emancipatory aspects of liberalism, while also helping to explain the suspiciousness in countries like Britain about ideas of social reconstruction. This also helps explain a cultural antipathy towards sociology, and towards social theory in general, if it does not see society in strictly liberal terms as a collection of individuals.

Protestantism has helped people to trust their own vision and judgement. Its more democratic impulse comes through in the recognition that individuals can themselves legislate what is moral, even if at some level morality still remains something essentially separate and independent. But once it has been discerned people have to be ready to submit themselves to it.

This maintains the authority of the moral law as existing independently of people's feelings, desires and inclinations. Somehow the moral law, like knowledge in general within a rationalist culture, contains within itself a 'higher' notion of people's interests, knowing better than they do themselves what is best for them. It is because people have to submit voluntarily to this law, that liberal democratic society can continue to think of the law as an expression of people's freedom.

This is different from the character of subordination, another feature of the empiricism which is closely connected as a tradition informing our social theory in a liberal moral culture influenced by the Enlightenment. Empiricism has a similar double-edged contradictory character. On one hand it helps people form and maintain a trust and confidence in their own sense-experience, legitimating a belief that truth has to be somehow validated in the experience of people themselves. At the same time it tends to restrict our conception of genuine knowledge to sense-observation.

In this way our vision and cultural sensibilities are narrowed, as are the forms of our social theory, to 'generalisations from the facts of sense-experience'. In a subtle and generally unrecognised way people learn to subordinate their understandings, feelings and insight to 'the facts' which are presented as having some kind of neutral authority. So, somewhat paradoxically, empiricism tends to *undermine* people's beliefs in themselves and in their own feelings and intuitions in a different kind of way. Somehow empiricism would almost deny, in contrast to what Derrida might suggest, the presence of the person themselves in the knowing situation.

Within an empiricist tradition knowledge becomes externalised and essentially depersonalised, somehow radically divorced from people's deepening understanding of themselves and their histories. This systematically undermines the significance of self-knowledge and self-awareness. These become subsidiary features divided somewhere between the private and the public realms.

So the only 'real' knowledge is knowledge of the objective world, where if the self is not obliterated within this process without understanding what is happening to it, it is often reduced to psychological knowledge of the 'individual self'. This is objectified in psychology into the 'self' as 'object of scientific observation'. Again Gouldner helps us grasp how readily we have been brought up within modernity to accept unthinkingly what he identifies as a tradition of objectivism:

Objectivism . . . cannot understand personal presence as a concealed and consequential thing in all efforts to know social worlds.
Objectivism then is the very antithesis of reflexivity.

The objectivist thinks that 'objective' truth is that which exists apart
from the men who constitute it, and thus as existing *apart* from their
values, interests or 'attitudes'. He assumes that truth is that
knowledge of the world which would be cleansed of the impurities
presumably brought by men's presence . . . Those who believe that
their selves are not worth knowing, or are already known, can only
make history with a false consciousness . . . Knowledge is not
simply a hammer with which to make the world yield; knowledge
of the world and of self-in-the-world is an aspect of our very
humanness.

(Gouldner 1972: 87, 124)

If we are to restore a vision of the self-in-the-world as an aspect
of our very humanness' *without* losing grasp of the integrity of
difference and diversity we need to understand what has made such
a vision so difficult for us today – this means coming to terms with,
as Weber did, the relationship of Protestantism to the spirit of
capitalism. Traditions of post-structuralism have also made this form
of self-knowledge hard for us to value. Recasting the terms of social
theory is not something we can accomplish as an act of will, but is
something that we might be able to begin as we turn to explore some
of its historical and cultural sources.

Chapter 4

Authority

CAPITALISM AND RATIONALITY

We need to be aware of some of the implicit Christian sources of the morality and politics of capitalist society. These influences have been largely submerged through our self-conception of living in a secular society. Within liberal moral culture, we are encouraged to think of our moral and political ideas as matters of individual opinion and reasoning. This can make it more difficult to appreciate the social and historical conditions for the moral ideas we so easily take for granted as common sense.

Gramsci can help us towards a different kind of awareness and self-consciousness which appreciate the significance of a particular kind of historical investigation of culture:

> In acquiring one's conception of the world one always belongs to a particular grouping which is that of all the social elements which share the same mode of thinking and acting. We are all conformists of some conformism or other, always man-in-the-mass or collective man. The question is this: of what historical type is the conformism, the mass humanity to which one belongs? ... The starting-point of critial elaboration is the consciousness of what one really is, and is 'knowing thyself' as a product of the historical process to date which has deposited in you an infinity of traces, without leaving an inventory.
>
> (Gramsci 1971: 324, note 1)

In its own way this helps explain the importance of Max Weber's *The Protestant Ethic and the Spirit of Capitalism* (1930). Weber partly wrote this as a critique of orthodox notions of historical materialism and of a form of economic determinism. Rather than treating it as a text essentially antagonistic to Marxism, we should realise that Marx would also have questioned the orthodox version of his work.[1] Certainly Weber helps us challenge liberal self-conceptions which think of the structure of social relations as growing out of individual moral decisions.

Weber understood how capitalist society presents itself to people as an 'unalterable order of things' which seems part of a common-sense 'normality' we are brought up to take very much for granted:

> Still less, naturally, do we maintain that a conscious acceptance of these ethical maxims on the part of the individuals, entrepreneurs or labourers in modern capitalistic enterprises, is a condition of the further existence of present-day capitalism. The capitalistic economy of the present day is an immense cosmos into which the individual is born, and which presents itself to him, at least as an individual, as an unalterable order of things in which he must live. It forces the individual, in so far as he is involved in the system of market relationships, to conform to capitalistic rules of action. The manufacturer who in the long run acts counter to these norms, will just as inevitably be eliminated from the economic scene as the worker who cannot or will not adapt himself to them will be thrown into the streets without a job.
>
> (Weber 1930: 54–5)

Weber concludes that the capitalism of today 'has come to dominate economic life' and 'educates and selects the economic subjects which it needs'. This in turn helps us understand the context in which Weber investigates 'the social ethic of capitalist culture'. Without ignoring the enormous significance of changes in capitalist society, Weber helps us to an understanding of fundamental features of a culture we so readily see in historical terms. He helps us *ground* our individual and personal experience as a social and historical experience we share with others, without reducing this experience.

Weber helps us understand forms of subordination and self-denial we take very much for granted within liberal morality while assuming that we are free and equal rational beings able to determine our own lives. Social life within capitalist society is not organised around the satisfaction and nourishment of human needs, even if we are often misled about this through the utilitarian idea that production is organised around consumer preferences. So when Weber helps us think about the 'irrationality' of capitalist production he is helping us to a deeper critique, though one he fails himself to develop.

Since Weber also seemed to believe in the inevitability of capitalist rationalisation reorganising most areas of human life, this remains one of the abiding contradictions in his writings:

> In fact, the *summum bonum* of this ethic, the earning of more and more money, combined with the strict avoidance of all spontaneous

enjoyment of life, is above all completely devoid of any eudaemon-
istic, not to say hedonistic, admixture. It is thought of so purely
as an end in itself, that from the point of view of the happiness
of, or utility to, the single individual, it appears entirely transcenden-
tal and absolutely irrational. Man is dominated by the making of
money, by acquisition as the ultimate purpose of his life. Economic
acquisition is no longer subordinated to man as the means for the
satisfaction of his material needs. This reversal of what we should
call the natural relationship, so irrational from a naïve point of view,
is evidently as definitely a leading principle of capitalism as it is
foreign to all peoples not under a capitalistic influence. At the same
time it expresses a type of feeling which is closely connected with
certain religious ideas. If we thus ask, *why* should 'money be made
out of men', Benjamin Franklin . . . answers . . . with a quotation
from the Bible, which his strict Calvinist father drummed into him
again and again in his youth: 'Seest thou a man diligent in his
business? He shall stand before Kings' (Prov. 22.29). The earning
of money within the modern economic order is, so long as it is done
legally, the result and the expression of virtue and proficiency in
a calling.

(Ibid.)

If we are less conscious and aware of these religious sources, we can
still recognise large parts of ourselves especially as men and what we
have been brought up to be in this picture. It is hardly surprising that
since male identities are largely defined within the public sphere of
work and men identify so strongly with individual success say, 'as
an end in itself', they lose touch with their individual wants and needs.
We readily assume that 'success' and 'individual achievement' will
bring 'happiness' and we focus our energies in these directions, barely
aware of the distance we move from a living sense of our individual
wants and needs.

Along with Kant's identification of human dignity and moral worth
with a moral law that is discerned through reason alone, Weber's
discussion of rationalisation helps us understand some of the other
processes through which individuality has become an abstract quality
in a liberal moral culture. Talk of individuality has become increasingly rhetorical and meaningless, since it is no longer grounded in
people's sense of their particular wants and needs.

LIBERALISM AND INDIVIDUALITY

John Stuart Mill recognised this deep contradiction between the self-
conceptions of liberal society, of individuals being free to make

individual choices, and the lived reality of conformism which is a denial
in practice of this very individuality. As the processes Mill identified
continued, liberal theory was bound to become increasingly rhetorical,
since it could no longer illuminate and express the everyday realities
of people's lives.

Mill realised that the real tensions being created in capitalist society
concerned not the lack of self-control individuals have, but the lack
of control individuals have over their lives. Mill was aware, as was
Weber, of the enormous dominance of social morality and social relations of power, over individual lives:

> Society has now fairly got the better of individuality, and the danger
> which threatens human nature is not the excess, but the deficiency,
> of personal impulses and preferences.
>
> (Mill 1964: 190)

Mill goes on to explain what he means by this:

> I do not mean that they choose what is customary in preference
> to what suits their own inclination. It does not occur to them to
> have any inclination, except what is customary. Thus the mind itself
> is bowed to the yoke: even in what people do for pleasure, confor-
> mity is the first thing thought of; they like in crowds; they exercise
> choice only among things commonly done: peculiarity of taste,
> eccentricity of conduct, are shunned equally with crimes; until by
> dint of not following their own nature they have no nature to follow:
> their human capacities are withered and starved: they become
> incapable of any strong wishes or native pleasures, and are generally
> without either opinions or feelings of home growth, or properly
> their own. Now is this, or is it not, the desirable condition of human
> nature!
>
> (Ibid.)

This is echoed somewhat paradoxically in the kind of detailed critique
of the personal and moral relations Marcuse was to hint at nearly a
century later in his *One Dimensional Man*.

This insight into the workings of individuality has existed as a strand
in liberal social theory since Rousseau's early essays but it has
often been silenced because it has rarely been appreciated that, far
from guaranteeing individual autonomy and independence, liberalism
has often left us with an abstract and attenuated conception of the
individual. Mill recognises the devastating truth that 'by dint of not
following their own nature they have no nature to follow: their human
capacities are withered and starved.

But Mill does not help us challenge enough the moral and political
relations of power which sustain these conceptions and which often

render liberal self-understandings abstract and rhetorical. Mill does not seem to recognise, as Weber does, the centrality of these moral relations to the workings of capitalist society, so he cannot appreciate just how much he is challenging prevailing social practices. If he does recognise a challenge to the fundamental conceptions of Calvinism, he does not grasp, as Weber does, how integral these have become.

Mill is clear about his direct challenge to the Calvinist notion of the 'desirable condition of human nature'.

> It is no, on the Calvinistic theory. According to that, the one great offence of man is self-will. All the good of which humanity is capable is comprised in obedience. You have no choice: thus you must do, and not otherwise: 'whatever is not a duty, is a sin'. Human nature being radically corrupt, there is no redemption for anyone until human nature is killed within him. To one holding this theory of life, crushing out of any of the human faculties, capacities and susceptibilities, is no evil: man needs no capacity, but that of surrendering himself to the will of God; and if he uses any of his faculties for any other purpose but to that supposed will more effectively, he is better without them.
>
> (Ibid.)

There is a powerful contradiction between the moral inheritance of a Calvinist tradition which works to negate people's own feelings, hopes and desires in preparing them to subordinate themselves to an external authority, and a liberalism that is ready to acknowledge that 'in the last analysis' people know themselves best and have to take responsibility for their individual lives.

The continuing influence of Kant, as I have argued in *Kant, Respect and Injustice* (Seidler 1986), determines the ways we learn to manage this contradiction. Kant maintains the authority of the external moral law, while giving a way for individuals themselves to validate this authority through the workings of the categorical imperative. A Kantian inheritance has also been important in legitimating the autonomy and independence of law within liberal society as the laws of a democracy which people have been able to legislate for themselves as citizens. This helps us believe in ourselves as self-determining rational beings free to make our own lives.

Mill was able, for a time at least, to focus liberal social theory upon the *lived reality* of the moral relations of capitalism. He was not prepared to take liberal notions at face value, but wanted to investigate the processes of invalidation of the crucial liberal idea that individuals should be left alone to develop their own potentialities and capacities. Mill knew that it was not enough to guarantee to individuals the right of not being interfered with by others if people were to be genuinely free to develop their capacities and potentialities. At some level this is a vision he seems to share with Marx.

Mill at least recognised the importance of challenging the prevailing moral conceptions of Calvinism, since these inevitably worked to undermine people's belief in their own powers, capacities and needs. He did also question the self-conception of people as rational, when this involved an implicit denial of their desires, emotions and feelings. Mill's *Autobiography* shows how deeply injured he was personally, through the narrow rationalist education he received at the hands of his father. Mill learnt a lesson that much Marxist theory has still to learn:

> I, for the first time, gave its proper place, among the prime necessities of human well-being, to the internal culture of the individual. I ceased to attach almost exclusive importance to the ordering of outward circumstances.[2]
>
> (Mill 1971: 111)

An Enlightenment tradition calls for a rational reconstruction of society in the name of reason. This prepares the ground for the identification of progress and civilisation with science and technology, the rationality of which we have to accept if we are not to stand in the way of progress. The consequences that flow from progress being identified with the control and domination of nature are rendered invisible within the 'common sense' of modernity. Somehow the reconstruction of society is in the fulfilment of some 'higher goal' that comes to have a reality independently of the quality of individual lives.

This goes back to the tradition of Plato's *Republic*, in which the question of the just ordering of society is taken to be prior to and independent of the fulfilment of individual lives. This is partly because it is not possible for individuals to treat each other justly if they live in an unjust society. Plato might have been right that the conception of justice cannot be generated through people learning to live individually just lives, but this does *not* mean that a just ordering of society can be legislated by reason alone.[3]

These thoughts can help us question the prevailing liberal idea that morality can be centred around the Kantian question of what an individual ought to do. This is influenced, as is clear in Kant, by the Protestant conception that the individual is working out his or her own individual salvation, in a relationship with God. So it is that a concern with morality rests firmly with individuals themselves and is separated from consideration of justice and equality as they are conceived in the distributive terms of social and political theory. Modernity has in large part been defined through a separation of morality from politics.

But if Plato, within the tradition of Greek thought, challenges the separation of morality from politics, he can think that justice has to do with the rational organisation of society because he could assume, in a way that has become difficult for us, that divisions within the city somehow reflect similar divisions within the individual soul. This means that justice was not being grasped in distributive terms alone, independently of his understanding of what is involved in people living fuller, happier and richer lives.[4]

AUTHORITY AND RATIONALISM

Since the Enlightenment, Western thought has separated questions of epistemology from politics, especially in our thinking that 'people are social products' and that if you change society people will change. A social theory which believes human nature can never be trusted and that people's wants and desires can only lead them morally astray, will easily think society has to be changed *for* people. This notion has deep roots in both liberal and Marxist social theory. J.S. Mill characterised this well, as the 'theory of dependence and protection':

> According to the former theory, the lot of the poor, in all things which affect them collectively, should be regulated *for* them, not *by* them. They should not be required or encouraged to think for themselves, or give to their own reflection or forecast an influential voice in the determination of their destiny ... The relation between rich and poor, according to this theory (a theory also applied to the relation between men and women) should only be partly authoritative; it should be amiable, moral and sentimental: affectionate tutelage on the one side, respectful and grateful deference on the other.
>
> (Mill 1985: 119)

Within Western philosophical culture both the rationalist tradition and the empiricist tradition can help prepare the terms of this subordination. Initially it was the radical impulse in Locke's writings against inherited privileges which developed the idea of people as blank slates waiting to be filled. So human nature was to be formed through the imprint of external forces.

This radical idea was somehow also used to establish the essentially authoritarian idea that children needed to be 'trained' and 'disciplined', since otherwise they would go wild. This could also be brought into line with the Kantian tradition which argued that people could only become moral if they listened to the authority of the moral law and struggled against the influence of their evil natures.

This Kantian tradition could at least recognise some inner tension and struggle within the individual, even if it legitimated denial and repression. In Durkheim's hands social theory was to take pride in the externality of social rules, putting greater pressure on individuals adapting to social rules which now themselves presented a higher vision of morality. Society had itself taken the place of reason and the moral law. Society was to be the source of moral authority itself.[5]

A rationalist tradition within modernity can be defined by its categorical distinction between reason and nature. Reason alone is a source of freedom and morality and means that people need to be saved from themselves, from the grip of their own natures. People cannot be trusted. Reason gave access to a 'higher truth' which had to be realised in social relations if people were to be free. In the end the dangers became clear as this was to take a distorted historical form in the self-righteousness of Robespierre or the tyranny of Stalinism.

This extreme form of rationalism, which seems to allow the legislation of a single path of truth and freedom, has often reproduced itself tragically in different forms within revolutionary traditions. An orthodox Marxism has in so many ways taken to heart a Western rationalist tradition and its identification of science with reason, progress and the domination of nature. If Marx is to be listened to and not discredited then any tradition of Marxism embodied in a sense of history as a source of truth and authority, has to be carefully investigated.

The Frankfurt School developed a critique of this Enlightenment tradition and the ways it encouraged the identification of progress with the domination of nature through the rule of science and technology. But the Frankfurt School failed to develop a full enough critique of the rationalist tradition, particularly the implications for questions of gender, sexuality, race and ethnicity that flowed from the systematic devaluation of nature and emotional life. They were too deeply influenced by rationalism themselves, wanting to investigate the irrationality of capitalist society, in terms of a broader vision of reason. But the Frankfurt School helps us to at least grasp how the realisation of reason becomes accepted as a 'higher ideal' which has to be striven for. Like Weber they had also learnt something from Nietzsche.[6]

They help analyse the essential contradiction of a tradition which is both democratic in its conception that we are all 'rational creatures', while at the same time preparing for the domination of instrumental reason in the idea that, if we are rational then we should be ready to accept the dictates of reason or the moral law. So it is that reason or the moral law can become an instrument of domination, when they legitimate the idea that somehow people can be 'forced to be free'.

For the Frankfurt School this was the iron fist concealed in the tolerance of liberalism. In Marcuse's terms, it establishes the limits of pure tolerance.[7]

This rationalistic tradition has influenced both liberal and Marxist theory in a pervasive way. This is why it is important to recognise its continuing hold over our thinking and feeling. It easily identifies 'freedom' in formal terms with living within a market economy and democratic social order, thereby separating it from our thinking about the quality and meaning of individual lives. We lose a sense of the importance of people asserting and empowering themselves as individuals.

We easily dismiss such thinking as 'selfish' or 'self-indulgent' because it refers to the individual rather than to collective existence. This is a damaging misconception even in Marx's terms since, already in the *German Ideology* of 1845/6, Marx wrote that:

> The proletarians, if they are to assert themselves as individuals . . . must overthrow the state.
>
> (Marx and Engels 1976: 80)

Marx recognised that people have to involve themselves in a struggle against the prevailing structures of power and dominance to assert themselves as individuals.

But as long as individuals are forced to live within these structures, their assertion is bound to be partial, even compromised. It might involve, for example, the recognition of a young worker on the assembly line of a car plant, realising how much better he feels if he shouts back at a foreman who is on his back to 'Fuck off', rather than swallowing it all and going back with a stomach ache or taking it out on his wife and children when he gets home. But people are often forced to endure indignities because they realise that if they speak up or protect in many situations, they will lose their jobs and so their very livelihood.[8]

If we can grasp these structures of power and dominance as social relations, we can begin to see how, for instance, the power of workers in a car plant is reflected in *how* they assert themselves against authority. If the company does not have orders to fulfil, workers are in a relatively weak position, especially if the company is looking to rid itself of people. The collective strength of a group of workers is also reflected in the self-confidence and assertiveness of individual workers.

This also relates to the freedom individual workers can feel while locked into these class, race and gender relations of power and subordination. We need to understand how individual self-confidence and collective strength grow in relation to each other rather than being

necessarily opposed. Too often we assume that a language of individualism has always to be replaced by a language of class for socialist
conceptions of freedom to develop. It has been a cruel and damaging
irony to realise how often the Left has readily sacrificed the notion
of 'freedom' as 'bourgeois' without fully grasping the significance of
the long and better historical struggles for these very rights and
freedoms.

Socialist thought has too often largely remained trapped within a
rationalist tradition. We need to recognise the importance and the limits
of this tradition, especially as we learn to appreciate differences of
gender, race and sexual identities. This involves a renewed recognition of the importance of a language of democracy, which was so
central within the movements in Eastern Europe against communist
rule. At the same time we need to realise how, in liberal moral theory,
democracy depends upon people being recognised as 'equal' only in
their capacity for rationality. It has been blind for too long to issues
of diversity and this is why it is largely expressed in terms of the
abstract rights of citizenship, since this is where, in the public realm,
people are called upon to use their rationality.

The recent historical experience of Portugal in 1976, Spain in 1978
and Eastern Europe and the Confederation of Independant States in
1987 and 1989 showed how people, freed from the controls of
authoritarian rule of long standing would rally around the institutions
of representative democracy. It was always damaging for the Left
simply to attack democracy as an instrument of capitalist rule. People
who had been silenced for so long valued the opportunities of
democracy, however limited. It was the Left which had still to learn
lessons about the meaning of freedom and democracy.[9]

AUTHORITY AND EXPERIENCE

In a very real sense the historical experience and traditions of the
Left have undermined our trust in democracy. The dominant Leninist
traditions in the Left still believe that the revolution is to be made
through 'correct leadership'. But we rarely recognise that it is
because rationalist traditions have been assimilated so uncritically
within orthodox Marxism that 'leaderships' can assume the authority of revolutionary theory to legitimate their assumption that they
'know best'.

The theoretical traditions of Althusserian Marxism have worked to
legitimate this instrumentalism long after its demise and pushed theory
further from the needs, aspirations and hopes of ordinary people.
Gramsci has warned us of this intellectualism:

The popular element 'feels' but does not always know or understand; the intellectual element 'knows' but does not always understand and in particular does not feel. The two extremes are therefore pedantry and philistinism on the one hand and blind passion on the other . . . The intellectual's error consists in believing that one can know without understanding and even more without feeling and being impassioned: in other words that the intellectual can be an intellectual if distinct and separate from the people-nation, i.e. without feeling the elementary passions of the people.

(Gramsci 1971: 418)

Gramsci had learnt from Hegal to challenge strains of rationalism that feed an instrumental attitude towards people, seeing them as objects needing to be shaped. Revolutionary theory, for Gramsci, was not simply to present people with truths they are forced to accept, but involved an inner transformation in the ways people think and feel.

This is made clear in Gramsci's critique of the underlying premises and conception of Bukharin's *Theory of Historical Materialism: A Popular Manual of Marxist Sociology*:

The first mistake of the Popular Manual is that it starts, at least implicitly, from the assumption that the elaboration of an original philosophy of the popular masses is to be opposed to the great systems of traditional philosophy and the religion of the leaders of the clergy – i.e. the conception of the world of the intellectuals of high culture. In reality these systems are unknown to the multitude and have no direct influence on its way of thinking and acting. This does not mean of course that they are altogether without influence but it is influence of a different kind. These systems influence the popular masses as an external political force, an element of cohesive force exercised by the ruling classes and therefore an element of subordination to the external hegemony. This limits the original thought of the popular masses in a negative direction, without having the positive effect of a vital ferment of interior transformation of what the masses think in an embryonic and chaotic form about the world and life. The principle elements of common sense are provided by religion, and consequently the relationship between common sense and religion is much more intimate than that between common sense and the philosophical systems of the intellectuals.

(Ibid.: 419–20)

Gramsci has restored the moral vision of Marx's work through helping restore our sense of people as subjects within the historical process, rather than simply as objects to be 'formed'. This should be a fundamental point of demarcation with positivist social theory as well as with aspects of Marx's theory which have tended to see people as objects to be produced in the image of the larger society. If Marxism has been too ready to prove itself in terms of a positivist tradition, we should not dismiss other strands within an idealist tradition which have been emancipatory. Often these are dismissed as 'individualistic' without an investigation of different forms of individualism.[10] Marx was aware of how class relations of power in capitalist society prevent the growth and development of a creative individuality, which could supposedly only come into its own within a socialist society.

FORMS OF INDIVIDUALITY

Socialism, rather than being a denial of individuality, is a critique of the particular forms of possessive and competitive individualism reproduced within capitalist society. This involves the creation of different conceptions of individuality, rather than their automatic negation, as structuralist Marxism has tended to assume. Again this is something we can learn from Gramsci:

> From the 'philosophical' point of view, what is unsatisfactory in Catholicism is the fact that, in spite of everything, it insists on putting the cause of evil in the individual man himself, or in other words that it conceives of man as a defined and limited individual. It could be said of all hitherto existing philosophies that they reproduce this position of Catholicism, that they conceive of man as an individual limited to his own individuality and of the spirit as being this individuality. It is on this point that it is necessary to reform the concept of man.
>
> (Ibid.: 352)

This is an insight which Althusser has falsely exploited to mount a general critique of the importance of individuality and subjectivity. In this way he has reproduced the obliteration of individuality, and its subordination to the larger structures of society, that has always characterised the positivist tradition of Comte and Durkheim. He reproduces in Marxist structuralism a theory of modes of production, not a theory of human emancipation. Gramsci's 'reform' of 'the concept of man' moves in a very different direction:

> I mean that one must conceive of man as a series of active relationships (a process) in which individuality, though perhaps the most important, is not, however, the only element to be taken into account. The humanity which is reflected in each individuality is

composed of various elements: 1. the individual; 2. other men; 3. the natural world. But the latter two elements are not as simple as they might appear. The individual does not enter into relations with other men by juxtaposition, but organically, in as much, that is, as he belongs to organic entities which range from the simplest to the most complex. Thus man does not enter into relations with the natural world, but actively, by means of work and technique. Further: these relations are not mechanical. They are active and conscious. They correspond to the greater or lesser degree of understanding that each man has of them. So one could say that each one of us changes himself, modifies himself to the extent that he changes and modifies the complex relations of which he is the hub. In this sense the real philosopher is, and cannot be other than, the politician, the active man who modifies the environment, understanding by environment the *ensemble* of relations which each of us enters to take part in. If one's own individuality is the *ensemble* of these relations, to create one's own personality means to acquire consciousness of them and to modify one's own personality means to modify the *ensemble* of these relations.

(Ibid.: 352)

Gramsci is challenging the very reduction of individuality to a mechanical conception of social relations that we find in Althusser. His understanding is deeply informed by Hegel, rather than presenting a break with his writing. He sees people in the process of becoming:

That 'human nature' is the 'complex of social relations' is the most satisfactory answer, because it includes the idea of becoming (man 'becomes', he changes continuously with the changing of social relations) and because it denies 'man in general'.

(Ibid.: 355)

Gramsci's recognition that 'the individual does not enter into relations with other men by juxtaposition, but organically.' amounts also to a critique of the processes of emancipation and freedom at the critical edge of liberal social theory.

If some of the liberal insights of John Stuart Mill can help us to avoid the reduction of individuality we find in positivism, and in orthodox Marxist writing, they often remain rhetorical and idealistic in their understanding of the social relations of gender, class and sexual and racial power which constitute determinants on this process of becoming. This is something Mill was increasingly to appreciate later in his life. In *On Liberty* he already has an important insight about human nature:

Human nature is not a machine to be built after a model, and set to do exactly the work prescribed for it, but a tree, which requires to grow and develop itself on all sides, according to the tendency of the inward forces which make it a living thing.

(Mill 1964: 188)

What are the conditions required for this growth? Liberalism has tended to think that people should be left alone to pursue their own ends. This recognises something important about the discoveries individuals have to make for themselves concerning the sources of their fulfilment and joy. But it does not appreciate how class, gender, ethnic and sexual relations of power within society determine the lives of individuals especially those in a position of powerlessness and subordination.

What is more, as I have argued in *Kant, Respect and Injustice* (Seidler 1986), it does not recognise the diversity of social relations people need to develop with others for them to be able to grow and develop their own individuality. This has to do with changed visions of authority as people distrust the traditional forms of authority and learn to trust their own judgement and discernment. It also involves an understanding of the *integrity* of differences so that we do not assume that there is a single path that people follow. In their own time people come to terms with the issues they need to deal with.

FREEDOM AND EMOTIONAL LIFE

Mill understood that the deeper workings of rationalism within a liberal moral culture were crucial. He introduces us to a fundamental issue which needs a more central place in our thinking about the meaning of human emancipation:

To a certain extent it is admitted that our understanding should be our own: but there is not the same willingness to admit that our desires and impulses should be our own likewise; or that to possess impulses of our own, and of any strength, is anything but a peril and a snare. Yet desires and impulses are as much a part of a perfect human being as beliefs and restraints; and strong impulses are only perilous when not properly balanced; when one set of aims and inclinations is developed into strength, while others, which ought to co-exist with them, remain weak and inactive. It is not because a man's desires are strong that they act ill; it is because their consciences are weak. There is no natural connection between strong impulses and a weak conscience. The natural connection is the other way. To say that one person's desires and feelings are stronger and more various than those of another, is merely to say that he has more of the raw material of human nature, and is therefore capable, perhaps of more evil, but certainly of more good ... A person whose desires and impulses are his own – are the expression of his own nature, as it has been developed and modified by his own culture – is said to have a character.

(Ibid.: 188)

This offers a fuller sense of the importance of emotional life in terms of what it means for people to have control over their own lives. It carries a truth that seems to resonate with some of Marx's early insights in the *Paris Manuscripts* of 1844. It is a challenge to the Kantian ethical tradition that has expressed itself in the 'common-sense' notions of duty and 'self-control' and which has provided the dominant moral psychology for both liberalism and orthodox Marxism.

Not only is this an insight that helps us rethink a relationship between reason and emotional life, but it also encourages us to think about freedom and empowerment in quite different terms, allowing us to recognise that individuality and autonomy have as much to do with recognising the integrity of our emotional feelings as they have with our thoughts and opinions. Mill introduces a language of *balance* between the different aspects of our being that enriches our conceptions of human nature and personal identity, but it also shows within Mill's break with liberalism a different conception of human liberation.

But Mill does not go on to investigate the sources of rationalism within a liberal culture, though he does make us aware of some of the consequences. He helps us identify the contradictions in a liberal moral culture between allowing that 'our understanding should be our own', and a positivist tradition wanting to assert the independence and authority of 'knowledge'. This is similar to a contradiction we have already identified in Kant's conception of morality, between moral law assumed to exist independently of human experience, and liberal conceptions of freedom whereby individuals are given a sense of their 'moral freedom' as their capacity to discover the dictates of moral law through the workings of the categorical imperative. This helps produce the contradictory character of liberal freedom, expressed in our readiness to submit to an external authority which has some how been presented as 'ours'.

The Enlightenment conception of reason declared that the 'morally right' could be discovered through the independent workings of the faculty of reason. We are brought up to take this very much for granted as the 'common sense' of a liberal moral culture, without recognising how this implicitly involves a form of *self-denial* through a subordination of our wants, feelings, emotions, desires and inclinations. This is why 'there is not the same willingness to admit that our desires and impulses should be our own likewise; or that to possess impulses of our own, and of any strength, is anything but peril and a snare'.

This is not simply a matter of changing our beliefs, but calls for some form of inner transformation in the way that we think and feel about ourselves. It has much deeper roots in a liberal capitalist culture than Mill helps us to grasp. Since Descartes we are very much brought up to identify our 'selves' with our 'rationalities'. Within modernity this has deeply informed both philosophical and popular conceptions of personal identity. In a very real sense within a rationalist tradition we can imagine our personal identities to be constituted by our thoughts, beliefs and memories. This is the 'higher self', or the 'true self'.

We learn to prove our dignity and moral worth, especially as men, by being prepared to subordinate our wants and desires, which are easily labelled 'selfish' or 'self-indulgent', to do what we ought to do. The conception of 'rational action' we are brought up to assume within a liberal moral culture involves setting ourselves certain 'goals' or 'ends' which come to provide the meaning of our actions. So we are often doing things because it is the 'right thing to do' or because it is 'expected of us', with little sense of what we want to do. As Mill has already reminded us 'they exercise choice only among things commonly done . . . until by dint of not following their own nature they have no nature to follow: their human capacities are withered and starved'.

This produces a very different set of moral concerns from those usually reflected in our moral and social theory. Mill helps us challenge the self-conception which haunts liberal morality, of people as being constantly overcome by strong feelings and desires. He makes us aware of a strong culture of moralism and selfishness. He helps us think in different ways from the prevailing discussions aroung post-modernity about the nature of the fragmentation of human experience. We learn to ask different questions as we link fragmentation of issues of self-denial. Thinking about self-denial can be tricky because we cannot often recognise ourselves within this characterisation. The language of wants and desires is so integral to the utilitarian tradi-tion that we easily think this does not refer to us. This relates to how understandings of 'wants' and 'desires' come to be reformulated within a liberal moral culture to refer to the 'ends' or 'goals' of action. This means, for instance, that, especially as middle-class men, we are encouraged to identify 'happiness' with 'individual achievement' and 'success'. We think of happiness as something that has to be 'worked for' or 'sacrificed for' if it is going to be 'worth having'.

DISDAIN OF NATURE

We grasp the character of these formulations, when we recognise how they are built upon an assumed subordination of our 'natures'. At another level our experience within a rationalist tradition is being organised around the assumption that when we act rationally we are acting against our 'animal' natures. A sense of hierarchy and superiority is written into the heart of this, since our identification with our 'rationalities' automatically involves us feeling superior to our 'natures'. There is, particularly for a dominant masculinity identified with self-control, implicit hierarchy built into our sense that 'self-control' involves control as a form of domination of our desires, wants and feelings. Supposedly only this allows us to do what is expected of us. This involves acting externally, in the sense of meeting the requirements of external authorities, be they parents, employers or teachers.

In the very self-conception of rational masculinities within modernity is hidden an implicit assertion of *superiority* over animals, and over the 'animal self' within us. This also works to devalue the experience of women and people of colour, Jews, gays and lesbians – people who were deemed in their different ways to be closer to nature and so excluded from the magic circle of humanity as this was redrawn within the terms of an Enlightenment modernity.

Within modernity claims to 'equality' as people are built upon our 'rationality'; and thereby assume the subordination of our wants, desires, emotions and feelings. So we prove our 'equality' with others through being ready to disdain our natures. This builds a deep fragmentation into our experience and into our relationship with the natural world. In identifying with our rationality and disdaining our natures, we almost have to rise above ourselves. For women, Jews, Blacks, Asians, gays and lesbians, who were excluded, this meant having constantly to prove that they were 'other' than they were – that they would be 'civilised' within the dominant terms of the West. This is *not* to argue against reason, but against a tradition of rationalism that would automatically set reason against our natures.

This fragmentation finds clear expression in Kant's ethical writings. We are encouraged to identify our very humanity with our reason and morality and so with controlling and subordinating 'natures', as these can only lead us astray from acting out of a sense of moral duty. This notion structures our very sense of identity. We are brought up assuming that individual dignity and moral worth can only be established through the workings of our reason and that this works independently of our wants, desires, emotions and feelings.

So in asserting our humanity, we find ourselves separated from and set against our 'natures'. Though cast in masculinist terms it also sets the terms for 'others' to judge and evaluate their experience. This produces a distrust of our feelings and desires, which we do our best to repress and conceal lest they threaten the image we have of ourselves. This is highlighted in the moral history of the notion of 'self-control' and the fear of 'losing control', within a liberal moral culture.[11]

In a similar sense to the ways reason is conceived as an independent faculty, set apart from our inner 'natures', we are also set apart from external 'nature'. As we are locked into a struggle within ourselves against the threat of our emotions and feelings, especially as heterosexual men, so we are involved in a struggle to dominate and control the unruly and uncivilised forces of nature. So that rather than learning about ourselves from a position within the natural world, we prove ourselves to be 'civilised' through our control and domination of nature. Since the Scientific Revolution of the seventeenth century, this has shown itself in the self-conception of science as involving the increasing control and subordination of nature. So it is that in Western culture, reason, progress and science have been set against the domination of nature. In the same way as nature is conceived of as 'unruly', 'chaotic', 'immoral', so too is that part of us which is said to be our 'nature'.[12]

Nature simply presents us with chaotic feelings and desires, and it is assumed that only the external intervention of reason can bring 'order' and 'discipline' into this chaos. The assumption is that we would otherwise be left as slaves to our natures, bereft of a freedom identified exclusively with reason, as our desires and feelings would be pushing us in whatever direction they wanted to go. Mill challenges this Kantian notion head on when he asserts that 'desires and feelings are as much part of a perfect human being as beliefs and restraints; and strong impulses are only perilous when not properly balanced'. But unfortunately this remains an insight that Mill never really develops. It is part of the contradictory inheritance that he leaves us with.

Chapter 5

Needs and desires

MORALISM AND PERSONAL LIFE

Mill is still helpful in challenging basic Kantian assumptions embedded in the ways we think and feel about ourselves within a liberal moral culture. But he does not grasp the *difficulties* of restoring trust and confidence in our own natures, unable as he is to connect his insight to the workings of relationships of power and subordination or to develop alternative visions of personal and political change.

This is something socialist critiques have often barely been able to recognise themselves, trapped as they have often been within the same Kantian moralism. Socialism has too easily presented itself in rationalist terms as an 'alternative ideal' which has to be worked for, involving a similar sacrifice and self-denial. Too often the socialist vision becomes a distant image, rather than something that can be lived in our relations with others. The Protestant ethic becomes assimilated into the everyday practice of 'political work', and similar criteria of 'success' are invoked.

If the politics of the New Left were important in questioning the distinction between 'private' and 'public', showing how forms of domination and control are equally being worked out in our private lives, it too easily replaced one abstract and moralistic code of behaviour with another. So 'ownership', 'possessiveness', 'exclusiveness', 'jealousy', 'individualism' were all identified within the libertarian politics in the 1970s as symptoms of bourgeois life we were unwittingly living out. These were to be replaced through an act of will which unknowingly reflected a Kantian moral psychology, by a contrasting morality which emphasised the importance of 'equality', 'community', 'independence', 'sharing' and 'collectivity'. But too often what have become known as the new social movements have been locked into their own moralism and dualities, as they hoped not simply for a new theorisation of social relations but their realisation as everyday practice. In a relatively short and intense period in libertarian politics of the 1970s, experiences involving not only joy and pleasure, but also pain and disappointment, were to force people to rethink the terms of socialist politics.[1]

Unfortunately the libertarian Left had enormous energy and hope, but little understanding and experience of the difficult process of personal and political changing. We reproduced what we knew unwittingly, which were Kantian traditions of moralism that remained fundamentally unquestioned because they lay in all of us. This had left us with little relationship to our ongoing emotions, feelings and desires and often with a brittle and externalised relationship to self.

It is worth asking why the generation of the late 1960s which was the generation born at the end of the war, was so susceptible to feelings of guilt and moralism. Was this because we were brought up in a period of such high and artificial hopes? Why did we expect so much from ourselves, and how could we at the same time be so hard on ourselves? These questions are worth asking, since they marked the historical experience of a generation. The rationalist tradition itself created and fosters a certain form of wilfulness. We easily assumed that if we wanted to change the ways we were, we could do this solely through effort and acts of *will* and without attention to the historical sources of our feelings.

It was easy to reproduce versions of the Calvinistic ethic in which it was our supposedly 'bourgeois' feelings of 'possessiveness', 'exclusiveness' and 'competitiveness' that had to be killed within us. This was a different version of the idea that human nature was radically corrupt, even though we thought it could easily be saved if we worked hard enough at it. This helps explain the peculiar combination of self-denial, living up to these high standards we set ourselves, masculinity and the bouts of Saturday-night hedonism. There were many moments of intense joy, but also times when we were very hard on ourselves. At some level the latter were often fuelled by a feeling of self-hatred and a lack of self-acceptance in which we did not like the way we were, and wanted very much to be different.[2]

The women's movement learnt to use consciousness-raising as a way of exploring the structures of feeling that women, at least, were living through. It provided a space within which the historical sources of these feelings could be grappled with as well as the contemporary relationships that sustained them. It gave women a context in which they could learn greater self-acceptance as they recognised that their individual feelings were shared by others. It also provided a source of support and solidarity which strengthened women to make changes in their relationships and living situations.

As men we had learnt to identify with a dominant form of masculinity which meant feeling deeply competitive, ambitious, jealous and possessive, especially within white middle-class, heterosexual forms of masculinity. At some level there was an understanding that these values did not bring the happiness they promised. They would more often bring much frustration, hard work and endless hopes, but little fulfilment. This was something that many people had learnt from watching their parents lives slip away. But locked into competitive relationships with other men it felt threatening to share our vulnerability. It was too easy to conceal our difficulties and to continue feeling, in a very different historical context, that we were unacceptable as we were, and that somehow we had to change.

This pervasive belief, which is never far from the surface of our public male identity and has an important source in Protestantism, that at some level, we are 'useless', 'worthless', 'inadequate' or 'unlovable' is reproduced and so carefully manipulated within the competitive male institutions. Far from the conservative idea that this helps the development of men's best qualities and capacities, competitiveness often plagues men with feelings of fear and inadequacy that are never far from the surface. This was part of the New Left's critique of competitiveness. Even if you have been 'successful' you are susceptible to feeling either that 'you should have done better' or that 'others are better than you'. At some level it is the insecurity encouraged by the Protestant conception of the corruptness of our natures that feeds our moralism. This partly explains how, especially as men, we can be so hard on ourselves.

MORALISM AND CRITICAL THEORY

Why has it been so difficult for Marxist writings to question this moralism? The Frankfurt School recognised the importance of this question. Horkheimer thought that the stress on labour within Marxist work had unwittingly produced an ascetic ideology. In *Dämmerung* he wrote:

> To make labour into a transcendent category of human activity is an ascetic ideology . . . Because socialists hold to the general concept, they make themselves into the carriers of capitalist propaganda.
> (Jay 1984: 57)

Marcuse, in contrast, was ready to defend hedonistic philosophies for preserving a 'moment' of truth in their stress on happiness. Both Horkheimer and Marcuse agreed that a liberal moral culture tended to go wrong when it accepted the competitive individual as the model of highest personal development.

But they themselves tended to remain trapped within a rationalist framework, wanting to make judgements about different kinds of wants, pleasures and enjoyments, almost without serious regard for the growth and development of individuality. In a very real sense their rationalism prevented them from developing a politics and morality which could explore the contradictions of our lived experience. Sometimes they fell back on more or less utilitarian formulations. So Marcuse could write in his essay 'On Hedonism':

> The apologetic aspect of hedonism is located at a deeper level. It is found in hedonism's abstract conception of the subjective side of happiness, in its inability to distinguish between true and false wants and interests of individuals as simply given and as valuable in themselves. Yet these wants and interests themselves, and not merely their gratification, already contain the stunted growth, the repression, and the untruth with which men grow up in class society. The affirmation of the one already contains the affirmation of the other.
>
> (Marcuse 1968: 168)

This is an important reminder that we cannot accept 'the wants and interests of individuals as simply given and as valuable in themselves', but nor can we so easily discount them. We need a way of engaging with these wants and interests, rather than the simple but misleading clarity of a rationalist judgement which would be able to legislate 'true and false wants and interests' and 'true and false enjoyments'. At the same time it is the strength of a rationalist tradition that it can allow us to develop a critique of the demands and feelings of our natures.

We do not simply have to accept our needs, wants and desires as defining a socially acceptable 'normality' we cannot question. A positivist sociology has always wanted individuals to be ready to subordinate wants and needs to the requirements of the larger society. It was society as a larger entity that somehow 'knew best'. But it is threatened by any questioning of the fundamental values and relations of power and dominance within society. It wants to settle with the conviction that 'the way things are, is somehow best for everyone'.

The rationalist tradition has always sustained a subversive edge, though it has often lacked a sense of the historical character of prevailing relations of power and subordination. Nevertheless it helps us ask about the 'rationality' of the prevailing social order, enabling us at least to think about whether societies are organised to allow the realisation of individual lives. At least the Frankfurt School were working for the reinstatement and enlargement of fundamental terms of criticism within this rationalist tradition. They were working for a substantial notion of rationality rather than the formalistic and instrumental notions of rationality as a means–end relationship which had come to predominate within liberal social theory.[3]

But the Frankfurt School were also limited within their rationalistic notion of critique, though they were always stretching it to express insights that in reality questioned their fundamental framework. Sometimes they seemed aware that the Enlightenment involved the destruction and domination of the natural world, but they stopped short of an ecological awareness that could have sustained a different relationship to nature. They were ready to settle for a more planned relationship with nature. Their rationalism still assumed a fundamental distinction between 'reason' and 'nature' which has important consequences for both conceptions of 'reason' as an independent and autonomous faculty separated from experience, and conceptions of nature as made up of fixed wants, needs and desires.

This made it difficult to develop a less 'abstract conception of the subjective side of happiness'; even if they sensed its importance their vision of identity and fulfilment remained thin and attenuated. Liberal social theory tends to see wants and needs as fixed within the individual's nature, while a shared sociological and orthodox Marxist conception tends to see our wants and needs as socially and historically produced. Both conceptions tend to see wants, needs, desires and feelings as aspects of a 'nature' which, in Kant's terms, is part of an empirical world of determination and unfreedom and is fundamentally separated from 'reason'.

The very autonomy of reason as an inner faculty which is itself the source of our freedom and independence denies reason and rationality to our wants, feelings, desires and needs, which are seen as 'fixed' even if they are socially produced. This means that reason's critique has the fundamental character of an *external* intervention into a 'nature' which has been independently constituted.

IDENTITIES AND DESIRES

A rationalist tradition makes it difficult within social theory to resist an external judgment which gives insufficient weight to the awareness, sensitivity, and developing consciousness of people themselves. This might also be in relation to class, ethnicity and gender, as well as issues of sexual identities. Even if we are ready to take the opinions and concerns of people into account, our sense of democracy and empowerment is in constant tension with the authority of positivism. It becomes easy to fall into thinking that we 'know best' in our ability to make rational judgments on the basis of impartial and objective evidence and without reference to people's diverse conceptions of their own identities, needs and wants.

If we think for a moment of the denial of sexuality that has been so deeply embedded in Western culture, it has been too easy, despite our best liberal intentions, to deny the validity of different forms of sexual practice as 'abnormal' or 'illegitimate' on the assumed understanding of heterosexuality as 'normal'. This is done within a culture in which, until very recently, the whole question of sexuality was regarded as 'unseemly', as a 'necessary evil' which it would be better to do without. This is something we only talk about with a great deal of unease and embarrassment. Even though people are ready to admit that sexuality is a 'natural part of life', we cannot help having very ambiguous feelings about it.[4]

Rather than sexuality being an area of our lives in which we can supposedly be most spontaneous, we must recognise that we are constrained by ideas of how we should be and with the fear of AIDS this has become even more fraught. Often heterosexual men feel that they are living up to certain images of themselves. Our sexuality, for all its supposed privacy, becomes as goal-oriented as all other areas of our lives. We realise, much to our disappointment, that we do not suddenly become different people once the bedroom door is shut behind us. It is difficult to break with the idea of sexuality as something that happens in the bedroom. A friend recently confirmed this when he admitted how his sexual relationship had been limited by his moving from a bedsitter, in which his sexuality had almost of necessity become a part of everything else, to a one-bedroom flat, in which it had been firmly placed back in the bedroom. This process had happened without his even realising what was changing.

We seem to require a different epistemology which post-modern theory also is seeking which does not simply accept naturalistically the wants and needs that people have as unchanging and fixed, but nor does it rush to the security of independent rational judgements without reference to the *quality* of people's experience. This touches a limit in the idea that identities are 'socially constructed' or provided by available discourses. Questioning the identification of masculinity with reason can open up issues of identity and desire in ways which help feminism and queer theory to develop a critical social theory without having to denigrate somatic and emotional lives. In developing fuller conceptions of personal identity we also set the terms for a richer account of the impact upon notions of self-identity of social relations of power and subordination. The Frankfurt School could never have developed such a politics of experience which was not empiricist, and which did not concede to the rationalism and essentialism of conventional phenomenology.[5]

Even Marcuse was often trapped in the ungrounded judgements of rationalism in his critique of needs and wants as 'ultimate data in their present form'. This idea makes it difficult to recognise the historical and dialectical formation and potential transformations of our wants, needs, desires and hopes. Rather we are left to judge them once and for all 'as to their "right"' at the bench of reason:

> The designation of happiness as the condition of the comprehensive gratification of the individual's needs and wants is abstract and incorrect as long as it accepts needs and wants as ultimate data in their present form. For as such they are neither good and evil nor true and false. As historical facts they are subject to questioning as to their 'right': Are they of such a sort that their gratification can fulfil the subjective and objective potentialities of individuals? . . . Pleasure in the abasement of another as well as self-abnegation under a stronger will, pleasure in the manifold surrogates for sexuality, in meaningless sacrifices, in the heroism of war are false pleasures, because the drives and needs that fulfil themselves in them make men less free, blinder, and more wretched than they have to be. They are the drives and needs of individuals who were raised in an antagonistic society.
>
> (Marcuse 1968: 189–90)

When Marcuse says that these 'false pleasures' work to 'make men less free, blinder, and more wretched than they have to be' does he think that, at some level, people experience this themselves? Can we not recognise the contradictory character of people's experience of their needs and desires? Is not the tension and contradiction within our lived experience something Marcuse is forced to think about more when he asks whether 'their gratification can fulfil the subjective and objective potentialities of individuals'? This involves developing a language of needs, wants and bodily experience which is sensitive to issues of gender and sexual identities and can connect to and illuminate our understanding of the 'potentialities of individuals' without having to conceive these needs and wants 'as ultimate data in their present form'.

INTEGRITY AND DESIRES

This involves a fundamental reworking of our Kantian understanding of the rationality of the person, which has informed both Durkheimian and Weberian traditions within social theory. This is a problem Marcuse is aware of in his essay 'On Hedonism', even if he does not fully come to grips with it:

> Insofar as the individual partakes of universality only as a rational being and not with the empirical manifold of his needs, wants and

capacities, this idea of reason implicitly contains the sacrifice of the individual. His full development could not be admitted into the realm of reason. The gratification of his wants and capacities, his happiness, appears as an arbitrary and subjective element that cannot be brought into consonance with the universal validity of the highest principle of human action.

(Ibid.: 159–60)

The issues are complex if we are to discover ways of reinstating within our social theory the integrity and dignity of our emotional and somatic lives as sources of knowledge as much as of enjoyment and fulfilment. Our questioning takes place within a particular cultural and political context. If we think for a moment about the social taboo about masturbation, we can bring some of these issues into sharper focus in an area of silence and concealment.

Until very recently heterosexual men have been brought up to think that is wrong to masturbate, so we have often been left to feel guilty and ashamed. This has come to be symptomatic of the shame we often feel for our bodies. It is harder to recover fully from feeling that sex is dirty, even if you have come to question this rationally. We are dealing with deeper experiences that are hard to change at simply a mental level.[6] It is not simply a question of an act of will, but of learning, as Freud rediscovered, to develop a different kind of relationship with one's body and one's self. This is more than a matter of changing what we think about masturbation so that we no longer think and feel it is harmful and damaging.

Certainly it can involve dramatically questioning the Cartesian idea that, as men, our mind is always supposed to control our bodily responses, to realise that our bodies have memories and responses of their own even if we are largely unaware of them. This is a realisation Tony has in Judy Blume's novel *Then Again Maybe I Won't*:

When I read Joel's paperbacks I can feel myself getting hard. But other times when I'm not even thinking about anything it goes up too. I don't know what to do about that. I mean, if my brain is working right it's supposed to control my whole body. But if I don't have any control over that part of me, what good is my brain? It's getting so I don't have anything to say about what goes on. I think that part of me has a mind of its own.

Suppose it decides to go up in school and everybody notices? Or at a Junior Youth Group meeting? What will I do to get it down? I think from now on I'm going to carry a raincoat with me every day. Then, if anything happens I'll have something to put over me in a hurry.

(Blume 1979: 38–9)

If men begin to see masturbation as a way of developing a deeper relationship with ourselves, even as a way of making love to ourselves, we are fundamentally challenging the idea that sexual fulfilment has only to come from a relationship with someone else. We are challenging the Freudian notion that we deepen our fulfilment by developing a relationship with a 'better object' if we think that it is partly through becoming more familiar with our own bodies and sexuality that we will be able also to deepen our contact and intimacy with others. This involves redefining our sense of the relationship between self and others as well as the ways we think about sexuality and about our sexual needs.

So this is not simply a matter of accepting our wants and needs 'as ultimate data in their present form'. Nor is it simply a matter of thinking that masturbation is not something we need to feel guilty about, or that enjoying masturbation is necessarily a matter of being narcissistic. This is partly a question of redefining and challenging the cultural notions we have inherited of sexuality. This can involve recognising how mechanical and goal-oriented we have become in heterosexual practice, so that we can become totally focused upon the quality of an orgasm.

But this also involves recognising how our deepest and most private experiences have been transformed in the images of the larger culture, so that we cannot help thinking of others in possessive terms. It also sets different terms for our discussions of identities and desires for it encourages us to think in terms of the *quality* of contact that we have both with different aspects of ourselves and in our relationships with others.

In a very real sense, people have to be able to discover this for themselves, in the changes that it brings about in the quality, intimacy and meaningfulness of their experience and relationships. This is part of a process involving a transformation, for instance in the ways heterosexual and gay men might think, feel and experience. It is to begin to heal the fragmentation between reason and nature which has come within modernity to organise so much of the way we think and feel about ourselves and others. It can involve difficult moments as, for instance, we acknowledge our disgust of sexuality and our bodies as part of the process of learning to accept and respect who we are rather than condemning ourselves for not meeting some external standards. This reformulation of our sense of what we need for ourselves is historically special, for in relation to class, race, gender and sexual identities it involves mental, emotional and bodily processes. These cannot be separated out as independent processes, but are to be understood as part of a process of individuation. We learn from the understandings of others, but we have to feel and experience for ourselves the truth of what they say. This is a process which can recognise that individuals have very different wants, but also that they share certain needs. We nourish ourselves in different ways.

NEEDS AND EMOTIONS

This does not involve accepting the needs and wants that capitalist and patriarchal culture has brought us up to assume. This does not simply involve an intellectual critique, but also an emotional and bodily understanding and transformation. I suppose a fundamental difference is that a rationalist critique, which has informed so many of our liberal and Marxist traditions but which is directly opposed in so many other ways, tends to build upon a Calvinistic inheritance which says that we should eradicate those parts of ourselves which are judged 'unworthy' or 'unacceptable'. It seems to remake our identities from the *outside* working in as we seek to conform and adapt to the standards and ideals that we set ourselves.

In this way notions of morality within a Marxist tradition have tended to remain fundamentally idealistic, simply establishing different standards for people to live up to. This reproduces the attentuated individuality of liberalism. Orthodox Marxism does not help people trust in themselves, and in their processes. Rather it tends to make people feel that they have everything to learn and little to give. This is different from a process of change that involves people accepting as part of a reworking of taken-for-granted class, race, gender or sexual identities what they want and need as part of the process of changing. Reinventing identities is a process which is built upon the validation of human experience rather than, for instance, the manipulation of inadequacy which as Weber grasped is central to the social relations of capitalist society.[7]

Recovering the self can involve, for instance, recognising the ways that our own individual and personal experience has been influenced through the society's manipulation of sexuality as a commodity. So that, as heterosexual men, we can experience ourselves caught in the notion of sexuality as performance, which often leaves us disappointed or unfulfilled. Or we can recognise ourselves trapped in a pattern where we are excited in a potential relationship as conquest, only to find ourselves bored and uneasy when we have succeeded. Sometimes it is almost as if the conquest proves that the person was not worth struggling for and simply confirms our low estimation of ourselves.

If these are personal experiences, they are also cultural and political, since they grow for example out of particular relationships of power within a heterosexual culture between the sexes that, before the theoretical and practical challenges of feminism and gay liberation, men were brought up to take for granted. We begin to learn for ourselves the meaning of Marcuse's words, already quoted, that 'these wants and interests themselves, and not merely their gratification, already contain the stunted growth, the repression, and the truth with which men grow up in class society' (1968: 168). We learn this through the pain and joy of our own experience. We learn that we want more for ourselves, even if this brings us into fundamental opposition to the dominant relationships of the society we live in.

This has been shown in practice, in the history of the contemporary women's movement. Women came together in the practice of consciousness-raising to share their experience as women, and to discover the sources of sisterhood and solidarity in this shared revelation. This gave women new sources of power and identity to struggle against the structure of power within the larger society. Although this movement has had to struggle against its own forms of moralism, which would create alternative uncompromising images that women felt they had to live up to even if they were not true to their own individual experience, it could always draw, when it was not deeply divided itself, upon its deeper sources of strength, upon the validity that it sought to give to the experience of each individual woman. As the movement fragmented it had to discover ways of acknowledging differences of race, class and sexual orientation while not losing contact with what is also shared.

Heterosexual men have more rarely been able to experience some of the same validity and sharing of experience through consciousness-raising, though this exists as a different practice because of the different situation of men and masculinities within a patriarchal capitalist society. But it is still true that feminism, and the politics of experience more generally, have provided a way of reconnecting with sources of identity which have so often been displaced within the abstract conceptions of the rational self that have controlled our visions of modernity. As issues of class, race, gender and sexuality are brought into focus there is a fear of fragmentation, fuelled by post-modern doubts of historical visions of women as a unified subject. But if there is a celebration of differences there are also dangers of a fragmentation that loses touch with the possibilities of personal and collective emancipation.

As Gramsci also knew, recalling a Greek tradition so hard to sustain in a modern culture that denies the value of self-knowledge and inner transformation, it is through accepting the *validity* of one's own individual and personal experience, grasped also as a social experience shared with others, that one gains new strength to challenge the larger structures of power and control.

CHANGE AND INSTRUMENTALITY

I want to explore connections between rationalism, moralism and a certain form of instrumentalism towards people. This has had a deep but largely unacknowledged influence upon both liberal and socialist traditions. While helping to reinstate the relationships between epistemology and politics familiar in the writings of the Frankfurt School, I want to question its rationalism through drawing upon some crucial feminist insights.

This is something a tradition of critical theory can learn from the feminist idea that 'the personal is political', which helps to reinstate the emotional along with the rational, the private and intimate along with the public and political. Still, the exploration of Adorno and Horkheimer into the contradictory inheritance of the Enlightenment is much more than an exercise in the history of ideas. Critical theory provides an exploration of some of the contradictions in cultural ideas of reason, science and progress within modernity, which we still take for granted. Contemporary discussions into the post-modern unwittingly still very much live in their image.

We need to renew critical traditions of social theory if we are to understand relationships between changes in structures of power, the social relations of everyday life and the processes of identity politics. Relatively little has been assimilated into socialist theory and culture for so long mesmerized by questions of Leninist state power. Until the revolutionary upheavals in Eastern Europe little had been learnt from the social experiments of the years immediately following the Russian Revolution, the experience of Spanish Anarchism and the experiences in the West following the explosion of 1968. In the 1990s it is as if Marxism is to be dispensed with as discredited rather than engaged with critically almost as if we do not know *how* to learn within a theoretical tradition which in its orthodox forms so closed in upon itself, secure in its vision of history and science.

Politics has often become too easily trapped into rationalist judgements of 'success' and 'failure', rather than grasping and learning from the processes of social transformation it is tempting to leave politics behind as part of a discredited modernity. Values and morality have too often been lost in the rush towards the post-modern. Hopefully, with recent events in Eastern Europe and the former Soviet Union precipitating a crisis in the language of socialism, this is beginning to change. Feminism and sexual politics can still provide a sense of the contradictions within lived experience and the dignity and validity of our emotional and somatic experience. They can help us challenge forms of social theory that treat individuals as social products, as with functionalism, or identities as 'socially and historically constructed'.

These traditions in their different ways prove incapable of illuminating tensions between what individuals want or need for themselves and the prevailing social relationships.

Within Marxism it has been easier to focus upon the 'laws of capitalist development', especially in periods of working-class defeat. This can give a sense of power and control, allowing politically conscious intellectuals to think that the difficult task of developing ongoing contact with working-class people struggling against oppression is unnecessary if these laws are operating to shape and influence people's lives without people being consciously aware of them. With this reading of Marx, which comes more into focus with the growing pessimism of his later years, it becomes possible to continue a similar instrumentalism towards people to that which we inherit within positivistic traditions.[8]

This encourages a conception of 'scientific Marxism' which tempts political activists into thinking that a social revolution can also be made over the heads of people. We find parties on the Left confident in the 'correctness' of their analysis, assuming that it is the theoretical 'backwardness' or working-class people which somehow explains why they are not ready to follow their lead.

Again it is Gramsci who dares to pose the fundamental question. He pushes us back into wondering about the cultural sources which encourage such a misreading of Marx:

How did the founder of the philosophy of praxis arrive at the concept of regularity and necessity in historical development? I do not think that it can be thought of as a derivation from natural science but rather as an elaboration of concepts born on the terrain of political economy, particularly in the form and with the methodology that economic science acquired from David Ricardo. Concept and fact of determined market: i.e. the scientific discovery that specific decisive and permanent forces have risen historically and that the operation of these forces presents itself with a certain 'automatism' which allows a measure of 'predictability' and certainty for the future of those individual initiatives which accept these forces after having discerned and scientifically established their nature. 'Determined market' is therefore equivalent to 'determined relation of social forces in a determined structure of the productive apparatus', this relationship being guaranteed (that is rendered permanent) by a determined political, moral and juridical superstructure ... whereas pure economists conceive of these elements as 'eternal' and 'natural': the critique analyses in a realistic way the relations of forces determining the market, it analyses in depth the contradictions, evaluates the possibilities of modification connected with the appearance of strengthening of new elements and puts forward the 'transito' and 'replaceable' nature of the science being criticised; it studies it as life but also as death and finds at its heart the elements that will dissolve it and supersede it without fail.

(Gramsci 1971: 410–11

Gramsci warns us about isolating 'the merely economic facts from the combinations of varying importance in which they present themselves in reality'. This helps us question certain concepts of 'economic laws' that could encourage a blind and damaging instrumentalism towards people. But it should also help us question a notion of 'economic rationality' that abstracts from the quality and experience of people's lives, thinking that economic relations can be conceptualised independently. This is the error we find reproduced in Althusser.

Max Horkheimer's work *Eclipse of Reason* (1974) helps us think about some of the cultural sources of an instrumentalism we take very much for granted. He helps us identify certain polarities of thinking and feeling.

There is a fundamental difference between this theory, according to which reason is a principle inherent in reality, and the doctrine that reason is a subjective faculty of the mind. According to the latter, the subject alone can genuinely have reasons: if we say that an institution or any other reality is reasonable, we usually mean that men have organised it reasonably, that they have applied to it, in a more or less technical way, their logical, calculative capacity ... to co-ordinate the right means with a given end.

(Horkheimer: 1974: 9)

In this way reason has become a technical conception. It does not any more relate to the ends and purposes of human action. As Horkheimer says, 'There is no reasonable aim as such, and to discuss the superiority of one aim over another in terms of reason becomes meaningless.'

REASON AND VALUES

Subjective conceptions of reason have become integral aspects of the 'common sense' we grow up with in a liberal moral culture, where it becomes easier to think of moral and political questions as matters of individual opinion and values. This limits our social and political consciousness. We find echoes of such a relativism in the ways postmodernity is often theorised as a break with a Cartesian conception of reason and its unified vision. It becomes much harder to grasp our individual experience within the context of the larger society, and its organisation and formation within social relations of power and dominance.

Our thinking becomes fundamentally fragmented as we can no longer connect issues of epistemology and politics and as we find it increasingly difficult to think historically and socially. This has a profoundly crippling effect upon our critical consciousness:

> Since ends are no longer determined in the light of reason, it is also impossible to say that one economic or political system, no matter how cruel and despotic, is less reasonable than another. According to formalised reason, despotism, cruelty, oppression are not bad in themselves; no rational agency could endorse a verdict against dictatorship if its sponsors were likely to profit from it.
>
> (Ibid.: 31–2)

> The present crisis of reason consists fundamentally in the fact that at a certain point thinking either becomes incapable of conceiving such objectivity at all or began to negate it as a delusion. This process was gradually extended to include the objective content of every rational concept. In the end, no particular reality can seem reasonable *per se*; all the basic concepts, emptied of their content, have come to be only formal shells. As the reason is subjectivised, it also becomes formalised.
>
> (Ibid.: 7)

This way of thinking has had a profound effect on our liberal moral and political consciousness. It makes it more difficult to investigate the structures of class, race, gender and sexual power and dominance within society, since these simply dissolve into a plurality of different discourses with each identifying its own sources of subjectivity. So, for instance, when people think about the meaning of 'success', they quickly think that this is a 'relative' concept, which very much depends upon what people want for themselves. So one person might regard herself a 'failure' if she becomes a bus driver, while others regard this as a sure sign of success. This kind of liberal relativism has come to have a strong hold over 'common sense', particularly since the Second World War.

Possibly such relativism before the Second World War is a response to the kind of cultural absolutism that legitimated different forms of imperialist and class domination. This tends to work to individualise the structures of power in society, so that they are simply conceived as the expression of individual wants and needs. Sometimes the relativism of 'common-sense' consciousness stands in contrast to the positivist truths of science, as if science can provide the only secure ground and escape. At other moments, particularly with the growth of phenomenology and more recently discussions around post-modernity in sociology, this liberal relativism has supported the challenge to the authority of positivism.

Phenomenology has usefully helped question the assumed distance between 'common sense' and 'science', showing the ways science often assumes and tacitly builds upon certain common-sense understandings of the social theory of the early 1970s which helped challenge the positivism which still dominated much of Marxist writings.[9] But it also fed a kind of subjectivism in the ways it challenged the gulf between the 'ignorance' of common sense and the 'truths' of science. It did help restore a validity and importance to *how* individuals understand the social world, recognising that knowledge is socially produced within a community. But it tended to see the 'social world' as somehow constituted through the conceptions of individuals, while at the same time being impotent to illuminate the existing structures of institutional power. It reproduced its own rationalist assumptions in the ways it reduced experience to the conceptual forms in which experience is intellectualised.

The critique of particular forms of instrumental rationalism remains important because it helps us rethink the assumed distinction between 'reason' and 'experience' and so opens up the possibility of bringing social theory more in touch with the contradictions of lived experience. Reason so easily becomes an instrumental notion because we find ourselves trapped in a fundamentally instrumental notion of purposive action. Rather than finding a place for purposive action within our more general understanding of human experience, this becomes the form according to which all areas of personal and social life have to be reorganised.

This was the significance of Weber's principle of 'rationalisation', which he saw as inevitably reorganising every area of social life in capitalist society.[10] We find that our lives become instrumentalised, without our even being aware of these transformations or having a moral language in which to illuminate them. We find that whatever we do we do it for a purpose, since we are constantly left with a feeling that we have to prove ourselves to others as well as to ourselves. This is what gives our lives meaning as we sense our weeks slipping away in endless lists of what we have to do. This is built into our social relations from an early age.

It is not too difficult to recognise some of the effects of competitive social relations of schooling, in the challenge from the schoolchildren of Barbiana:

Social climbers at 12. But your students' own goal is also a mystery. Maybe it is nonexistent; may it is just shoddy.

Day in day out they study for marks, for reports and diplomas. Meanwhile they lose interest in all the fine things they are studying. Languages, sciences, history – everything becomes purely pass marks.

Behind those sheets of paper there is only a desire for personal gain. The diplomas mean money. Nobody mentions this, but give the bag a good squeeze and that's what comes out.

To be a happy student at your schools you have to be a social climber at the age of 12. But few are climbers at 12. It follows that most of your people hate school. Your cheap invitation to them deserves no other reason.

(School of Barbiana 1970: 27)

We need a much fuller understanding of how this instrumentality can limit, injure and distort experience, giving it a particular form. This is not simply a question of developing an external critique from the point of view of impartial reason, nor simply of developing the more substantial rationality Horkheimer was after, to evaluate the goals and ends of our actions. Nor is it a matter of accepting an alternative moralism if this involves creating an alternative set of ideals people can only aspire to, if this is already bulit upon the subordination of our emotions, feelings, wants and needs.

A different kind of social and moral theory is needed which must be able to recognise an ongoing tension between language and experience rather than falling into the temptation of conflating experience into language, which post-structuralist theories have so often done. This must allow the possibility of an internal critique and development of people's experience, not simply an external critique in the name of reason. It must find ways of granting *validity* to people's own experience rather than treating experience as exclusively articulated through language or discourse, while granting the possibilities of living differently. Nor must this separate the transformation of people's sense of themselves, their wants and needs, from the struggles against the structures of class, racial and heterosexual and patriarchal power.

Rather this should help us give content to the vision Marcuse sketched out in his essay 'On Hedonism'. He warns us of the difficulties of pleasure and of recognisng our capacities and potentialities while we live with the everyday brutality, oppression and injustices of a capitalist society:

In this form of society, the world as it is can become an object of enjoyment only when everything in it, men and things, is accepted as it appears. Its essence, that is, those potentialities which emerge as the highest on the basis of the attained level of the productive forces and of knowledge, is not present to the subject of enjoyment. For since the life process is not determined by the true interests of individuals creating, in solidarity, their existence through contending with nature, these potentialities are not realised in the decisive social relations. They can only appear to consciousness as lost, atrophied and repressed.

(Marcuse 1968: 163)

These potentialities can only be regained in the transformation of social relations of oppression and subordination.

Traditional forms of social theory have not broken free from the overarching structures of rationalism. Too often they silently reproduce these Protestant structures which have been given a secular form. These focus our energy outside ourselves as we look towards judging and evaluating our behaviour and feelings according to standards and ideals that we have played no part in making. We have failed to recognise the dangers in learning to identify 'being good' with doing exactly what we are told. Judging in this way serves to undermine our sense of individual dignity and integrity. Social theory needs to find new ways of engaging with issues of individuality.

Similarly, visions of socialism have to include questions about the fullness and quality of individuals' experience. In this way politics has to be able to connect with questions of identities as it learns to challenge a rationalism which too often structures modes of domination of experience externally. Most importantly, a viable language of socialism involves illuminating and transcending the structures that weaken and undermine individuals by, for instance, rendering them passive or by turning them against themselves. It needs to help people identify for themselves a rationalistic tradition that has worked to erode their inner resources, arresting their development, and so blocking a fuller contact and relationship with their inner selves and emotional lives. If phenomenology cast in Cartesian terms has attempted the task of validating people's experience it can only do this within a rationalistic framework that sees people's differences in conceptual terms alone.

Chapter 6

Ideology

IDEALS

People were encouraged within orthodox Marxism to emulate certain 'ideals' in the sacrifices they were to make for socialism. In its own way, as I've argued, this tended to reproduce certain conceptions familiar within capitalist society and bourgeois morality. It served as a mechanism through which subordination of the self is established. The very weakness of a critical moral consciousness within an orthodox Marxism which tended to see morality as part of the 'superstructure' allowed for the reproduction of basic moral conceptions of self-denial and the devaluation of emotional life.

Capitalism has already been able to invoke the Protestant ethic to prepare people to subordinate themselves to the needs of production. Marxism has rarely grasped the workings of this ethic in the formation of character and personality. Its notions of 'ideology' have often tended to be too intellectualist, asserting that it is simply a question of the ideas social classes and individuals develop.[1] This has weakened our understanding of what is involved in a genuine social transformation. It has also made it relatively easy to assimilate mechanical conceptions of the ways people change.

An understanding of the significance of the Protestant ethic would help towards a much richer conception of the contradictions within a liberal moral culture. It would also help illuminate tensions between certain liberal conceptions of autonomy, freedom and individuality with underlying conceptions of self-denial and moral character.[2] This might have been one thing Marx was hinting at in his misleading talk of the 'progressive character of the bourgeoisie'.

It has certainly been damaging to the credibility of Marx's work for an orthodox Marxism to dismiss all liberal ideas as 'bourgeois ideology' without having carefully investigated how they work. Orthodox forms of critique have often become crudely ideological, failing to grasp differences in the reality of people's everyday experience of subordination and oppression. What is more, a dismissive critique of liberal notions of individual dignity, well-being and rights as 'bourgeois' has served to discredit Marx and can all too often disarm people in the face of powers which would seek to disempower and subordinate them.

We have to distinguish between different forms of subordination to the state. In Russia and Eastern Europe, for example, these have historically, until the revolutions of 1989, been very different from the subordination Protestantism serves to legitimate within capitalist society. But important lessons can still be learnt as long as we are ready to think about the relationship of the individual to class, ethnic, sexual and gender experience.

Althusser misleads us when he states in *For Marx* (1970) that Marx was replacing one kind of language with another, individualistic concepts with class concepts. In the end his reduction of the language of individual experience, which continues to be so influential in unwittingly shaping post-structuralist forms of thought in a shared antagonism to essentialism, too often supports a tacit subordination of individuality. Althusser also serves to disorganise an understanding of ethnic, gender and sexual forms of oppression, making us see them as bringing a regrettable fragmentation into rationalistic forms of social theory.

We can still learn something crucial from Erich Fromm's description of the effects of Luther's conception of Protestantism, in *Fear of Freedom*:

In making the individual feel worthless and insignificant as far as his own merits are concerned, in making him feel like a powerless tool in the hands of God, he deprived man of his self-confidence and of the feeling of human dignity which is the premise for any firm stand against oppressing secular authorities. In the course of the historical evolution the results of Luther's teaching were still more far-reaching. Once the individual had lost his sense of pride and dignity, he was psychologically prepared to lose the feeling which had been characteristic of the medieval thinking, namely, that man, his spiritual salvation, and his spiritual aims, were the purpose of life; he was prepared to accept a role in which his life became a means to purposes outside himself, those of economic productivity and accumulation of capital.

(Fromm 1991: 71)

These influences are working to undermine the trust and confidence people can have in themselves and so undermine the empowerment of their individuality. This is bound to render the liberal talk of individual freedom and self-determination rhetorical, abstract and ideological.[3] This can be compared to how individualistic liberal self-conceptions often work to mystify people about the workings of class, gender, sexual and racial relations of power and subordination. A liberal vision encourages people to think that they exist as abstract individuals who have control over their lives, since their position in society grows directly out of their individual abilities and talents. So it is that if people are poor, powerless and oppressed, they only have themselves, individually, to blame.

One reason why our grasp of our experience remains so abstract is that we are barely aware of how our lives, in a liberal moral culture, are shot through with ideals, with images we set for ourselves. Unless we develop a much more internal understanding of the workings of capitalist democracies, we are likely to reproduce its assumptions and ideas unwittingly. This will also help clarify our understanding of Marx's critique of morality.[4]

Marx understood how utopian thought sets itself an abstract ideal of socialism, assuming that if an ideal came to be shared it would help bring it into realisation. Marx was crucially aware of the need also to investigate the workings of the forces and relations of production which could bring this into realisation. So for Marx struggling for socialism was not simply a matter of the rational inculcation of a shared ideal, but also of coming to terms with the class relations of power and dominance in capitalist society.

It was the reality of these relations of class power and subordination which proved the insufficiency of showing the injustice and immorality of capitalist society. But this has been mistakenly interpreted to show the irrelevance to Marx of moral critique and moral education, as if the real material struggles exist independently on a level of their own. This error has been reproduced within Althusserian work which argues for the 'materiality' of ideological struggles, only to isolate them into a sphere of their own.

All this helps us understand why the moral critique of different phases of capitalist development has remained so sparse. The languages of socialism have largely failed to illuminate the very different moral relations of welfare capitalism. Its discussion seems abstract and remote. Often it fails to connect with the realities of people's lives. This made it so much easier for conservative libertarians in the 1970s to legitimate attacks on the welfare state. And it became part of the moral and political initiative that centred itself around Thatcherism in Britain and Reaganism in the United States.

Many working-class people had increasingly experienced being objectified and manipulated by the bureaucratic and depersonalising institutions of the state, including health and education. This frustration, exacerbated in a period of declining resources, is explained by many people as there being 'too much red tape', so that the libertarian Right's talk of 'individual choice' seems to offer working people a chance of regaining some of the power they have lost with the decline in public services over the 1970s.[5] It can give working-class people a sense that they are going to get their own back. In this crucial discussion the Left, confused about the place of individual choice and rights, is still too often caught up in an abstract defence of bureaucratic state institutions, often themselves identified with socialism.

INSECURITY AND SELF DENIAL

Within the period of the Reformation it became important for individuals to prove themselves in the eyes of God. Each individual was to develop his or her own relationship to God. Max Weber helps us understand how significant Protestantism has been in the formation of the 'common sense' of capitalist society. Life becomes a trial or contest in which we are continually having to prove our worth. We take this so much for granted that we are barely conscious of the religious sources of these ideas and conceptions that define our individuality and help give meaning to our lives.

Weber was aware of how easily we are deprived of our historical consciousness. This makes it easy to assume that the social world we know is the only 'realistic' way the social world can be. This tends to make absolute the existing structures of power and dominance and makes it difficult to imagine alternatives:

> One is tempted to think that these personal moral qualities have not the slightest relation to any ethical maxims, to say nothing of religious ideas, but that the essential relation between them is negative. The ability to free oneself from the common tradition, a sort of liberal enlightenment, seems likely to be the most suitable basis for such a business man's success. And today that is generally precisely the case . . . The people filled with the spirit of capitalism today tend to be indifferent, if not hostile, to the Church . . . religion appears to them as a means of drawing people away from labour in this world. If you ask them what is the meaning of their restless activity, why they are never satisfied with what they have, thus appearing so senseless to any purely worldly view of life, they would perhaps give the answer, if they knew any at all: 'to provide for my children and grandchildren'. But more often and, since that motive is not peculiar to them, but was just as effective for the traditionalist, more correctly, simply: that business with its continuous

work has become a necessary part of their lives. That is in fact the only possible motivation, but it at the same time expresses what is, seen from the view-point of personal happiness, so irrational about this sort of life, where a man exists for the sake of his business instead of the reverse.

(Weber 1930: 70)

Weber grasps how the 'common sense' we take for granted is 'irrational', when 'seen from the view-point of personal happiness'. So Wever, learning from Nietzsche, is clear that in accepting the 'rationality' of the moral culture of capitalism, we are implicitly accepting a form of self-denial and subordination. It is with the benefit of historical understanding that we become aware of what is 'so irrational about this sort of life'.

Our awareness of the historical formation of our 'individuality' shows the dominance of these notions within a liberal moral culture. Somehow self-denial and irrationality 'seen from the view-point of personal happiness' has been able to identify itself with 'freedom' and 'rationality'. It is at this level that we can begin to appreciate the working of ideology, not simply in abstract terms but somehow grounded in the organisation and texture of our everyday experience. Socialists have often been blind to the moral contradictions of liberal capitalism, either assuming this discussion is 'idealistic' or else that it reflects a 'necessary stage' that capitalism had to move through.

Weber also analyses the relationship between capitalism and democracy and the kind of moral culture and character formation which help sustain this relationship:

The capitalist system so needs this devotion to the calling of making money, it is an attitude towards material goods which is so well suited to that system, so intimately bound up with the conditions of survival in the economic struggle for existence . . . it no longer needs the support of any religious forces . . . In such circumstances men's commercial and social interests do tend to detemine their opinions and attitudes. Whoever does not adapt his manner of life to the conditions of capitalistic success must go under, or at least cannot rise. But these are phenomena of a time in which modern capitalism has become dominant and has become emancipated from its old supports. But as it could at one time destroy the olds forms of mediaeval regulation of economic life only in alliance with the growing power of the modern state, the same, we may say provisionally, may have been the case in its relations to religious forces . . . For that the conception of money-making as an end in itself to which people were bound, as a calling was contrary to the ethical feelings of whole epochs, it is hardly necessary to prove.

(Ibid.: 72–3)

Money-making as an end in itself becomes a way in which individuals prove themselves. It is almost as if people can *prove* themselves to have dignity and moral worth through subordinating and denying their wants and desires. In a similar way, salvation comes to exist as a kind of proving oneself before God, where people's everyday experiences and activities exist only as means towards salvation, rather than having any intrinsic value for themselves. The goal of life is firmly set in a salvation which lies outside life. It is this goal which gives our activities and experiences whatever meaning they have. Our every-day activities and practices come to have whatever meaning they have only through this external reference.

We can explain, for example, how this works if we think for a moment of how our interest in different subjects at school gets under-mined as we focus our attention simply on the marks we get. We can begin to feel that we learn in order to get marks. So we become aware of how the competitive organisation of schooling, rather than develop-ing our learning tends to instrumentalise it. We become adept at knowing what the teacher wants to hear rather than identifying and articulating what we understand.

This is a familiar situation but one in which we are perhaps not used to thinking and learning about effects of capitalist rationality. But our schooling experience has been organised very much in the image of the larger society, preparing people for a particular kind of experience at work. So it is that work increasingly gains whatever meaning it has from the wages we earn, just as in school we learn to do whatever is expected of us to get marks without fully recognising the process. We often lose a sense of the joy or fulfilment of learning as we do from the routinisation of work. We learn to expect very little for ourselves for at some level we are often haunted by an abiding sense that we are underserving.[6]

These notions themselves no longer express concrete expectations but become empty or rhetorical as we learn to identify our 'happiness' or 'fulfilment' with whatever 'success' we have gained. As salvation implicitly involves the subordination of our needs, wants and desires so that we can prove ourselves before God, so 'success' and 'individual achievement' often involve similar sacrifices to goals outside our every-day experience and relationships. So we begin to accept as almost second nature the idea that 'happiness' has to be sacrificed for. It is only sweet if we have really had to work hard for it. Personal fulfil-ment becomes a matter of realising goals that exist outside ourselves as we lose any ongoing sense of our individual needs and desires.

FAILURE AND INADEQUACY

Constantly feeling, particularly as men, that we have to prove ourselves, is connected to another aspect of liberal moral culture which we take so much for granted that its workings are rendered invisible. This is the underlying Protestant feeling that our 'natures' are somehow 'rotten' and 'evil'. Often this Protestant conception operates at an unspoken level, which makes it hard to grasp how it subverts liberal talk of individual freedom and self-determination, which can so often feel hollow and empty.

If liberalism has a more hopeful conception of people, it is continually being undermined by these deeper structures of feeling, as J.S. Mill recognised even if he could not fully connect them to the social relations of achievement and competitiveness. People often experience this in their everyday lives as a lack of confidence or as an insecurity, continually questioning the value of what they are doing. Of course not everyone is plagued by these feelings and they are mediated through class, gender, race and sexuality but often there is a *fear of failure*, of being made to feel put down in front of others, that can make it hard to take even the smallest risks in our relations with others.

Possibly with the development of feminist conciousness it is more easily recognised in the subordination women experience in a patriarchal society. For men it is often concealed, as we escape any recognition of vulnerability or weakness out of a fear that it will threaten our male identities. It is only with difficulty, in the private spaces of our lives, that we can, as heterosexual, middle-class men, sometimes admit the reality of our feelings and acknowledge the strains of 'keeping ourselves together' at work.

The Protestant writings of Luther and Calvin assumed that people's natures were essentially evil. This argument is at the heart of dilemmas that we have shown Mill to be struggling with. This assumption makes it impossible for people to perform any good deeds on the basis of their natures. We cannot trust ourselves. As Erich Fromm has pointed out, 'The depravity of man's nature and its complete lack of freedom to choose the right is one of the fundamental concepts of Luther's whole thinking' (1991: 63).

It is this emphasis on the fundamental evil and powerlessness of human nature that is continually undermining a liberal notion of 'freedom'. Mill recognised that as long as liberal conceptions of freedom and autonomy are tacitly built upon foundations which are continually undermining people's confidence and trust in their own feelings, desires and natures, they remain profoundly contradictory.

Fromm helps us understand a pervasive contradiction of liberal freedom, which is that it allows us to talk of freedom while experiencing subordination:

Luther's picture of man mirrored just this dilemma. Man is free *from* all ties binding him to spiritual authorities, but this very freedom leaves him alone and anxious, overwhelms him with a feeling of his own individual insignificance and powerlessness. This free, isolated individual is crushed by the experience of his individual insignificance. Luther's theology gives expression to this feeling of helplessness and doubt ... The member of the middle class was as helpless in the face of the new economic forces as Luther described man to be in his relationship to God. Luther's relationship to God was one of complete submission. In psychological terms his concept of faith means: if you completely submit, if you accept your individual insignificance, then the all-powerful God may be willing to love you and save you. If you get rid of your individual self with all its shortcomings and doubts by utmost self-effacement, you free yourself from the feeling of your own nothingness and can participate in God's glory.

(Ibid.: 69)

Liberal discussion of individual freedom, equality and happiness makes it difficult to recognise and identify these proceses of self-effacemeent. But in many ways we can be so used to living with these tensions that they are rendered invisible. Since we are brought up to identify our 'selves' with our individual success and achievement, we are constantly suspicious, especially as heterosexual men, of needing the help of others. As Mill knew, this also leaves us with an often unacknowledged fear of being too different from others even while continuing to talk of freedom and individuality.

Our self-image as white, middle-class heterosexual men becomes increasingly rhetorical and unreal, as we become aware of how hard it has become even to *identify* individual wants and needs. It is as if we have learnt to protect ourselves against the competition of others by not having strong enough individual desires, passions and feelings. This makes it easier to maintain a masculine self-control and so accommodate our behaviour to the expectations of others.[7]

In social theory this is theorised in Goffman's terms as the 'naturalness' of role-playing and the 'presentation of self'. The self becomes something we learn to manipulate to our advantage, rather than something we need and want to express in our everyday lives. These contradictions have such a long history that we easily lose touch with the fact that there is anything lacking or else we learn to celebrate within much post-modern theory. Rousseau talks about this in is *Discourse on the Sciences and Arts*, showing the ancestry of Mill's vision:

> While government and laws provide for the safety and well-being of assembled men, the sciences, letters, and arts, less despotic and perhaps more powerful, spread garlands of flowers over the iron chains with which men are burdened, stifle in them the sense of that original liberty for which they seemed to have been born, make them love their slavery, and turn them into what is called civilized peoples . . .
>
> Today, when subtler researches and a more refined taste have reduced the art of pleasing to set rules, a base and deceptive uniformity prevails in our customs, and all minds seem to have been cast in the same mould. Incessantly politeness requires, propriety demands; incessantly usage is followed, never one's inclinations. One no longer dares to appear as she or he is; and in this perpetual constraint, the men who form this herd called society, placed in the same circumstances, will all do the same things unless stronger motives deter them.
>
> (Rousseau 1964: 36, 37–8)

One no longer dares to appear as she or he is because we partly feel that we are not 'acceptable' as we really are.

SELF-DOUBT AND ISOLATION

We can sometimes get in touch with an uncomfortable feeling that 'if people knew what we were really like, they wouldn't like us'. This would leave us alone and friendless. The culture of modernity shaped through a secularised form of Protestantism makes us doubt ourselves, and we cannot help feeling, in our personal and private moments, that at some level we are fundamentally mean and selfish. These feelings are given a different inflexion in the experience of men and women. These are not simply individual feelings we share with others in private moments, but are systematically reproduced within a liberal moral culture.

We are often scared of being thought 'selfish' and 'self-indulgent', as we mistakenly identify this with pleasing and fulfilling ourselves. This partly explains why we sometimes find it easier to give to others than to give to ourselves, contrary to the self-conceptions we have internalised. As feminism has explored it this can be particularly true of women who have been brought up to find meaning in serving the needs of others. At some level both women and men can still recognise something of themselves in Calvin's words:

For it is an ancient and true observation that there is a world of vices concealed in the soul of man. Nor can you find any other remedy than to deny yourself and discard all selfish considerations, and to devote your whole attention to the pursuit of those things which the Lord requires of you, and which ought to be pursued for this sole reason, because they are pleasing to him.

(John Calvin's Institutes of the Christian Religion,
Book 3 Ch. 7,2, quoted in Fromm 1991)

This can continue to exert a deep, if unacknowledged, hold on our private conceptions of ourselves, though it is also something we feel ashamed of feeling in more permissive times so it can also be something we hide from others. This creates a pervasive if ill-defined sense of doubt and inadequacy that continues to affect people's often uneasy and insecure sense of self. In the desire to avoid being recognised as the 'selfish' person we feel ourselves to be, we more anxiously devote our energies to external activities expected of us.

This trait tends to be particularly marked in the formation of dominant masculinities. As men, we are more often encouraged to define ourselves through competitive relations with others. It is often a matter of seemingly inescapable feelings as we compare whether we are as good as others. In schooling, for instance, this can mean developing only those talents in which we can prove ourselves better than others rather than those difficult for us. We can be plagued by feelings of low self-esteem, doubting the value of anything that we do, fearing that others will put us down or ridicule our efforts. It can seem preferable not to take any risks and certainly not to risk ourselves emotionally with others. We want to avoid at all costs being made to look silly in front of others. We are always on guard against other men, since life so easily becomes a grand competition in which, as men, we cannot help feeling that others are going to put us down if they get the slightest chance.

But as heterosexual men, this also means that we often develop little ongoing relationship with or understanding of ourselves, since we have been brought up to identify so closely with the goals of our actions and with individual achievements. This is connected to the cultural identification within modernity of masculinity with an independent faculty of reason. It is in our very control over our emotions and feelings that we assert our masculinity as well as prove our implicit superiority over women.

But in estranging ourselves from our emotions and feelings, as heterosexual men we barely identify the injury and damage we do to part of ourselves. Rather, it becomes easier to feel threatened, whatever self-image our rational self would want to sustain, by our wants and desires, assuming they are part of 'a world of vices concealed in the soul of man'.

IDEOLOGY AND SUBORDINATION

We can say something about the prevailing structures of 'identity-formation' within a liberal moral culture without denying difference and saying that we all individually feel this way. I want to identify certain tendencies of thinking and feeling, showing their sources in the historical development of a modernity shaped by a Protestant culture and morality. This argues for a historical and cultural dimension in the formation of 'identity' and theories of difference, while also recognising the workings of social relations of power and dominance within which people grow up and live their lives.

So, for instance, when we think about the diverse ways the nature of 'success' relates to people's identities and sense of self, we are not simply thinking in Weberian terms about a 'value' that people share.[8] Social theory has often conceptualised these issues in Weberian terms as a matter of individual 'values' and 'beliefs'. This unwittingly undermines a social and historical consciousness, making it difficult to grasp the historical and social relations that form an understanding of 'success'.

We cannot, for instance, appreciate the cultural reproduction of values of 'possessive individualism' without realising how this is structured into dominant masculinities and into the social relations of family, school and production. So as middle-class boys we might feel individually good that we have done well at school, without beginning to understand the social and historical sources of our feelings. We might not even be aware of the connection between 'feeling good' and 'knowing that we are doing better than others'. In a similar way, we might not have begun to realise how we have tended to like subjects we are good at and get good marks for. I remember, back in the 1950s, being good at different subjects at school without really being able clearly to say what I was interested in. It is as if I had lost this capacity somewhere in the process. This made it difficult to choose subjects I wanted to carry on with.

It can be difficult to become aware of connections we take so much for granted, as part of our everyday lives in school. We do not think about how as boys our relationships to others and to our own learning are formed and organised through a structure of hierarchical and competitive relations. This is not an experience that traditions of social theory have usefully illuminated, especially the fear and insecurity that is so often structured into identities. Too often theories of ideology have presented these issues in intellectual terms, and so have been unable to illuminate the emotional and somatic dimensions of the workings of relations of power and authority.

Since this school reality is often presented to us in terms of a liberal language of choice, these relationships are mystified. This does not mean that an ideology serves to 'cover over' or 'veil' an underlying structure of relations that can be independently described. Althusser has helped us think about the very 'real' influence of these conceptions and ideas. They have a reality of their own. They are not simply a 'veil' for 'underlying material interests' which are assumed to have the only genuine 'reality' in the situation. But, paradoxically, Althusser has also made it harder to understand the workings of ideology.[9]

So, for instance, at school we were encouraged, as middle-class boys, to feel we could choose whatever relationships with other pupils we wanted. The depth and meaningfulness of these relationships would simply depend on a sharing of interests and on individual commitment to these relationships. This is very much the way friendship is presented to us within a liberal culture. It is a question simply of individual liking and disliking.[10] We are not given any way of understanding how the particular form and quality of these relations is affected by the competitive relations in which they operate. If this created all kinds of tensions, fear and suspicion, this is something we have been made powerless to understand. Again it is the case that we only have ourselves to blame.

We are left to assume that any difficulties in our friendships have to be of our own making. We can even blame ourselves for not trusting enough the friendships we make at school, preferring to rely on friendships we have made in the neighbourhood. This can be the way we live these relations as white, middle-class boys, while being mystified about how they are influenced by the hierarchical and competitive social relations within the school. This can show itself as tension and contradiction within these relations, especially as we become dimly aware of how our feelings of mistrust are reproduced.

So, for instance, I can recall how at the moment history essays were handed back at school by the teacher, I noticed how all my energy was directed towards the mark I had got. I can also recall how jealous and envious I felt if someone did better than me. But I might not even want to become aware of such feelings, ready to blame myself for having them. The processes of mystification includes the ways our experience is individualised and internalised, so that we blame *ourselves* for these negative feelings. This only confirms the underlying feeling of our 'rottenness' as boys and our sense of not really deserving to have friendships when we feel this way about them. This works to invalidate our experience as we resist the reality of becoming aware of our jealousy. This is especially true if this threatens a sense of friendship built around the implicit conception that 'in friendship you don't feel envious or jealous of people'.

In a similar way we might be unaware of why it can be hard to make choices about subjects we are really interested in. The workings of a liberal moral culture can make us individually internalise what is in reality partly a socially produced situation so that we think it reflects our individual weakness and incapacity. Again we easily blame ourselves. We take it as further confirmation of our worthlessness and inadequacy. This binds us to the processes making us feel this way and limits our awareness of how this situation is sustained and reproduced through the social relations of schooling.

So often we have little grasp of how different subjects are brought into equivalence, as virtual commodities in the production of marks. We can find that we do subjects we are 'good at', thinking somewhat externally 'we must enjoy them because we are good at them'. We can lose a sense of what we really enjoy learning. Rather, a process of *inversion* takes place as our thinking involves a conclusion or deduction of what we 'must enjoy' because we get high marks. It becomes hard to think of the creativity of learning, since so much of our satisfaction now comes from knowing we are better than others. Often we are not even aware that there could be an alternative. This simply becomes the way we learn to feel good about ourselves.

FREEDOM AND POWER

Paulo Freire helps identify the social processes through which education becomes a process of pacification. He helps us understand relations of teaching and learning as relations of power. But he goes further in giving us a way of investigating how we were made to feel through schooling. He shows how our freedom to learn is limited without us being aware of the social processes undermining our self-esteem and integrity. We learn to see this as 'normal':

> The teacher talks about reality as if it were motionless, static, compartmentalized, and predictable. Or else he expounds on a topic completely alien to the existential experience of the students. His task is to 'fill' the students with the contents of his narration – contents which are detached from reality, disconnected from the totality that engendered them and could give them significance. Words are emptied of their concreteness and become a hollow, alienated and alienating verbosity . . . This is the 'banking' concept of education, in which the scope of action allowed to the students extends only as far as receiving, filing, and storing the deposits. They do, it is true, have the opportunity to become collectors or

cataloguers of the things they store. But in the last analysis, it is men themselves who are filed away through the lack of creativity, transformation, and knowledge in this (at best) misguided system.

(Freire 1974: 57–8)

This challenges a liberal self-conception that at school we are 'free to learn whatever we want to learn' since we are offered a whole variety of subjects to choose from. A vision of freedom as market choice rather than as effective power over our learning becomes established. We can be left feeling that it is our fault if we have not learnt at school. This has become centrally important in legitimating the structures of power and class domination in post-1945 social democracies. The notion of 'equality of opportunity' has become crucial in organising our expectations and vision of human equality.

It means that, for example, a man stuck on the assembly line, say, at Ford's plant at Dagenham in East London, can think 'if I had only worked harder at school, then I would have a better job'. This builds upon a liberal moral culture in which a person is left to feel that he only has himself to blame. If he has limited job choice, and so limited freedom, he should not blame the structure of class, race or sexual power and dominance but only himself.

Responsibility is placed firmly on the shoulders of individuals for whatever misery and oppression they experience. In this way the very structures of power and authority are explained as growing directly out of the differences of ability and talent between individuals. Society itself is individualised as social inequalities are *legitimated* flowing directly out of individual differences within a liberal moral culture.

Freire helps us understand the importance of education as a process of pacification. He helps us grasp how we are objectified through the social processes of learning, while we continue to talk about 'freedom' and 'learning':

It follows logically from the banking notion of consciousness that the educator's role is to regulate the way the world 'enters into' the students. His task is to organize a process which already occurs spontaneously, to 'fill' the students by making deposits of information which he considers to constitute true knowledge. And since men 'receive' the world as passive entities, education should make them more passive still, and adapt them to the world. The educated man is the adapted man, because he is better 'fit' for the world. Translated into practice, this concept is well suited to the purposes of the oppressors, whose tranquility rests on how well men fit the world the oppressors have created, and how little they question it.

(Ibid.: 62–3)

This is the process of pacification that we cannot easily rebel against, since it only proves, as Durkheim has it, our individual pathology. If we are not happy with this situation, this only proves there is something wrong with us. We are to be classified as either 'naughty', 'disobedient', 'lazy', 'stupid', 'inadequate', or 'unruly'. More is involved here than simply challenging a particular concept of education, since we are forced to think about how our experience of education is formed and maintained within the larger social relations of power and subordination that we learn to take for granted as 'rational' and 'fair'.

Our understanding of social relations also has to involve, if we learn from Gramsci, grasping how 'character' is formed within these relations. This involves developing critical forms of social and moral theory which can contextualise a psychological understanding of the ways people are injured, hurt, limited, damaged and distorted in the adaptations they are forced to make to prevailing relations of power and subordination.

This does not have to involve assuming an original conception of 'human nature' that has been 'distorted' and has somehow to be 'returned to'. But it does involve understanding the moral and psychological workings of social relations. This is something Fromm illuminates when he talks about a boy's relationship to his strict father:

> By dynamic adaptation we refer to the kind of adaptation that occurs, for example, when a boy submits to the commands of his strict and threatening father – being too much afraid of him to do otherwise – and becomes a 'good boy'. While he adapts himself to the necessities of the situation, something happens to him. He may develop an intense hostility against his father, which he represses, since it would be too dangerous to express it or even to be aware of it. This repressed hostility, however, though not manifest, is a dynamic factor in his character structure. It may create new anxiety and thus lead to still deeper submission; it may set up a vague defiance, directed against no one in particular but rather towards life in general.
>
> (Fromm 1942: 12)

When Fromm says that 'it would be too dangerous to express it or even to be aware of it' he is drawing upon Reich's pioneering study *Character Analysis* to help us realise the importance of psycho-social processes that are rendered invisible within the dominant rationalist traditions of social theory, which in seeing the social world as collectively constituted give no significance to emotional 'injury' and 'damage'. Yet these processes, which Fromm never manages to characterise theoretically within his developing liberal moral framework, are a determining factor in the ways we relate to each other.[11]

This does not mean that we cannot become aware of these processes as we can become aware of our feelings towards, say, our fathers. The boy Fromm is talking about cannot be completely satisfied or in balance with himself as the 'good' boy. For one thing, he might become aware of the difference in how he relates to his father from how he relates to others. Part of him might well become aware of the *inappropriateness* of his responses in a number of different situations. He might become aware, for instance, that he does not really get what he needs for himself since he is too sensitive to the needs of others.

Certainly a liberal moral culture does not make it easy for him to acknowledge the hostility he feels towards his father. We are brought up to control and conceal these negative feelings, often even from ourselves. This creates its own sense of 'unreality' in our relationships. We cannot acknowledge the feelings we have. This means we cannot acknowledge part of ourselves. We can easily be trapped into thinking that 'he's my father so I should love him'. The negative feelings will be denied since they can only show how ungrateful and unworthy we are, or so we are made to feel. The liberal culture formed within a secularised Protestant inheritance very much teaches us to 'control' these feelings, since otherwise they will control us. But in denying these feelings we are denying a significant aspect of our reality.[12]

IDEOLOGY AND EMOTIONAL LIFE

It is partly because a rationalist culture subordinates so systematically our emotions and feelings as genuine sources of insight and knowledge that we have so little relationship with and experience of them. This is also what makes it so easy, for men especially, to think that if they are given any space they will easily get out of hand. So if, for instance, John becomes aware of the depths of his rage for his father at the ways he has constantly humiliated and mistreated him, he can feel terribly afraid as soon as he lets himself become aware of these feelings. It is partly because he has never allowed himself to express any of the resentment he feels when his father orders him to do things that he feels so easily overwhelmed when he touches these feelings.

We might imagine for instance that, at some level, these feelings remain somehow underneath the surface of the relationship as some kind of echo, but then we have to make sure that this picture of a relationship with different levels does not mislead us about how this resentment can be lived out in some form in the ongoing relationship. So, for instance, the very willingness with which John is ready to comply with his father's wishes can carry the 'unreality' of obsequiousness about it. This could build its own kind of tension and uncertainty within the relationship. It might also come out as a kind of reserve or coldness in the relationship.[13]

Liberal social theory has been too ready to draw a sharp distinction between psychology as the study of individual experience and sociology as the study of society. Different forms of orthodox Marxist theory have tended to collude in this mystification, because of the idea that individual experience is essentially 'bourgeois'. This idea has sometimes led, in the work of Lukács, possibly in reaction to his own early work, to the same reductions of individual experience as echoes of the social totality. Even if his vision of totality is quite different, in this regard it still shares a rationalism with positivistic and Durkheimian traditions within sociology.[14]

This has made it difficult adequately to conceptualise that class relations of power and dominance in capitalist society do not simply rest on exploitation of the workforce through the extraction of surplus value, but daily limit, injure, hurt and damage people's everyday lives. A socialist transformation has to involve far more than a redistribution of wealth or an adequate analysis of forms of class exploitation. It also requires a fuller vision of equality and justice than that carried within a distributive theory:[15] a vision which also can illuminate and give weight to diverse forms of gender, race, ethnic and sexual oppression.

It is an essential strength of Lukács' dialectical theory in *History and Class Consciousness* that it does not separate out the different elements of a class analysis but grasps them as aspects of a more total transformation. But, critical social theory should also be able to *illuminate* people's experience at the same time as it brings into focus the structures of class, gender, racial and ethnic power and hetero-sexual domination. So, to give an example which brings out issues of class, John might be told by his father that he can 'choose whatever career makes him happy' while knowing that if he decides to go to art school, his father is going to accuse him of 'wasting his talents'. This source of tension is not only in his relationship with his father, drawing upon patriarchal assumptions about what fathers can expect from their sons, but also exists as a social contradiction continually reproduced as dominant masculinities within a liberal moral culture. It systematically denies the reality and significance of structures of power in people's lives, through a liberal relativism which makes people think that 'success' is simply a matter of individual values, of what individuals happen to regard as 'success'.

Gramsci helps us think differently about what is involved:

Self-deception can be an adequate explanation for a few individuals taken separately, or even for groups of a certain size, but it is not adequate when the contrast occurs in the life of great masses. In these cases the contrast between thought and action cannot but be the expression of profounder contrasts of a social historical order.

(Gramsci 1971: 327)

So when John is told by his father that he is thinking of doing something 'beneath himself', this points out to John something about his class background and gender expectations. The nature of class superiority is often left implicit. But it is no less insidious and powerful for all that. So John is left feeling guilty not only for 'letting his father down' but also for somehow 'letting himself down'.

If John responds by reminding his father that 'you asked me to say what I would be happy doing' this is likely to annoy his father, as if he were wilfully misunderstanding what his father is trying to say to him. Nor will his father be placated if John quotes back that 'each individual has his own conception of success and happiness', even if this provides the general framework within which we are brought up to think and feel about ourselves within liberal society. His father might dismiss this as barely relevant in the current situation, knowing that there are certain 'realities' to be taken into account. But nor will his father want to be told that he is denying John the right to choose his own career, or to follow his own interests. This is not the point here.

If John is older his father may be uncomfortable ordering John to do things. He may want to reason with him, and persuade him to 'see sense'. He wants John to know that he has 'his best interests at heart'. He wants John to make up his own mind. The power in the situation is left implicit. John is just left feeling that he will deeply disappoint his parents' class, gender and sexual expectations if he decides to go to art school. He is told that he has to face the reality of his responsibilities, and 'he needs a career that will enable him to support a family later'.

This begins to expose the tensions and contradictions between the ways we are brought up to think within a liberal moral culture, and the realities of class, gender and racial and heterosexual power within which we have to make our lives. It brings out, in the context of a single example, how we have to develop the cultural notions of individualism and difference we inherit, to illuminate the workings of ideology within the realities of class, gender, ethnic and heterosexual power and domination. If these are not simply to exist as 'uncomfortable realities' that liberal relativism protects us from facing we have to explore our inherited liberal conceptions of the individual.

To do this we have to develop less abstract and reductive conceptions of ideology as we learn to identify and name the ways that we *live out* ideology in our everyday experience. As we learn to separate out what we want and need for ourselves individually in order to sustain our integrity, difference and sense of self-worth, so we challenge what the prevailing authorities, whether they be our parents or teachers, expect of us.

If we are to live lives respecting our insights and understanding so must we question forms of social theory which would construct our identities out of the prevailing social images and discourses. If our subjectivities are too easily imagined to be socially and historically constructed this threatens to *close up* the space within which we can learn to define ourselves and so learn to grow in our own authority and wisdom. So much of our prevailing forms of social theory leave us unable to illuminate the tension between our different experiences and the terms and discourses in which we are supposedly to render them intelligible.

Chapter 7

Identities

THE EXTERNALISATION OF SELF

If we return to Max Weber's writings on *The Protestant Ethic and the Spirit of Capitalism*, he helps put some of these ideas into the broader context they need. We can return to the crucial questions already quoted since we have hardly begun to explore their depth and meaning for us:

> If you ask them what is the meaning of their restless activity, why they are never satisfied with what they have, thus appearing so senseless to any purely worldly view of life, they would perhaps give the answer, if they know any at all: 'to provide for my children and grandchildren'. But more often and, since that motive is not peculiar to them, but was just as effective for the traditionalist, more correctly, simply: that business with its continuous work has become a necessary part of their lives. That is in fact the only possible motivation, but it at the same time expresses what is, seen from the viewpoint of personal happiness, so irrational about this sort of life, where a man exists for the sake of his business, instead of the reverse.
>
> (Weber 1930: 70)

This is still an important question to ask. With the development of capitalism it comes to have more meaning for more people. It shows for Weber the irrationality built into the inversion whereby 'a man exists for the sake of his business, instead of the reverse'. The culture and morality of capitalist society work to make this 'irrationality' the normal and taken-for-granted situation. This does not simply affect the ways that people understand or conceptualise their experience. It helps form and legitimate the very relations of class power that exist at the heart of capitalist society. Work is not a matter of the satisfaction of human needs, even for the capitalist class.

Weber does not really help us understand the relations of class power that mean that the working class is forced to work for its very means of livelihood. If the conditions of working-class life have changed, particularly in the 1950s and 1960s, this says something about the rewards of wage-labour, not something about the meaningfulness of work for working-class people. If anything, the de-skilling of many jobs with the development of assembly-line production since the 1900s has tended to undermine whatever skill and pride existed in many working-class jobs.[1]

It is clear that many people simply work for the wages they get. They do not expect to get anything else from work. In some ways this has brought the experience of work closer to what Marx initially describes in the *Economic and Philosophical Manuscripts of 1844*:

> *First, the fact that labour is external* to the worker, i.e. it does not belong to his essential being; that in his work, therefore, he does not affirm himself but denies himself, does not feel content but unhappy, does not develop freely his physical and mental energy but mortifies his body and ruins his mind. The worker therefore only feels himself outside his work, and in his work feels outside himself. He is at home when he is not working, and when he is working he is not at home. His labour is therefore not voluntary, but coerced; it is *forced labour*. It is therefore not the satisfaction of a need; it is merely a *means* to satisfy needs external to it.
>
> (Marx 1975: 69)

Marx's discussions of alienated labour have often been quoted, but it has been strangely difficult to integrate his powerful understandings into social theory. The language is unfamiliar. Sometimes the language is reproduced without any appreciation of the difficulties it presents to a liberal and empiricist understanding. Many people, even in clerical, service and professional work, can recognise themselves in these opening lines.

An aspect of the power of capitalist ideology is that it makes it hard for people to identify the ways they often do not affirm themselves at work. It is almost as if people do not *expect* to affirm, or realise themselves, at work. It is easy to lose a sense of what this language means in a society where it is so generally appreciated that you only work for the money you get.

It is almost as if the kind of double life Marx suggests when he says 'the worker therefore only feels himself outside his work, and in his work feels outside himself. He is at home when he is not working, and when he is working he is not at home', has become a general aspect of what Harry Braverman has called 'the degradation of work in the twentieth century'. This is not to minimise the reality and sharpness of class relations, but to identify processes that have been involved in the transformation of processes of work. Marx anticipated some of these developments in *Capital*.

Weber helps us grasp some of the moral and cultural relations in the formation of 'identity' that make people unaware of these processes. So, at one level, liberalism encourages us to feel that we 'choose' the job we do, when we could have chosen others. We can acknowledge the reality of this choice while also understanding that, for many working-class people, it is a matter of choosing to work in very similar conditions, under very similar relations of power and subordination.

If people continue to have 'choice', it is not the kind of broad and open choice we tend to assume. At another level that we have already tried to illustrate, we are brought up in a society organised around the social relations of competitive individualism, where our very sense of self is externalised, through the processes of *identifying* our sense of self with 'individual achievement' and 'success'. This means that the different things we do, especially as men, including work, become different ways of proving ourselves.

I have already hinted at some of the sources in the ways that the religious culture of Protestantism, which remains formative within the moral culture of modernity, tends to make men in particular feel that our natures are 'rotten' and 'evil' so that it is only through what we do that we can redeem ourselves. We have continually to prove that we are not the good-for-nothings that our parents accused us of being. This has a particular resonance in the experience of boys.

Although this has obviously been moderated within more liberal practices of child-rearing it is still common, particularly within the middle class, that children have to prove themselves to earn their parents' love. Love is often unwittingly used as a form of manipulation and control. Love has to be earned because at some level we are not lovable, or so we are made to feel. It has been partly through the understandings of Freud and psychoanalysis that we have a fuller language to help us express some of the processes Marx was hinting at back in 1844.

When Marx says that the worker 'only feels himself outside his work', he is aware that we are more able to feel ourselves when we are doing things which satisfy our needs. Through the very processes by which our sense of self is externalised, we tend to think that we must be happy because we have, for instance, 'done well at an exam at school', 'had a good day's work' or 'finally passed our exams to become a lawyer'. These are all things that we have worked for, assuming that 'happiness' comes with 'individual achievement'. This can be particularly illuminating in the context of thinking about the ways we conceive our 'needs' in relation to dominant forms of masculine identities. It is partly because someone has put all his hopes on becoming a lawyer that he has worked so hard for the exams. He needs to have his sense of achievement validated partly because of the ways he has organised his life, but also because of the structure of power and reward that exists in the larger society.

It is also because he has so identified himself with 'becoming a lawyer' that nothing else will satisfy him. This is the way that he proves his worth, not only to others, but also to himself. In Weber's terms, you could say that 'a man exists for the sake of his business, instead of the reverse'. Somehow his very sense of 'personal happiness' has been *identified* with achieving this goal he has set himself. Here we only get misled if we think about whether this can be a 'genuine' need or not. All we can reflect upon for the moment is the process through which this kind of 'goal' was set. Was this something that he wanted for himself, or something to do with winning the approval of his parents? More centrally, how did he come to assume that 'happiness' was a goal to be struggled for even if it meant systematically denying feelings, wants, desires, emotions and passions?

NEEDS AND IDENTITIES

Marx understood that work could not involve the satisfaction of human needs if it is an 'unfree activity', in which people are subordinated to the power of capital to gain the means of livelihood. It is because capital and labour have such fundamentally opposed interests in capitalist production that universal conceptions of morality are bound to be ideological. They unwittingly deny the reality and significance of these relations of power and subordination.

If the product of labour does not belong to the worker, if it confronts him as an alien power, this can only be because it belongs to some *other man than the worker*. If the worker's activity is a torment to him, to another it must be *delight* and his life's joy. Not the gods, not nature, but only man himself can be this alien power over man.

We must bear in mind the above-stated proposition that man's relation to himself only becomes *objective* and *real* for him through his relation to the other man. Thus, if the product of his labour, his labour *objectified*, is for him an *alien*, hostile, powerful object independent of him, then his position towards it is such that someone else is master of this object, someone who is alien, hostile, powerful, and independent of him. If his own activity is to him an unfree activity, then he is treating it as an activity performed in the service, under the dominion, the coercion and the yoke of another man.

(Marx 1975: 74–5)

Marx recognises the significance of talking about 'man's relation to himself' knowing that this 'only becomes *objective* and *real* for him through his relation to the other man', but he does not really help us identify the different forms that this relationship can take. Marx needed a deeper encounter with the ways the Protestant tradition worked to divide people against themselves if he was to question his focus on work as the exclusive domain in which meaningful relationships take place.

Protestantism has had a deeper historical influence on the meaning of socialism, tying its vision of self-realisation to work and so implicitly subordinating other areas of life. For all the depths of Marx's insights, which have still been barely assimilated within social theory, his discussion of human needs remained relatively inadequate.[2] This is partly because of the ease with which he assumed that 'the productive life is the life of the species'. This was too uncritically assimilated into Protestant conceptions of the need to subordinate the different part of our lives to work.

It is the subordination of our 'natures', our wants, desires, feelings and emotions that Marx did not question deeply enough. He remained within an Enlightenment framework that, in broad terms, set reason against nature, even if this was in tension with aspects of his stress on practical activity and 'free, conscious activity'. Challenging secular rationalism, for more than its ignorance of practical activity, would place a challenge to the capitalist control of the means of production, and thereby over the lives of working people, in a very different context:

> For in the first place labour, *life-activity, productive life* itself, appears to man merely as a *means* of satisfying a need – the need to maintain the physical existence. Yet the productive life is the life of the species. It is life-engendering life. The whole character of a species – its species character – is contained in the character of its life-activity; and free, conscious activity is man's species character. Life itself appears only as a *means to life*.

(Ibid.: 71)

Thinking in terms of 'means' shows the continuing influence of Kantian thought on Marx's moral thinking. This was something Marx tended to assume, and which had a considerable influence over the ways he conceived human fulfilment and realisation. Marx tended to identify 'life-activity' with 'productive life', though he had a much broader conception of the nature of 'productive life' than that related to our experience of work. Sometimes he is talking more generally about 'free, conscious activity' as 'man's species character'. This meant it was easy for Marx to slip into accepting the notion of 'purposive action' as defining our very humanity.

Marx tended to share some of the assumptions of the Enlightenment modernity of his day about the ways you draw a distinction between 'animal' and 'human'. This is crucial, because defining certain ends for ourselves through an autonomous reason alone is generally taken within modernist forms of social theory to define our very humanity. In its antagonism to nature as somehow given and unchanging, we can discern a source of its ecological blindness.

In large part an Enlightenment vision of modernity has accepted uncritically the notion that progress involves the control and domination of nature. Some of Marx's contradictory inclinations are brought out when he discusses the consequence of estranged labour:

> In the same way the worker's activity is not his spontaneous activity. It belongs to another; it is the loss of his self.
>
> As a result, therefore, man (the worker) no longer feels himself to be freely active in any but his animal functions – eating, drinking, procreating, or at most in his dwelling and in dressing-up, etc.; and in his human functions he no longer feels himself to be anything but an animal. What is animal becomes human and what is human becomes animal.
>
> Certainly eating, drinking, procreating etc., are also genuinely human functions. But in the abstraction which separates them from the sphere of all other human activities and turns them into sole and ultimate ends, they are animal.
>
> (Ibid.: 69)

Again the tensions that seem to be pulling Marx in different directions tend to get expressed in terms of 'means' and 'ends'. We can value Marx's recognition that sexuality, for instance, has to be understood in the context of other aspects of human relationships, so that it should not be conceived of as a 'sole and ultimate end'. But this is to open a discussion about the meaning and significance of sexuality within human relationships; Marx is prepared to sidestep this since he finds it hard to shake off the notion that sexuality is private and emotional and so marginal when it comes to a fulfilment and self-realisation that comes from creative labour. The way that he talks about sexuality as a 'genuinely human function' seems to block adequate recognition of it as a form of self-expression.

Marx seems powerless to challenge the objectification of sexual relationships even if he recognises that sexuality should not be separated out. So, for instance, Jane might challenge John for seeing her simply as a sexual object, so that everything that he does is directed towards getting off with her. This is sexuality as conquest. Jane might feel that he is not really interested in her as a person, in what she thinks, feels and hopes for. She might be left feeling that he is simply feigning interest, but at some level does not really want to know. It might be hard for John to respond to this challenge, since he is so used to relating to women in this way that he thinks it 'normal' and 'natural'. He does not really recognise the ways that he objectifies her, nor what the processes of change could be. This opens a discussion about the form that heterosexual sexual relations take, as long as women are seen as sexual objects.

OBJECTIFICATIONS

It has been in the theory and the practice of the women's movement that Marx's early discussions of objectification, of the ways people are estranged and no longer feel themselves, have come to have a peculiar contemporary relevance. This movement opens up the possibility for a level of political, cultural and personal critique that was generally lost in the traditions of orthodox Marxism.

The ways that Marx describes the worker's relationship to his work in conditions of capitalist production resonates deeply with some of the understandings of the women's movement, which have identified the fact that the more women devote themselves to their relations of subordination to men, the less worthy and secure they feel in their own individual identities. In a very real sense they are undermined as individuals in their own right.

It is this understanding of sexual relations as relations of power and subordination that has complemented the insight into the centrality of processes of objectification in the human and social relations of monopoly capitalism:

So much does the appropriation of the object appear as estrangement that the more objects the worker produces the fewer can he possess and the more he falls under the dominion of his product, capital.

All these consequences are contained in the definition that the worker is related to the *product of his labour* as to an *alien* object. For on this premise it is clear that the more the worker spends himself, the more powerful the alien objective world becomes which he creates over-against himself, the poorer he himself – his inner world – becomes, the less belongs to him as his own. It is the same in religion. The more man puts into God, the less he retains in himself. The worker puts his life into the object; but now his life no longer belongs to him but to the object. Hence, the greater this activity, the greater is the worker's lack of objects. Whatever the product of his labour is, he is not. Therefore the greater this product, the less is he himself. The *alienation* of the worker in his product means not only that his labour becomes an object, an *external* existence, but that it exists *outside him*, independently, as something alien to him, and that it becomes a power of its own confronting him; it means that the life which he has conferred on the object confronts him as something hostile and alien.

(Ibid.: 67)

Marx assumed that work should somehow be the expression of the self. The different things that we do should be an expression of our individuality. This is the process through which we identify and clarify the very meaning of our individuality.

Capitalist production denies this essential condition for the growth and development of our humanity. It forces the worker to relate to the 'product of his labour as to an alien object'. Marx was very impressed with the analogy of people's relationship to God. This helped organise and focus his thinking about work, but it also limited his thinking. So it was crucial for Marx to develop the insight that 'the more man puts into God, the less he retains in himself'. This helped him say that 'the worker puts his life into the object; but now his life no longer belongs to him but to the object', which in turn expresses a profound social and psychological understanding that implicitly challenges the more Kantian language of 'means' and 'ends', within which Marx was also sometimes trapped.

Marx can speak to us, but often we lack a more general framework which would allow us to integrate his insights. Often they remain challenging insights that disturb us at the margins of our consciousness. Many people have experienced the depths of Marx's moral and psychological understanding, without really being able to learn fully from it.[3] It has been the recent historical experience of the women's movement, and of sexual politics more generally, that has brought these insights into some kind of contemporary focus. It has been recognised as a feature of the dependency and subordination of women in sexual relations, that the more of themselves they put into the relationship, the less they have of themselves.

Women have talked within feminist consciousness-raising groups about the ways they have unwittingly been forced to give up their own individual wants and needs to take on the responsibilities of partners and children. It becomes difficult to define individual needs without feeling 'selfish' or 'mean' because women learn to *accept* blame and responsibility. In this way women are brought up to subordinate their own wants and needs automatically and to put others first. It has been less clear that this personal relation is also a social relation which undermines women's sense of their own individual and collective identities.

For women to become individuals in their own right often involves challenging the social relations of domesticity and childcare. Liberal talk of equal respect for differences has often shown itself to be ideological. It has made it even harder for women to see the power relations they have been brought up within. This is not a matter of getting others to 'see you differently' or to 'value you more highly', but of changing the everyday relations which continually reproduce this subordination, and which are continually undermining women's sense of their self-esteem and self-worth.

Rather than reaching for an abstract conception of equality feminism began to appreciate and take responsibility for the way in which relationships of power are working to *undermine* a woman's sense of self-worth and identity. It is not simply a question of dealing with results, but with the actual relations of power lived out in everyday life. This is something else that, paradoxically given a widespread sidestepping of Marx in the 1990s, echoes what Marx recognised about work relations:

> But the estrangement is manifested not only in the result but in the *act of production* – within the *producing activity* itself. How would the worker come to face the product of his activity as a stranger, were it not that in the very act of production he was estranging himself from himself. The product is after all but the summary of the activity of production. If then the product of labour is alienation, production itself must be active alienation, the alienation of activity, the activity of alienation.
>
> (Ibid.: 68)

Marx shows that the very social relations of work in capitalist society involve a process of a person 'estranging himself from himself'. This is a process through which people lose a sense of themselves. So people lose a sense of the costs and sacrifices they are making and gradually come to take them for granted. This is not simply the description of a psychological process, but of the workings of social relations which are also relations of power and subordination.

Marx is not simply describing processes of, say, 'estrangement' as a consequence or 'result' of these social relations of work. To believe this would be to sacrifice the critical edge of Marx's writing. Sociology has been very anxious to understand processes of alienation in these terms, which make it possible to shift responsibility on to the shoulders of workers themselves for being affected in these ways.

The alienation which grows out of the class relations of power of capitalist production too often gets reduced to talk about 'job satisfaction'.[4]

Marx tended to assume the centrality of expressing ourselves through work. This is partly because of the centrality of capitalist control over the means of production in organising class relations of subordination and dominance, which means that working-class people are forced to work under the rule of capital to gain means of livelihood. They have to work for capital to earn the very 'means for life'. As Marx says, 'The extremity of this bondage is that it is only as a *worker* that he continues to maintain himself as a *physical subject* and that it is only as a physical subject that he is a worker' (Ibid.: 67).

In this way Marx is showing how capitalist society *reduces* people, so that people only count as 'workers'. This is the only value and identity that people can have within the capitalist economy. It is the very workings of the social relations of capitalism that make rhetorical and ideological Kant's claim that people should not be treated merely as means but only as ends in themselves. Marx's critique of the social relations of liberalism is important in that it shows that in a class society people *cannot* simply choose to have whatever relationships they want to have with others.[5]

Marx recognises the ways people become commodities for capital. This is not because of the evil nature of individual capitalists, but because of the workings of the capitalist economy, something Marx understood in the *Paris Manuscripts* as much as in *Capital*:

> The *value* of the worker as capital rises according to demand and supply, and even *physically* his *existence*, his *life*, was and is looked upon as a supply of a *commodity* like any other. The worker produces capital, capital produces him – hence he produces himself, and man as *worker*, as a *commodity*, is the product of this entire cycle. To the man who is nothing more than a *worker* – and to him as a worker – his human qualities only exist in so far as they exist for capital *alien* to him.
>
> (Ibid.: 79)

Marx is aware of the social processes through which people are reduced to labour power. Exploitation creates the fundamental ambivalences in the liberal ideology of capitalism, in which legal and civic relations have to sustain visions of freedom and equality within the public realm of citizenship.[6] The institutions of social democracy have to restore a sense of individual dignity and worth, which are systematically being undermined through the workings of the capitalist economy, which treats people as commodities.

The working of state socialist institutions as we knew them in Russia and Eastern Europe, denied people even these civil rights on the assumption that they are merely formal so would make no difference to people's lives. Orthodox Marxism argued that because the means of production were not in private hands but were owned by the state there could be no exploitation, since any surplus was supposedly used for the benefit of the whole community. Similarly, since there was supposedly no exploitation there was no justification for any right to strike. These notions as Simone Weil recognised are also crucially ideological in the sense that they work to mystify the social relations of domination and subordination in the labour process.

IDENTITIES AND ACTIVITIES

Marx understood the central importance of the forces and relations of production in capitalist society. He recognised the centrality of the ownership of the means of production in establishing the social relations of class power and dominance. This rested on an assumption for Marx that 'the productive life is the life of the species'. Marx meant this in different senses he never really distinguished.

Sometimes he is talking in an epochal sense about the need to understand the centrality of how a society reproduces its very means of livelihood, if we are to understand its history. But sometimes he is talking more ontologically about the needs of people to express themselves through their activity. Here he is challenging the contemplative conception of people that was shared by traditional philosophy. So we find Marx writing, as one of the 'Theses on Feuerbach' that 'the highest point attained by that materialism which only observes the world, i.e. which does not conceive sensuous existence as practical activity, is the observation of particular individuals and of civil society' (Marx and Engels 1976).

So Marx is challenging forms of materialism which see social reality in terms of 'objects of observation, but not as human sense activity, not as practical activity, not subjectively'. This is also a critique of the 'common-sense' ways we relate to the social world which are very much encouraged in the social theory of positivism. This common sense produces a respect for 'the facts' as some kind of totally independent reality and limits our understanding of the ways the social world can be changed, since we assume that social reality is something that we have to be ready to adapt to since 'this is the way things are'. Marx helps us understand the centrality of 'practical activity' in a transformed understanding of 'social reality'. The social world becomes something that we can change and transform, not something to which we are forced to accommodate ourselves.

Marx is also aware that when he talks about the needs for people to express themselves through their activities, this is largely determined by their position within the mode of production. No doubt there is a flexibility that did not exist before now and that some working-class people can use education to remake their lives. Again, many people do not have the choice that liberalism promises, since they are obliged to find their place within the social relations of production that exist in their communities. But this sometimes pushes Marx to identify people with their place within production. We find this in *The German Ideology*:

> The way in which men produce their means of subsistence depends in the first place on the nature of the existing means which they have to reproduce. This mode of production should not be regarded simply as the reproduction of the physical existence of individuals. It is already a definite form of activity of these individuals, a definite form of expressing their life, a definite mode of life. As individuals express their life, so they are. What they are, therefore, coincides with their production, with *what* they produce and with *how* they produce it. What individuals are, therefore, depends on the material conditions of their production.
>
> (Marx and Engels 1976: 10–11)

This is a crucial passage. It challenges some of our common-sense assumptions about identity, freedom and expression and makes us realise how much people are formed and maintained through their work relations. But this also has to be understood historically. It was no accident that led Dennis, Henriques and Slaughter to call their analysis of a Yorkshire mining community 'Coal is our life'. Working as miners was clearly 'a definite form of expressing their life, a definite *mode of life*'.[7] But Marx tends to assume something more general about the ways individuals express themselves through their work, when he says that 'as individuals express their life, so they are. 'What they are, therefore, coincides with their production.'

At one level we can think about, say, workers on the assembly line at Fords, Dagenham. Relatively few people in the younger generation of workers identify themselves with the work they do. They see it as something they are forced to do to get money. This does not mean that the shift system does not dominate the everyday organisation of their lives. But we also have to take seriously the changes that have taken place in the ways that people identify with work. This is something that Marx also recognised when he said that 'the worker therefore only feels himself outside his work, and in his work feels outside himself'.

There is a different explanation for the direction Marx seems to be pushed in. In opposition to a more contemplative conception of people, it was an enormous discovery for Marx to realise that as individuals express their life, so they are. Marx was recognising the fact that our understanding tends to change as changes take place in our experience. This invokes a *practical* conception of 'experience' that is very different from the passive relationship to the social world that is assumed in the empiricist tradition.

But Marx never really develops this idea. Sometimes he assumed too easily that people express themselves through their 'life-activity', which Marx was too ready to identify with 'productive life' and so with production. This also resonates with a dominant heterosexual masculinity that is identified with activity and so feels threatened by a passivity that is all too often identified with the feminine. This sustains homophobic feelings since men often fear connecting with their softer feelings which are identified with gayness. Since Marx had other reasons for recognising the centrality of production and productive relations, it was easy for him to settle the problem of human needs and individuality in this way. This served to invalidate other areas of human life and other activities through which people need to express themselves. It also served to reinforce a dominant form of masculinity.

Marx recognises that the individual has to express his or her life through the social relations that are available. This is to challenge the liberal conceptions which would isolate the individual, seeing his or her development in terms of the satisfaction of certain pre-giving qualities and needs. Marx challenges this conception, which does not recognise the ways we express our lives through what we do and how we relate.

Nor does it recognise *how* we discover our needs and clarify our wants as we change through the social relations we have with others. Marx challenges the abstract separation of 'the individual' from 'the society', and from the social relations of class power that people live out in their everyday lives:

> We must above all avoid setting up 'the society' as an abstraction opposed to the individual. The individual *is* the social entity. The expression of his life . . . is therefore the expression and verification of the life of society.
>
> (Quoted in Dunayevskaya 1971: 65)

Marx makes us aware of the fundamental insight that, as we express our lives, so we are. This takes us to the heart of the ways we relate to others in our everyday lives and challenges inherited liberal self-conceptions which treat the self as somehow safely preserved in its integrity in our inner lives. Within modernity cast in secularised Protestant terms this can make us feel that others 'don't really know' who we are since all they know is our social persona. We only really know ourselves and we carefully choose whom we share ourselves with.

This privatisation of the self can serve as an important protection, if it is also at some level a mystification. It offers false consolations and blinds us to how we are continually being 'read' in our relationships.[8] It can make us feel safely in charge of our 'real life' that takes place in the privacy of our own homes. We can supposedly remain untouched by the humiliations and compromises of social life, secure in the knowledge that our 'true self' has barely been exposed. This is the sense of freedom that early existentialism is built upon.[9] It tends to make us oblivious to the demands of social life as we withdraw further into ourselves.

Marx says something interesting about this Protestant conception when he describes as a very condition of alienation that the objects we produce confront us as something 'alien', as having a 'power independent of the producer'. Because we are forced to work for others, our labour is no longer an expression of ourselves:

> In the conditions dealt with by political economy this realisation of labour appears as a *loss of reality* for the workers; objectification as *loss of the object* and *object-bondage*; appropriation as *estrangement*, as *alienation*.

> (Marx 1975: 66)

It is partly because we do not even expect to be able to express ourselves in our work that we suffer this 'loss of reality'. Our sense of self becomes isolated and estranged from our everyday activities, and we do not even expect to be able to express 'who we are' in our relations with others.

Marx conceived that we express ourselves through our 'life-activity'. Not only does he sometimes relate this too narrowly to work and production, but he has a particular vision of how it works. Marx recognises that it is a need for people to be able to express themselves in the way they are living. The capitalist control over the means of production means that work becomes for the worker a way of 'estranging himself from himself'. So the activity of labour becomes a form of alienation.

This relates to how Marx conceives the building up of our identities as the building up of activities in which we can express ourselves. The more the worker produces in alienating relations, the poorer he or she becomes. This shows that *forms of expression* are crucial for Marx. It is worth quoting again the passage which shows how influenced this belief is by Marx's thinking about people's relation to God:

the more the worker spends himself, the more powerful the alien objective world becomes which he creates over-against himself, the poorer he himself – his inner world – becomes, the less belongs to him as his own. It is the same in religion. The more man puts into God, the less he retains in himself. The worker puts his life into the object; but now his life no longer belongs to him but to the object.

(Ibid.: 66–7)

NEEDS AND EXPRESSION

Marx's very rich sense of people as creative beings is closely identified with a conception of people as productive beings. Somehow this is related to his critique of the traditional philosophical conception of people as 'rational creatures', which have often been rendered as contemplative and active only in their mental life, through which the social world is categorised or classified.

Sometimes it seems as if Marx is saying that we make ourselves through our activities, through our practices. Marx did not assert this contrast too sharply, but nor did he say enough about it. Sometimes it is as if food, clothing and houses are conceived of as the 'means of life, just as nature provides labour with the *means of life* in the sense that labour cannot *live* without objects on which to operate' while 'life-activity, productive life itself' should be the 'end'of life (Ibid.: 67, 71).

It is because labour in capitalist society is 'forced labour' that it is 'therefore not the satisfaction of a need, it is merely a *means* to satisfy needs external to it' (Ibid.: 69). It seems to be precisely because the most fundamental human need is for people to express themselves through their work, that the more workers in capitalist society spend themselves, the less belongs to themselves as their own. But, partly because Marx did not develop a discussion of the ways that people could express themselves in the different areas of their lives, he does not develop a full enough understanding of the diversity of human needs and their relationship to human growth and development. The social relations in other parts of our lives are so fundamentally transformed as commodity relations, that it seemed important for Marx to focus directly on the central role of the social relations of production.

When Marx says, 'The more man puts into God, the less he retains in himself', this tends implicitly to build upon the assumed Protestant notion of the 'evilness' of human nature. Marx tends to see our 'natures' as animal, and he tends to share the cultural assumption that we only rise above our 'animal natures' because of our conscious powers of reasoning. He seems also to share the Kantian assumption that, in our emotions, feelings, wants and desires, we are largely determined by forces over which we have little control. Our freedom comes from our rationality, even if Marx does talk about our 'sensuous existence'. This is still a profoundly contradictory theme in his writings.

Recovering the self is not simply a matter of reinstating our emotions, feelings, wants and desires in a more central role in our experience. It also involves recognising the crucial significance of sexuality, intimacy and personal life in our understanding of 'human nature' and the ways it can change and transform attention to different areas of life. This also clarifies weaknesses in how Marx conceives what people need and want in their lives, for all the insight contained in his notion of expression. It is because the culture and morality of Protestantism make it so hard for people to trust themselves that they are ready to put so much into God. We have already connected this to what Fromm identifies as 'the development of a frantic activity and a striving to do *something*'.

Human relations involve giving, but they also involve receiving. Within the morality and culture of capitalism there is a ceaseless task to prove ourselves through activities. Passivity is experienced as threatening, especially to our dominant senses of masculinity. To be effective means to be actively in control of any eventuality, able to deal with whatever the world presents us with. At some level the culture undermines our sense that we deserve to receive, since it soon makes us feel that if we are passive we are 'worthless', 'inadequate', 'rotten' or 'not good enough'.

We are always judging ourselves with modernity, cast within Protestant terms, by external standards, since it has become difficult to *believe* in our own sense of what we might need for ourselves. Liberal discussions about individual freedom and choice can sometimes only make it harder for us, since we are so aware of how little control we seem to have over our own lives. We are anxious to prove ourselves, which often means doing the 'right thing', conforming to the standards of external authorities. There is something in Marx's writings that goes along with this tendency rather than challenging it and revealing its historical and cultural sources.

Marx certainly helps us understand the need for us to express ourselves through our activities. He makes us aware of the class character of work in capitalist society, organised around production for profit and not need. He makes us aware of the need to challenge the class relation of power at work if work is to become a meaningful expression. If Marx was clear how empty workers are made to feel, as they put themselves into the production of objects which are not theirs, he does not develop a full enough sense of how important it is for people to satisfy their creative needs in their everyday lives. He also sways little about gender relations at work which might, for instance, open up concerns about sexual harassment since there is supposedly not space for sexuality which supposedly belongs to the personal realm alone.

In this regard, Marx says little about friendship, love and sexuality, for he inherits a somewhat dismissive attitude to the subjective and personal aspects of life. It is because justice has to do with the public realm that Marx inherits, partly through Hegel, a classical belief that human beings, as intrinsically social beings, can only realise themselves fully within the public realm. Emotional life has its place, but it is within the sphere of personal life alone.

It is certainly difficult to theorise about human needs, since we are continually being reminded that they are so fundamentally socially and historically conditioned or else the effects of prevailing discourses. Marx wanted to avoid this kind of empty discussion by focusing his attention on

> the real process of production, starting out with the simple material production of life, and on the comprehension of the form of intercourse connected with and created by this mode of producton, i.e. of civil society in its various stages as the basis of all history, and also in its action as the State.
>
> (Marx 1976: 27–9)

This can provide us with a very different starting point but it should not make redundant questions about the diversity of human needs, even if it challenges the abstract ways that these have traditionally been framed.

Human needs cannot be defined in some kind of abstract discussion, but involve recognising, for instance, the historical contradictions that exist in the ways needs are being continually contested, say for instance between the way that capital would define people's needs in terms of individual achievement and success, and the ways different gender, racial and sexual groups, and individuals, in society would challenge definitions of their needs. Again possibly the clearest recent examples have come from the women's liberation movement and the attempts on the part of women to define their own meanings and values as they discover their own diverse voices.

The morality and culture of a patriarchal and heterosexist society has very much defined women into a subordinate position in relation to men. Capitalist ideology has been inherently patriarchal, and has wanted to define the fulfilment of women in terms of their serving the needs of men and children. It has been argued that it is 'natural' for women to find their happiness and fulfilment in this way. This can only mean that there must be 'something wrong' with a woman who is not happy to settle down with husband, housework and children.

This has rightly made feminism suspicious about arguments that flow from what is 'natural', since they have so obviously been used to legitimate the subordination and oppression of women. But this has also made us question certain accepted notions of cultural relativism, since these have sometimes worked to legitimate the oppression of women in different cultures. At the same time, feminism makes us potentially far more sensitive to the different forms this oppression can take.

HISTORY AND NEEDS

The women's movement has sharpened conflict as women have challenged the social power of men. Many women have rejected the notion that domesticity and childcare are somehow 'natural' to women. They have discerned the subtle workings of a legitimation for the subordination and oppression they experience as women. They have challenged the socially defined and sanctioned roles for women and so, in their own way, they have forced a reconsideration of the idea that needs are completely socially and historically conditioned. For feminists have not simply argued that women used to be quite satisfied with their subordination to the desires and needs of men but now want more for themselves; rather they have identified continuous and diverse histories, which have largely gone unrecognised, in which women have been resisting this subordination.[10]

They have identified a continuous history of contradiction, tension, guilt, suffering and oppression, as some women have continually rejected the gender and sexual identities that society has prepared them for. Often this has shown itself in the hidden history of tension, compromise and emotion, as well as physical and psychological violence which have also been a part of the history of marriage and heterosexuality as institutions.[11] It has been crucial to uncover some of the pain and acute difficulty of these herstories, so that it is not assumed that women simply accommodated themselves to their subordination without different forms of resistance.

Feminisms force us to invoke some notion of gendered and individual needs, needs that have been systematically *denied* through the processes of subordination. We have to recognise, for instance, the ways women's sexuality has been systematically denied as if sexuality were a possession of men that they could cast exclusively in their own image. As women learn to explore their sexualities they learn to clarify what brings satisfaction and fulfilment in both heterosexual and lesbian relationships. This is both an individual and collective process as women find strength and courage through their relationships with other women to give voice to what they want and need for themselves. This does not mean that we can define these needs abstractly as somehow pre-given. But nor can we begin to gain a sense of the realities of these herstories unless we also question the notion that human needs are completely socially and historically created, a belief that also serves those who would mystify the reality of human histories as a long struggle against different forms of exploitation and oppression.

So, for example, a woman might recognise that she wants to have more of her individual life, and she does not want to continue living simply in relation to her husband and children. She wants to get a job as a journalist. She needs the work, and she needs the everyday social interaction that she has badly missed. She knows that her husband will not object, since he has always said that she should have a fulfilling job. But she also knows that it will be impossible if it all stays on her shoulders. This is how Jennifer Curry has described the situation in which this leaves a middle-class woman:

> So we struggle on, trying to pack one week's work into everyday, encouraged by the sort of magazines I write to strive to be a perfect lover for our husband, a perfect mother for our children, a perfect wife for our house, a more-than-perfect worker in our chosen career.
>
> Of course, we fail. We fall into bed too weary for more than a chaste kiss, we nag our children, we don't find time even to banish the cob-webs, and sometimes we put in a less than perfect performance when we're out at work.
>
> (*Guardian*, 20 November 1979)

This extract gives you a sense of the variety of standards that middle-class women are forced to live up to. It is a more general feature of the social relations of patriarchal societies that both men and women, if in different ways, can be continually plagued with feelings of failure and inadequacy for not living up to these standards. It is worse within a liberal modern culture because we cannot help feeling that we set these standards for ourselves. We cannot help feeling that, if we worked harder and more conscientiously, we should be able to meet them, so that we really only have ourselves to blame if we fail. This is an aspect of the moralism that is deeply embedded: we feel that we should be capable of meeting all these standards we set ourselves. In part it is a problem that is created because we have learnt to take for granted particular values and beliefs.

This is clear to Jennifer Curry, when she compares her experience with that of her middle-class mother:

> Where I live there's no difficulty in finding a home-help. Jobs are scarce and money tight, and there is many a woman willing to do

housework to supplement the family income. No, the difficulty lies deep in myself. I can't get rid of the feeling that I should clean up after myself, and that it is somehow demeaning to ask someone else to do it for me.

My mother had no such scruples. As soon as I was at school she went back to full-time teaching and engaged a 'maid' as they were called then. My remonstrations that it was unfair to expect someone else to do her dirty work, and that the mistress–maid relationship was both anachronistic and anti-social, cut no ice. 'What nonsense,' she said. 'I'm a good teacher, so I teach. Sally's a good housewife, so she cleans the house. And I give her some of my earnings. It's as simple as that.'

For her, it has worked. But my generation, brought up on ideals of equality, democracy, and a classless society, can't rid itself of the concept that 'work' is a virtue, but 'service' is a dirty word.

(Ibid.)

We can sense the ease with which she can even blame herself for feeling this way, as if it would almost be better if she felt different. This touches a raw nerve of liberalism which exists in its dealings with class relations of dependency and power. If it is a question of individual morality, relations and values, it is also a question of the class, gender and sexual relations within which she feels obliged to live and make her life.

If Jennifer Curry feels that 'it was unfair to expect someone else to do her dirty work' then it is hard to be convinced by her mother saying that 'Sally's a good housewife, so she cleans the house.' At one level her mother can feel that she is getting on with her teaching, what she wants to do, and that she is providing Sally with an income that she very much needs. She does not recognise the moral dilemmas that face her daughter. But nor is it a situation that Jennifer can solve individually, even if she begins to understand it more.

Possibly it would be made easier if the social relations of domesticity and childcare were more generally challenged in the household. Why should her husband not take a more equal role? Why does the responsibility remain firmly on her shoulders, if he really means what he says? There are no easy solutions within these patterns of relationships and often it is a matter of making the best possible compromise, giving due recognition to the demands that face the individuals concerned. It is also that there is no 'right' solution that can be worked out by reason alone, for needs change and individuals learn to identify what they want and need for themselves in different terms.

In a different society, in which more recognition and value was given to our relationships with children, childcare might not be organised

around the primary demands of work. If we as men were less identified with work we might learn to value our relationships with children
in different ways. As the boundaries between public and private begin
to soften it might become easier to take on fuller responsibilities. This
might come to be a 'need' that we identify, so learning to question
the organisation of work that so often costs us a close and intimate
relationship with children. Similarly, as women learn to balance their
needs for work with their desire to be with their children, patterns
of work will have to change. In this context different visions of equality,
freedom and responsibility might well emerge as identities become
less exclusively fixed within particular realms of activity.

If this means people straddling different worlds, this fragmentation
is not simply to be welcomed as a feature of a post-modern world.
It can too often leave people feeling frustrated, empty and exhausted,
as they recognise that they are doing nothing well and that their
energies are dispersed beyond recognition and is a situation that needs
to be reorganised so that some sense of integration and fulfilment is
possible. The point is that people have to be ready to acknowledge
their felt needs in the situation, which might be very different from
what they suppose them to be or even how they think they ought
to be, so that meaningful negotiation can take place. This involves
a break with a rationalistic tradition that supposes that a solution is
to be found through putting our feelings and desires aside, rather than
bringing them honestly and openly into the situation, and then, of
course, they can always change.[12]

Chapter 8

Contradictions

MORALITY AND SELF-DENIAL

The dominant moral traditions within a liberal moral culture can make us assume that morality is very much centred around an individual quest concerning 'What ought I to do?' So morality concerns the ways in which *I* decide what would be the morally correct thing to do in any situation. This bears the influence of a Protestantism in which the individual is very much working out his or her own individual relationship with God. So morality is traditionally a matter of proving ourselves in the eyes of God. It is a matter of doing 'the right thing', which will bring salvation in a world to come even if it does not bring happiness and fulfilment in the present.

Rather, within a secularised culture of modernity implicitly shaped by a Protestant ethic, we cannot help feeling influenced by the notion that we very much prove our 'moral worth' by showing a readiness to sacrifice our individual wants and needs. So, for instance, we talked about the ways that John can feel proud of himself, within the terms of a traditional masculinity, because of all the sacrifices he takes himself to be making for his wife and children. This is an implicit morality of self-denial which has been deeply influenced by Kant, and which has become part of the common sense of a patriarchal society.[1]

This tradition has created its own notions of moral strength. It has helped individuals believe in themselves in a way that has strengthened their oppositions to external authorities. In its own way too it has formed within liberalism a powerful tradition of individual resistance against injustice. But at the same time it has worked to individualise and desocialise our moral consciousness. Morality becomes a matter of individual decision, conscience and witness. As Kantian morality involves us living up to the moral law out of a sense of duty, whatever sacrifices this calls for in our wants and desires, we inherit a tradition in which the full weight of moral decisions rests on individual shoulders.

Morality becomes very much a matter of living up to standards that we have supposedly set for ourselves. We develop little sense of how society sometimes places us in contradictory, if not impossible situations where, because of the class, gender, ethnic and sexual relations of power and dominance, it often becomes a matter of balancing irreconcilable demands. This is a pervasive feature of liberal society, which creates frustration and tension in individuals' lives and leads us to assume that if we only use our reason it is more possible to live a moral life in an unjust society or to relate more equally to others than was possible within older more traditional and authoritarian cultures.

It is important to identify *changes* taking place in liberal society and culture, so that we can explore the moral tensions and contradictions that individuals face. These are too easily dismissed within traditions of social theory that leave little space for moral considerations. So, for instance, we should think about how liberal teacher education encourages student teachers to relate individually to each child's individual needs and abilities. Liberal ideas find it difficult to focus upon individuals without at the same time tending to mystify the significance of class, ethnic and racial differences. In its anxiety not to discriminate, liberalism can mystify people about the sources of their own individual identities, cultures, histories and experience.

This mystification can make it harder for people to gain a sense of themselves, they feel the need to identify themselves as 'individuals with particular abilities', rather than as coming from a particular class, gender, ethnic or racial background and experience. What is more, this can create an impossible situation for a teacher in, say, an inner-city school who is trying to relate individually to his or her large and overflowing class. Often the teacher has not been adequately prepared to understand the significance of class, ethnic and racial background and, unable to cope, he or she is plagued by a sense of failure, feeling that he or she 'isn't good enough'. It is easy to feel that the teacher should be able to respond to each child, since this is what he or she has been taught to do. It is not surprising that so many young teachers give up after their first year of teaching. Often they are barely prepared for the contradictory situation they are able to face. There is little grasp of how the 'problems' are created and sustained within the social relations of power.[2]

FEMINISM AND MORALITY

The women's movement and sexual politics generally have worked to challenge a number of our inherited moral conceptions. Women have become aware that to begin to exist as individuals in their own right, they have to challenge the subordination they are brought up to accept almost as 'second nature'. This is a challenge to functionalist forms of social theory that have assumed that no man would find individual fulfilment through adapting to roles and duties that have been socially prescribed. So women, for instance, have learnt to value their own relationships with other women, rather than being ready to put them aside to be available for men. This involves recovering a sense of their own individual needs and wants, rather than being ready to subordinate them to look after the needs of others.

Instead of simply caring for others, women have also learnt to care for themselves. But this also involves, as feminism has discovered, changing the traditional pattern of relationships between men and women. For, if this individuality is to be expressed in everyday life, it means sharing more of the responsibility of domestic life and childcare, which involves challenging the traditional power of men in the home, as well as the forms of social theory which have legitimated these forms of inequality.

But there is bound to be a tension in setting up a new idealised conception of the 'free and equal woman'. This ideal in itself can become a tyranny if it creates in women a renewed sense of inadequacy and failure for not being able to live up to this new image of themselves. This would reproduce within feminism the same moralistic structures, rather than challenging them. It is only when women begin to express this new identity in the ways they live, refusing to accommodate themselves automatically to the demands of their partners and choosing at times to prioritise other aspects of their lives, that they are forced to realise how threatening these changes are to traditional male power. As men, we are often ready to support feminism as long as we think it means leaving women alone to sort out their lives. It is difficult when sexual politics is seen to challenge our privileges as men.

But feminism has also created its own kind of envy amongst heterosexual men. It is quite common for men to admit that they have their own close and trusting relations with women, since their relations with each other tend to be so full of competition and struggle. At another level it has been hard for heterosexual men, to find closeness, love and intimacy with each other, without feeling threatened by homophobic feelings that have not been worked through. We have often used women to contact the warmth and tenderness in ourselves. We are often so closely identified with our work and careers, our male identity having been established in the public realm, that it is easy to feel out of touch with ourselves.[3]

Often, as men, we can feel trapped into acting and responding in ways expected of us, living up to certain externalised images of ourselves, rather than out of any inner sense of our wants, desires and feelings. Because of this, a dominant masculinity has increasingly been experienced as an artificial construction that has somehow come to stand in the way of men developing an *inner* connection with themselves.[4] In contrast to this, the women's movement seems to have given women more of a sense of their individual needs and collective strength. This is not to romanticise a fragmented women's movement which has moved in many diverse directions, but rather to recognise the potential challenge it creates for our inherited conceptions of morality.

Because masculinity is closely identified within an Enlightenment vision of modernity with 'rationality' and with notions of 'purposive action', to investigate its roots is to expose crucial sources of modernity which have been set in its image. We learn to prove ourselves as heterosexual men by setting certain goals and ends for ourselves through reason alone which we then struggle to realise. This involves the systematic subordination of our wants and feelings, which are construed as 'weaknesses' or as 'interferences' in pursuing these 'rational' goals. In this way, notions of 'purposive rational action', which for Weber present us with sone kind of standard against which other forms of action are to be assessed, have built into them certain implicit moral conceptions, drawn largely from a Kantian tradition. Weber is explicit in his debt to Kant, though the moral implications for his theory of action are rarely explored.

It is the general assumption that these goals, ends and ideals are to be set through reason alone, and are thereby separated from the workings of our emotions, feelings, wants and desires. The gender implications require the devaluation of affective action, usually identified with women.[5] Consciousness is too easily identified with rationality and intellectuality, and so separated from emotions, desires and other aspects of our 'natures'. Following Kant purposes and ends that we choose through reason only, and which are supposedly untainted by emotion, can alone express our autonomy and freedom. To a great extent both Weberian and Durkheimian traditions within social theory take for granted a Kantian tradition in which the promptings of nature defined as egoistic and selfish stand in contrast to the demands of freedom.[6]

CONTROL AND EXPRESSION

Some of the contradictions and tensions in Marx's writings lie in his unresolved relationship to this Enlightenment tradition. He was often anxious to distinguish people from animals and so privilege the rationalised notion of consciousness that has so deeply marked the Marxist tradition:

The animal is immediately identical with its life-activity. It does not distinguish itself from it. It is *its life-activity*. Man makes his life-activity itself the object of his will and of his consciousness. He has conscious life-activity. It is not a determination with which he directly merges. Conscious life-activity directly distinguishes man from life-activity. It is just because of this that he is a species being or it is only because he is a species being that he is a Conscious Being, i.e. that his own life is an object for him. Only because of that is his activity free activity.

(Marx 1975: 71)

So our rationality becomes the source of our 'freedom'. This encourages people to identify freedom with control over nature, just as rationality assumes a certain control over our emotions and feelings, which are seen as aspects of our 'natures'.

This has often meant a very unholy alliance between the history of socialism and of a capitalist society, ready to compete amongst themselves in the domination and control of nature. Within modernity we no longer think of the importance of living 'in tune' with nature, finding our place within it. This has been the important insight of an ecology movement that is challenging to both traditions. Charles Taylor in his book *Hegel* says something illuminating about this:

We rather see the control as valuable not so much in itself as in its confirmation of a certain view of things; a view of the world not as a locus of meanings, but rather of contingent, *de facto* correlations. Manipulability of the world confirms the new self-defining identity, as it were; the proper relation of man to a meaningful order is to put himself in tune with it; by contrast nothing sets the seal more clearly on the rejection of this vision than successfully treating the world as an object of control. Manipulation both proves and as it were celebrates the vision of things as 'disenchanted', to use Max Weber's famous phrase.

(Taylor, C. 1978: 8)

But Marx was also influenced by a tradition critical of the anthropology of the Enlightenment and of the calculative notion of reason divorced from emotions, feelings and will. The central notion of this tradition, largely influenced by Herder, was to see human activity and human life as expressions.[7] We have already seen how central this is to Marx's discussion of alienation. It also develops a powerful critique of the ways we have generally accepted within modernity that the goals and purposes we set ourselves should be externally established through the workings of reason alone. In this way it challenges common-sense conception of purposive action and encourages us into a different vision:

> To talk about the realisation of a self here is to say that the adequate human life would not just be a fulfilment of an idea or a plan which is fixed independently of the subject who realises it, as is the Aristotelian form of a man. Rather this life must have an added dimension that the subject can recognise as its own, as having unfolded from within him. This self-related dimension is entirely missing from the Aristotelian tradition. In this tradition a proper human life is 'my own' only in the sense that I am a man, and there is thus the life fit for me . . . the expressivist view sees this development more as the manifestation of an inner power striving to realise and maintain its own shape against those the surrounding world might impose. Thus the ideal realisation is one which not only conforms to the idea, but is also internally generated; indeed these two requirements are inseparable in that the proper form of a man incorporates the notion of free subjectivity.
>
> (Ibid.: 15)

This conflict has been articulated recently in the practice of the women's movement, where the desire to be treated as a person, rather than simply as a sexual object, has encouraged women to challenge the social relations of patriarchal power. This is not simply a question of women learning to express their ideas, or even of getting others to change the ways they see women: women have recognised the connection between questions of identity and relations of power and subordination.

As women have changed the ways they *relate* to men, say in refusing to be paid for on an outing, men have been forced to rethink how they have conceived women. Even if it is not possible for individual women to find this freedom and equality without a fundamental transformation of gender relations of power, it is important not to underestimate the changes that can happen. Even if it is painful to make changes when facing the reality of power relations, it can be possible for women to learn to draw strength and support from each other in the process.

Social theory has often failed to appreciate the importance of feminist insights. Feminism has *not* assumed a pre-given set of human qualities simply waiting to be expressed, but rather sets a challenge to an Aristotelian tradition, for which the ideal a person seeks to realise is wholly determined beforehand. A strength of feminist theory is that it often recognises an openness in the ways women identify, define and clarify their wants and needs, given the structures of power and dominance within which they live.[8] In contrast, orthodox Marxism

Marxism has been too ready to assume that it has got all the answers, or that it knows what it means to live a socialist life. Often it has been trapped by its own rationalism unable to *hear* what people have to say for themselves.

If we think that Herder's formulations tend to individualise our understandings, making it difficult to grasp the significance of class, gender and sexual and racial relations of power and dominance, there is still something important to learn. Herder can help connect with some insights of existentialism which recognise the importance of individuals learning to take greater responsibility for their lives in the here and now, as they learn to clarify *their* needs and goals. This helps provide an important criticism of certain Marxist notions that have had such damaging historical consequences in encouraging people to sacrifice themselves for a collective future before they have learnt how to take individual responsibility in the present:

> Thus the notion of human life as expression sees this not only as the realisation of purposes but also as the clarification of these purposes. It is not only the fulfilment of life but also the clarification of meaning. In the course of living adequately I not only fulfil my humanity but clarify what my humanity is about ... The realisation of his essence is a subject's self-realisation; so that what he defines himself in relation to is not an ideal order beyond, but rather something which unfolds from himself, is his own realisation, and is first made determinate in that realisation.
>
> (Ibid.: 17–18)

Marx was deeply influenced by this tradition and used it to make sense of class relations of power and subordination. He learnt that this 'self-realisation' could not be left up to individuals but that it involved a social transformation since capitalist society was unjust, organised as it is around a fundamental class oppression. But Herder can help ground the need for a social transformation in different terms from those concerned with an abstract goal of 'social revolution'. We too easily think of socialism as some kind of 'goal' or 'ideal' we have to sacrifice for. Revolution, as Simone Weil grasped, comes to have a life of its own, independent of the quality and meaning it has for the lives of people.[9]

Socialist language has often become abstract and disconnected, losing touch with the everyday reality of people's lives. If people are not political because they have not felt the injustices and oppression of the world it can be difficult to develop 'consciousness'. It is also possible to lose touch with the sources of our moral outrage that might have made us politically conscious in the first place. It is easy for considerations of means and ends to gradually dominate our thinking and feeling, so that gradually we organise politically towards a distant 'goal' that has little meaning in our own lives and experience.

MASCULINITY AND RATIONALISM

More personally, if I think about the link between the kind of man I was brought up to be, and the ways I was brought up to identify with individual achievement and success, I can grasp an inner connection to the workings of rationalism as I rethink and reword a dominant masculinity identified with reason and separated from emotional life. I have felt the ways it has limited and isolated me, making me suspicious of other men, who are always experienced as potential competitors.

Part of me is still trapped by an image of masculinity I grew up with, blaming myself for not doing it well enough. Another part is aware of how my identification with my rationality has separated me from my emotions and feelings as signs of weakness, making me more instrumental in relation to myself and to others. Identifying vulnerability with feminine aspects shows how growing into manhood involves coming to terms with homophobic feelings, learning how to draw support and love from other men. All of this is one aspect of the larger rationality of society, which only values those capacities and abilities that can be sold in the market.

Through 'consciousness-raising' groups I became more aware of the processes through which male identity is structured unknowingly according to market values. I began to learn the different ways I have unwittingly compromised myself, developing particular aspects of myself to win the approval of others. So, for instance, I discover how I had learnt to subordinate my friendships more or less automatically since it is necessary to move to different jobs. I had never really stopped to think what was really important for me, but assumed, as have other men, that I would make whatever sacrifices were necessary to get on in my individual career. As I have learnt how much of this experience is shared by other middle-class men, who have grown up with similar anxieties to prove themselves, I have begun to understand my individuality in more social and political terms.

I learn for instance how my uneasiness and reserve with other men, and my difficulty in trusting myself to them and making myself vulnerable, has a lot to do with homophobic feeling and the competitive organisation of schooling. I cannot help feeling that I have to conceal significant aspects which are then left without a form of expression, to prove myself with other men, since they will always be ready to put me down. This is not something that I was even consciously aware of. I had simply assumed that this was a given characteristic of my individual personality.

In sharing my experience with other men in the 1970s and 1980s I learnt how much I have been formed by a shared experience of schooling, CND, the Civil Rights movement in the US, and the Vietnam War, which have been influences on the formation of a whole generation. These have not simply affected the ways we think, but also *who* we are, and how we respond to life. Understanding this can also help me clarify what I want for myself individually, and why it has seemed so difficult to satisfy my individual needs. So I discover, for instance, that others who have been politicised through 1968 have often also inherited a deep sense of guilt and unease about reading and writing, feeling that these intellectual activities somehow have to be politically justified in the face of an awareness of class, gender, sexual and racial oppression and suffering in our society.

This clarification is not a process of recovering 'needs' that we have never fully acknowledged, though this can be an aspect of this process. It is part of a reworking of our individuality and identities within the social and political realities of class, gender, sexual and racial relations of power and dominance. This reworking helps to situate our contradictory experience socially and historically, in a way that liberal individualism tends to mystify us about. It becomes important to know *how* to live within these relations of power and dominance since they cannot be willed out of existence, nor are they the creations of our consciousness alone. Even so we often want and need to feel that we are also part of the challenge to them.

Such shifts in consciousness do not involve dissolving our individuality into definite social and historical categories, in the way that Althusser and the tradition of structuralist Marxism would have us do. To do this would simply make the moral issues we face both individually and collectively seem as if they have disappeared. It would also reproduce the subordination and self-denial that is such a central feature of modernist social theory. Sexual politics, in contrast, can potentially help us trust ourselves more, so that we understand how we have been formed and that we live a fundamentally fragmented social experience. These contradictions have to be faced directly, so that people can be helped to recognise the moral realities and difficulties of living more equal and human lives within the context of class, ethnic and sexual relations of power and dominance.

These are not problems that can be solved within the framework of a capitalist, patriarchal and heterosexist society, but contradictions that have to be lived with. A young teacher, for example, faces the difficulties of teaching in a school that is organised on competitive and hierarchical principles. This profoundly affects the kind of teaching and learning that can happen, as well as the relations she can develop with pupils. The teacher is inevitably working against the dominant social relations of power, possibly learning to use the liberal rhetoric of the school, which recognises, in theory at least, that the development of all the children should be given equal priority. This is frustrating and difficult work, especially in a period of heavy government expenditure cuts. It is important to recognise that these are not problems that she can solve individually, but that she needs the support and solidarity of other teachers to work out a 'politics' for the situation.[10] This cannot be achieved simply by realising abstract principles, but necessitates working through the difficult contradictions she faces in her everyday life, say as a politically conscious feminist teacher.

QUALITIES AND CONTRADICTIONS

Marx was very aware of the ways in which money works to distort human relations. This is a contradictory tendency in his writings, especially as it relates to the discussion of commodity fetishism in *Capital*. The source of some of these difficulties can be found in Marx's early writings:

> That which is for me through the medium of *money* – that for which I can pay (i.e. which money can buy) – that am *I*, the possessor of the money. The extent of the power of the money is the extent of my power. Money's properties are my properties and essential powers – the properties and powers of its possessor. Thus, what I *am* and *am capable* of is by no means determined by my individuality, I am ugly, but I can buy for myself the most *beautiful* of women. Therefore, I am not *ugly* for the effect of *ugliness* – its deterrent power – is nullified by money. I, in my character as an individual, am *lame*, but money furnishes me with twenty-four feet. Therefore I am not lame, I am bad, dishonest, unscrupulous, stupid; but money is honoured, and therefore so is its possessor. Money is the supreme good, therefore its possessor is good. Money, besides, saves me the trouble of being dishonest: I am therefore presumed honest.
>
> (Marx 1975: 128)

In this way it can easily look as if the power of money is able to replace one set of qualities with another, which can encourage people to think that the power of money allows a discourse of individual qualities to be replaced by a discourse relating to the qualities assumed through one's power over money. This would very much destroy the tension and possibilities of critique, since 'what *I* am and *am capable* of is by no means determined by my individuality'.

Marx can help explain some of the central contradictions of capitalist society, which is at odds with its liberal self-conception. At this

this level Marx resonates with some of the powerful ideas of the women's movement and sexual politics generally, which have been able to bring some of these contradictions regarding freedom and equality into focus. They have helped to open up an exploration of unacknowledged needs and desires, setting different terms for understanding the fact that the recognition and expression of our qualities is part of the growth of our individual self-worth and authority.

Marx seems to identify 'what I *am* and *am capable of*' with what power I have over money. This means that 'moneyed properties are my properties and essential powers'. It is only if we can express our needs and desires in terms of money that they cease to be 'imaginary'. Marx is expressing something significant about the social reality of capitalist society, but he also misleads us into thinking that if a need cannot be realised, then it disappears, or is 'a mere thing of the imagination'. It was Freud who was to open up the important investigation of repression through a language of the unconscious and the psyche. Marx seems to be trapped in his own rationalism:

No doubt *demand* also exists for him who has no money, but his demand is a mere thing of the imagination without effect or existence for me, for a third party, for the others, and which therefore remains for me *unreal* and *objectless*. The difference between effective demand based on money and ineffective demand based on my need, my passion, my wish etc., is the difference between *being* and *thinking*, between the imagined which *exists* merely within me and the imagined as it is for me outside as a *real object*. If I have no money for travel, I have no *need* – that is, no real and self-realising need – to travel. If I have the *vocation* to study but no money for it, I have *no* vocation for study – that is, no *effective*, no *true* vocation. Being the external, common *medium* and *faculty* for turning an *image* into *reality* and *reality* into a mere *image* (a faculty not springing from man as man or from human society as society), *money* transforms the *real essential powers of man and nature* into what are merely abstract conceits and therefore *imperfections* – into tormenting chimeras – just as it transforms *real imperfections and chimeras* – essential powers which are really impotent, which exist only in the imagination of the individual – into *real powers* and *faculties*.

In the light of this characteristic alone, money is thus the general overturning of *individualities* which turns them into their contrary and adds contradictory attributes to their attributes.

Money, then, appears as the *overturning* power both against the individual and against the bonds of society, etc., which claim to be *essences* in themselves. It transforms fidelity into infidelity, love into hate, hate into love, virtue into vice, vice into virtue, servant into master, master into servant, idiocy into intelligence and intelligence into idiocy.

(Ibid.: 129–30)

Marx seems to be limited within a too general distinction between what is 'image' and what is 'reality'. So Marx can also say that 'If I long for a particular dish ... money ... converts my wish from something in the realm of the imagination ... into [its] *sensual, actual* existence – from imagination to life, from imagined being into real being' (Ibid.: 129). But as Marx knew, my hunger is not any the less real for being unsatisfied. My hunger is *not* simply a feature of my imagination. It affects my life, and also my relations with others who might despise or reject me because of my poverty.

But it can also spur people into protest and revolt. It can be the cause of riots, as people insist on taking things which they cannot afford. If money has the power to turn 'the world upside down' to effect 'the confounding and compounding of all natural and human qualities', Marx does not clarify what is at issue, because he offers a too general distinction between 'effective demand based on money and ineffective demand based on my need, my passion, my wish'. Marx falls into the trap of seeing this from the point of view of 'effective demand', thinking that this is the only 'reality'.

If John, for example, had been effectively forced to leave school because his family needed his wages and could not afford to support him through two more years of education, then it does not really matter whether he was learning a great deal at school, because he knows he has to find a job. Marx is helping us question the liberal notion that we can say that John has had a 'choice' to stay at school and helps us challenge the 'effectiveness' of 'reality', of saying that John has benefited from equality of opportunity in education. We might say that John has had 'no effective, no true opportunity'.

But Marx is misleading us when he says that 'if I have the *vocation* for study but no money for it, I have *no* vocation for study – that is, no *effective*, no *true* vocation'. In saying this he denies us the possibility of making important distinctions, even if he helps us challenge the hypocrisy of those who would say that John is 'free to study if he wants to, since no one is stopping him'. This fails to recognise the reality of John's life, when he has gone out to work in the local factory. He simply does not have the time and peace of mind, nor the encouragement, to study.

But Marx gives too much transformative power to money, as if the needs and desires will simply disappear if they are not realised or fulfilled. Marx grants money too general a role for 'turning an *image* into *reality'*, as if our desires, wants, feelings, emotions and frustrations somehow lack'reality', and are simply to be thought of as 'imaginary', unless somehow money can bring them into 'reality'. This image and language does not capture the depths of Marx's understanding of the ways in which human relations and values are transformed as money comes to have a central meaning. We only value things and relations in terms of their monetary value. This brings about the degradation of the human world and allows Marx to state that: 'money is thus the general overturning of *individualities'*.

It might well be that John's true vocation for learning comes out later when he is able to go to night school. He learns enough to know that he has never really been given an 'equality of opportunity', and comes to grasp the class, gender and ethnic character of education in capitalist society.[11] He recognises that it is not simply that the sons and daughters of the middle class have been able to buy their education, though he realises that many would never have got so far in the state system. They have not really needed much learning in order to inherit their parents' wealth and position in society.

John knows that he has had a vocation for learning, but has never really been given the opportunities because of his background circumstances. He appreciates whatever opportunities he has now, though he knows how much talent and understanding of people is wasted because of the ways in which education is organised. John's desire to learn was not simply 'imaginary'. It has been a real driving force in his life. It has not only proved to him what others could do, but that the society is very much organised *against* those who are powerless and oppressed, with whom he now feels a much stronger identification.

CAPITAL AND NATURE

The Frankfurt School thought that the very development of the capitalist mode of production, particularly with the development of assembly-line production since the 1920s, highlights crucial questions concerning the enormous natural wealth produced with a simultaneous impoverishment of human society. This is the moment when questions about human needs, nourishment and fulfilment become more central, as a higher material standard of living is apparently not related to greater human happiness.

The Frankfurt School was talking about the experience of the industrialised countries. But as the revolutions in Eastern Europe have made us starkly aware of the human and ecological impoverishment within the state command economies, we are forced to ask again on what terms did Marx think that capitalist society should be judged? Was he right to talk about 'the great civilising influence of capital'? Did his treatment of human needs make it difficult for him to escape being trapped himself in this 'circle of social production and exchange'?

In the 1990s we cannot avoid this kind of fundamental questioning if we are to reassess Marx. Here it is not an issue of Stalinism, or even of Leninism, but of preparing for a sustained theoretical exploration of some of the tensions and contradictions within Marx's own work. I can give a couple of quotations from Marx's *Grundrisse* which might help focus such a questioning. Marx tells a story that he takes from *The Times*:

> The Times of November 1857 contains an utterly delightful cry of outrage on the part of a West-Indian plantation owner. This advocate analyses with great moral indignation – as a plea for the reintroduction of Negro slavery – how the Quashes (the free blacks of Jamaica) content themselves with producing only what is strictly necessary for their own consumption, and, alongside this 'use value', regard loafing (indulgence and idleness) as the real luxury good; how they do not care a damn for the sugar and the fixed capital invested in the plantations, but rather observe the planters' impending bankruptcy with an ironic grin of malicious pleasure, and even exploit their acquired Christianity as an embellishment for this mood of malicious glee and indolence. They have ceased to become slaves, but not in order to become wage labourers, but, instead, self-sustaining peasants working for their own consumption ... the relation of domination is the only thing which is reproduced on this basis, for which wealth itself has value only as gratification, not as 'wealth itself, and which can therefore never create *general industriousness*.
>
> (Marx 1973: 326)

Marx is not concerned here with making moral judgements, since he is simply describing historical processes. But this is different from saying that he does not have a moral and human understanding of these processes, though Marx does sometimes lose touch with this. He does seem to accept the inevitability of capitalism and, in the *Grundrisse* at least, seems to welcome what he calls this 'universal industriousness'. He sometimes falls into thinking that 'capital creates the bourgeois society', even if working-class resistance and struggle again assume a central importance in *Capital*:

> Thus, just as production founded on capital creates universal industriousness on one side – i.e. surplus labour, value creating labour – so does it create on the other side a system of general utility,

utilising science itself just as much as all the physical and mental qualities, while there appears nothing *higher in itself*, nothing legitimate for itself, outside this circle of social production and exchange. Thus capital creates the bourgeois society, and the universal appropriation of nature as well as of the social bond itself by the members of society. Hence the great civilising influence of capital; its production at a stage of society in comparison to which all earlier ones appear as mere *local developments* of humanity and as *nature-idolatry*. For the first time, nature becomes purely an object of humankind, purely a matter of utility; ceases to be recognised as a power for itself; and the theoretical discovery of its autonomous laws appears merely as an object of consumption or as a means of production.

(Ibid.: 410)

Marx seems to welcome the domination of nature as an aspect of the 'civilising influence of capital' which sets socialism within a framework of rationalist modernity that identifies progress with the domination and control of nature. Marx seems to welcome that, with capitalism, 'for the first time, nature becomes purely an object of humankind, purely a matter of utility'. It is as if Marx's recognition of the historical direction of these social processes tempts him into accepting these developments as laying the fundamental conditions for socialism. It is almost as if this involves welcoming the 'universal industriousness', being aware that the free Blacks' resistance to wage-labour can only be temporary. It is as if this denigration of nature in its autonomy and independence is a process that they have to go through to lay the material foundations for socialism.

I think this needs to be considered carefully for it is one of the sources of the difficulties of communication that still exists between socialists and Greens. It helps us understand why they are often talking past each other. Socialists find it hard to take seriously the Greens' challenge to productivism as well as their calls for a different relationship to nature. It is almost as if, for orthodox Marxism, moral critique has to be a form of idealistic nonsense, since it does not recognise the necessity of these historical processes, nor does it recognise how they are creating the very conditions for socialism. This led many people, particularly in the Second International, to recognise the increasing state control of the means of production under conditions of monopoly capitalism as somehow preparing the way for socialism.[12]

Arguments about decentralisation and the control of people over their own lives can, generations later, still appear utopian and idealistic.

But it is this very identification of socialism with state nationalisation that has created a crisis for many people about the meaning of socialism, given the historical experience of Russia and Eastern Europe. This is not an issue that can be dodged, especially after the popular movements that have brought revolutionary changes in Eastern Europe, even if it leads us to question certain fundamental ideas in Marx's writings.

Marx's critique of utopianism was largely a critique of the notion of setting up an abstract concept of socialism, thinking that this could then be brought into reality if people could be convinced of its moral justice. Marx thought that posing abstract visions in this way was bound to be an empty and rhetorical gesture, unless you were also fully aware of the social relations of productions that could make them a reality. But our evaluation of the place of utopian ideas in contrast to scientific notions of socialism still has to be rethought. Althusser's efforts in this direction easily lead us astray.

In reality Marx's writings seem more contradictory, even if we can identify certain developments. Sometimes it seems, especially in portions of the *Grundrisse*, that he seems to rely on the development of capital not simply for creating a material basis for socialism, but also for the development of human needs:

> Production of surplus value based on the increase and development of the productive forces, requires the production of new consumption, requires that the consuming circle within circulation expands, as did the productive circle previously. First quantitative expansion of existing consumption; secondly creation of new needs by propagating existing ones in a wide circle; *thirdly*: production of *new* needs and discovery and creation of new use values ... likewise the discovery, creation and satisfaction of new needs arising from society itself; the cultivation of all the qualities of the social human being, production of the same in a form as rich as possible in needs, because rich in qualities and relations – production of this being as the most total and universal possible social product, for, in order to take gratification in a many-sided way, he must be capable of many pleasures (*Genußfähig*), hence cultured to a high degree – is likewise a condition of production founded on capital.
>
> (Ibid.: 408–9)

There is little space left open for a critique of the form and character of these needs. Marx has not prepared the grounds for theorising the contradictory character of needs, and the kind of awareness and relationship we can have of them. If the social relations of class, sexual and racial power give us limited possibilities for changing, we should not negate the possibility of a critical transformation of our own sense of our needs, even if this brings us into sharper conflict with the prevailing relations of power.

A shift in ecological awareness in the 1980s that brought into different focus human relationships to nature as well as to planetary crisis, remains a significant ray of hope, especially with children. It is as if Marx, particularly within the *Grundrisse*, gets trapped in his awareness that 'there appears nothing *higher in itself*, nothing legitimate for itself, outside this circle of social production and exchange'. In his anxiety to critique abstract conceptions of morality and justice, Marx reproduces a form of his earlier distinction between 'image' and 'reality', saying that within the social relations of capitalist society the contract of wage-labour is *just*, since we cannot invoke abstract conceptions that are not *'effective'* within the society.[13]

In these less dialectical moments, Marx loses touch with whatever struggles might be continually going on around these conceptions of equality and justice, say, as working people refuse to subordinate themslves to the rule of capital, or women refuse to carry on doing the housework or emotional work for men when they get so little for themselves in return, or Blacks riot within the inner-city ghettoes or gay men and lesbians refuse the limitations of a heterosexist culture. This is partly because, at certain stages, Marx was too ready to admit that people were made in the image of the capitalist society since, at another level, he was too welcoming of the developments brought about by capitalism:

> Capital's ceaseless striving towards the general form of wealth drives labour beyond the limits of its natural paltriness (*Naturbedürftigkeit*), and thus creates the material elements for the development of the rich individuality which is as all-sided in its production as in its consumption, and whose labour also therefore appears no longer as labour, but as the full development of activity itself, in which natural necessity in its direct form has disappeared; because a historically created need has taken the place of the natural one. This is why *capital is productive; i.e. an essential relation for the development of the social productive forces*. It ceases to exist as such only when the development of these productive forces themselves encounters its barrier in capital itself.
>
> (Ibid.: 325)

Marx seems to rely on 'capital's ceaseless striving' to create the 'material elements for the development of the rich individuality'. This tendency in his thinking still needs caeful scrutiny and investigation.

Chapter 9

Empowerment

FREEDOM AND NECESSITY

Marx came to question his conception of communism as 'the *definitive* resolution of the antagonism between man and nature, and between man and man'. In his later writings he recognised that people would have to continue to struggle for their means of livelihood. Both Marx and Engels learnt that there was much less harmony in nature. They were sceptical about 'the true socialist' who 'proceeds from the thought that the dichotomy of life and happiness must cease' (Marx and Engels 1976: 533).

They found no such dichotomy in nature, and felt that 'since man, too, is a natural body and possesses all the general properties of such a body, no dichotomy should exist for him either'. In rejecting romantic conceptions of nature, Marx was never clear about how the 'antagonism between man and nature' could be resolved, other than by the control and domination of nature, or about the sense in which a person 'is a natural body'. Rather he tended, especially in his later writings, to fall back implicitly on expressing a Kantian notion which saw people's 'natures' as a necessity that they had to rise above.

This was an aspect of Marx's inherent rationalism, which sometimes subordinated our emotional and sexual lives as forms of unfreedom and determination over which we have little control. But this remains deeply ambiguous in Marx, especially in his conception of labour. In the *Grundrisse* Marx can also be found opposing Adam Smith's notion that labour in general is a curse, and that leisure is identical with freedom. Marx recognises the needs that people have for a certain form of work. He also expresses the contradictory tensions we have already tried to identify:

Adam Smith seems to have no idea that the individual, 'in his normal state of health, strength, activity, skill and agility' also has need of a normal portion of labour, and cessation of rest. Of course, the measure of labour itself appears externally given, through the aim to be accomplished and the obstacles to be overcome by labour on the way to its accomplishment. This surmounting of obstacles is in itself a manifestation of freedom. Furthermore, the external aims have shed the appearance of a merely external and naturally imposed necessity, and are posited as aims set by the individual himself. It is therefore self-realization, objectification on the Subject, and hence the activity of real freedom, whose action is labour. Of all this, Adam Smith has no conception. He is of course right to say that in its historical forms (slave-labour, serf-labour, wage-labour) labour always appears as repulsive, and as *labour under external compulsion*, and that as against this, the absence of labour appears as 'freedom and happiness'.

(Marx 1973: 505)

Marx is identifying something important when he says that the 'surmounting of obstacles is in itself a manifestation of freedom', but it remains unclear what situation he is talking about.[1] It is also possible to be misled by the Kantian resonances, as we remember how, for Kant, we demonstrate our freedom by struggling against our inclinations, our wants and desires, to do our duty. This often seems ambiguous in Marx, which is partly because there is such a pervasive tradition of moral thought that would see our emotional lives, our wants, and desires as a 'merely external and naturally imposed necessity'.

Recognising these Kantian resonances places in a very different context Marx's talk about 'the activity of real freedom, whose action is labour'. Somehow the very conception of 'labour' would involve a subordination of our wants, feelings, emotions and desires. This does not seem to be what Marx intends, though his banishment of morality and moral discussion in this context makes it painfully difficult to be clear. His vision of labour also makes it *difficult* to recognise the importance of the feelings that we have for what we do which mean that there is a significant difference between working mechanically and working with some feeling for our activities.

Certainly we are reassured, in terms of recovering the self, by his recognition of the importance of the fact that the 'aims' are not simply 'external and naturally imposed' but are 'posited as aims set by the individual himself', though we can still be worried about how this is to be interpreted. Are these aims to be posited in the full knowledge and awareness of our developing needs, wants and desires, or are they assumed to involve the subordination of these aspects of our 'natures'?

The discoveries of Freud have given us understanding of the emotional and psychological work that it can take to clarify our aims and purposes. This points to a different relationship to our natures, which no longer have to be controlled through the external intervention of reason alone. It opens up the possibility of a different relationship with our emotional lives. Similarly Reich helps to challenge a Cartesian mind–body dualism by making us more aware of bodily processes through which we can escape some of these necessities and come to have more control in the expression of our diverse emotional and sexual lives.[2]

So, for example, I can become aware of a pattern in which, whenever I'm beginning to feel sad, I avoid or displace these feelings into anger and resentments. I get irritated and frustrated with people. I do not seem to be able to help myself when in the grip of this pattern. In this sense I seem to act out of some necessity. But I can become *aware* of this pattern, and also of the ways it has been culturally reinforced through conceptions assimilated since childhood, that sadness is to be identified with 'weakness', and so should not have anything to do with 'masculinity'.

These are not simply 'ideas' I am aware of, but identifications involved in the ways I relate to others, as well as to my own feelings and experience. It is threatening for me to accept and express this sadness, so when it happens I prefer to deny it. This is an aspect of a long process of personal and emotional change, not simply a matter of becoming intellectually aware. It helps to set issues of freedom and necessity in less rationalistic terms, by reinstating the concept of emotional work as calling upon different aspects of the self.

Sometimes the investigations Marx was absorbed in, the developments of capital, mean that we lose a sense of the contradictory aspects of freedom. We lose touch with the dignity, endurance and joys, limited as they inevitably were, involved in ongoing struggles against the indignities of everyday subordination. This is something we can learn about from E.P. Thompson's *The Making of the English Working Class* (1970).

Marx makes this suffering central to the theory expressed in *Capital*. In periods when it seems easier to look to the development of capital itself to bring about significant changes, it is easy to be dazzled by consumerism and style. It is harder when we can no longer believe in the redemptive powers of history, to live with the recognition of injustice and oppression. It is easier to wish them away or to treat them as inevitable, as if it is naïve to think that the poor will not always be with us. It is partly because we lose touch with the everyday struggles against forms of class, gender, racial and sexual exploitation and oppression.

Rather than developing out of the contradictions of people's experience in a divided society, it is easy for freedom to become a distant goal, somewhat akin to the 'kingdom of ends'. Marx recognises that the necessities of organising for our material livelihood remain, even if they can now be brought under people's rational control. Production should no longer involve a system of domination and exploitation, but of 'associated producers rationally regulating their interchange with nature':

> In fact, the realm of freedom actually begins only where labour which is determined by necessity and mundane considerations ceases; thus in the very nature of things it lies beyond the sphere of actual material production. Just as the savage must wrestle with nature to satisfy his wants to maintain and reproduce life, so must civilized man, and he must do so in all social formations and under all possible modes of production . . . Freedom in this field can only consist in socialized men, the associated producers rationally regulating their interchange with nature, bringing it under their common control, instead of being ruled by it as by the blind forces of nature; and achieving this with the least expenditure of energy and under conditions most favourable to, and worthy of, their human nature. But it nonetheless still remains a realm of necessity. Beyond it begins that development of human energy which is an end in itself, the true realm of freedom, which, however, can blossom forth only with this realm of necessity as its basis. The shortening of the working day is its basic prerequisite.
>
> (Marx 1976: 799–800)

Marx seems trapped by a Kantian contrast between a 'realm of necessity' and the 'realm of freedom'. This partly seems at odds with Marx's hopeful words in the *Grundrisse*, that capitalism would bring with it the development of individuality. At other moments in the *Grundrisse* itself, Marx recognises that the freedom within the free competition of capitalism involves 'the complete subjugation of individuality':

> It is in fact only free development on a narrow and limited foundation – the foundation of the rule of capital. This kind of individual freedom is hence at the same time the most complete destruction of all individual freedom and the complete subjugation of individuality under social conditions, which assume the form of objective powers, indeed of over-powering objects – objects themselves independent of the individuals who relate to them.
>
> (Marx 1973: 545)

FREEDOM AND NEEDS

As Alfred Schmidt says in his important discussion in *The Concept of Nature in Marx*, Marx 'turned the tables on the ideologists of capitalism.

The free individual, who apparently was to have been protected from socialism, has never in fact existed in the sense proclaimed by the ideologists' (Schmidt 1971: 145). But Alfred Schmidt says something else that tends to identify Marx's discussion of individuality with a more Kantian notion of 'moral self-realisation'. I have hinted at something like this, though I am not sure how far to take it. It might be one of the costs of the later developments in his thinking and certainly suggests a much more complicated discussion of Marx's development.

It might also suggest that some of the reasons people still feel drawn to his earlier writings is that they help clarify a certain dissatisfaction, even if we fully grant the overwhelming strengths of the later writing. This is because the central moral questions which confront us with the historical experience of socialism, especially in Russia and Eastern Europe, are barely brought into focus in Marx's later writings. Even if Alfred Schmidt seems to overstate his conclusion, he opens up an important train of thought:

> Thilo Ramm is no doubt right to speak of a very strict conception of marriage on Marx's part. One must also agree, that in 'Engels' conception of freedom ... sensuality and instinctive activity are given far greater weight than in Marx, for whom these drives are restrained by the dictates of moral self-realisation.' The writings of Engels, even in their presentation, are reminiscent of the French Enlightenment, whereas the Marxist attitude belongs more to German Idealism, indeed to Kantian ethics, despite his cautiousness in the matter of uttering moral judgments.
>
> (Ibid.: 152)

This is a crucial issue in the current crisis of socialism because of the poverty of socialist discussions of freedom. We have been too ready to dismiss the very conception of freedom as 'bourgeois', as somehow distracting us from more basic material needs, rather than recognising in it one of the fundamental human conditions. It has been a central contribution of feminism and sexual politics to raise questions of the relationships between dependency, power, sexuality and individuality, setting a different framework for our thinking about freedom and necessity.

Feminism and psychotherapy have opened up the discussion of human needs, making us aware of the need for certain kinds of loving relationships to be relationships of equality. Sexual politics has also helped challenge liberal conceptions of 'equal respect', showing the underlying relations of sexual power and subordination, and has given new life and content to egalitarian and libertarian discussions, raising issues about the *quality* of human relationships and the need for individuals to learn how to give and receive of themselves, rather than to close off and withdraw into themselves.

Sexual politics has given a fuller context in which to develop Marx's critique of liberal conceptions of equal rights, through a fuller exploration of human needs. In Marx's *Critique of the Gotha Programme* (1875) he was returning to an insight that he had expressed in *The German Ideology*, even if he had often lost grasp of it:

> But one of the most vital principles of communism, a principle which distinguishes it from all reactionary socialism, is its empirical view, based on a knowledge of man's nature, that difference of *brain* and of intellectual capacity do not imply any difference whatsoever in the nature of the *stomach* and of physical *needs*; therefore the false tenet, based upon existing circumstances, 'to each according to his abilities' must be changed, in so far as it is related to enjoyment in the narrower sense, into the tenet, 'to each according to his need'; in other words, a *different form* of activity, of labour, does not justify *inequality*, confers no *privileges* in respect of possession and enjoyment.
>
> (Marx and Engels 1976: 606–7)

Marx helps challenge the framework which establishes a contrast between 'intellectual' and 'physical', which mirrors a distinction between mental and physical labour. This 'is related to enjoyment in the narrower sense', which produces its own conceptions of inequality.

Marx wants to reinstate needs as criteria for rewards, so breaking the link between abilities, work and rewards. Motivation has been an issue within Eastern Europe, although it may have seemed as if people were not regarded more for working more. Against this, capitalism argued that it is only through economic incentives that people will show initiative and enterprise. Questions about different forms of 'incentives' still need to be rethought in the context of the historical experience of different societies. Differences between different jobs need to be reworked if they are to confer '*no privileges* in respect of possession and enjoyment'. Marx's 'empirical view, based on the knowledge of man's nature', turns out to provide too narrow a basis for raising issues about justice and human needs.

Struggles against sexual and racial oppression have also deepened our grasp of the human costs of diverse forms of exploitation and oppression, which cannot be reduced to aspects of class and are always more complex than issues of distribution. Often socialist discussion is confined to distributive forms of justice. Recently it has been feminism and sexual politics that have made us most sharply aware of the differences and diversities within relations of subordination and dependency. It has also made us aware of the hidden depths of subordination and the difficulties of creating change.

To alter this we must transform more than current social relations; we must work through the difficulties and pain of past relations and identities. We still need a language that can identify and express these insights into power, desire and identities. We require a sustained questioning of our inherited philosophical traditions, which in modern times have too often echoed an Enlightenment opposition between reason and nature, tearing apart connections that need to be made if issues of need and desire are to be rethought. Post-modern theory has grasped such a task in its own terms but often it is too ready to turn its back on the aspirations of modernity. It helps us focus on issues of identity, but as I go on to show, fails to appreciate enough of what is involved in recovering the self. We also need a much deeper evaluation of both Marx and Freud in their contradictory relationships to an Enlightenment modernity than even the Frankfurt School realised.[3]

LOVE AND MONEY

If people return to some of the writings of the younger Marx, it is not always because they do not appreciate the strengths of his later writings. Possibly it is because the vision is still fresh, and the imagination was also alive to issues that have become more critical. We are more aware of how an increasingly technological capitalism has ravaged the psyches, bodies and emotions, as much as it has deprived people materially. This raises crucial issues of fragmentation of identities and individuality, but not exclusively in their possessive, acquisitive and competitive forms.

With the development of sexual politics and post-colonial writings we have grown more aware of notions of individuality which recognise sexual, cultural and class histories and formation. But within discussions around post-modernity, the fragmentation of identities is often celebrated in ways that fail to recognise our need for relationships with and love of others.[4] It becomes harder to recognise a need for certain forms of human community in which we can feel *recognised*, and have our differences and experiences validated. This awareness of ethnic and national identities, such as have re-emerged so sharply within Eastern Europe, disturbing as they are in their racist and anti-Semitic expressions, should not be understood solely negatively as a regression to past securities in a period of uncertainty. To do this is implicitly to invoke an Enlightenment vision of universality, even if it takes itself as a break with this very tradition.[5]

In his early writings Marx tended to think that it is money which 'as the existing and active concept of value, confounds and exchanges all things'. It turns 'the world upside-down – the confounding and compounding of all natural and human qualities' (Marx 1975: 130). Thus, money works to distort our human relationships in the ways that it 'serves to exchange every property for every other, even contradictory, property and object' (Ibid.: 130).

But Marx also at other times challenges this Enlightenment view of the weakening of traditional values and customs in the face of a single measure of reason and has a different vision of the nature of relationships. This is not an abstract conception of relationships that we somehow have to aspire to. Rather, it recognises and values the experience of individual people in their personal relationships. The letter of 21 June 1856 from Marx to his wife shows this strikingly: 'But love, not the love of Feuerbach's Man nor Moleschott's metabolism, nor again the love of the proletariat, but the love of the beloved and more particularly of you, makes a man a man again' (quoted in Schmidt 1971: 133).

In its own way this echoes sentiments expressed in Marx's *Economic and Philosophical Manuscripts* of 1844:

> Assume *man* to be *man* and his relationship to the world to be a human one: then you can exchange love only for love, trust for trust etc. If you want to enjoy art, you must be an artistically cultivated person; if you want to exercise influence over other people, you must be a person with a stimulating and encouraging effect on other people. Every one of your relations to man and to nature must be a *specific expression*, corresponding to the object of your will, of your *real individual* life. If you love without evoking love in return – that is, if your loving as loving does not produce reciprocal love; if through a *living expression* of yourself as a loving person you do not make yourself a *loved person*, then your love is impotent – a misfortune.
>
> (Marx 1975: 131)

Marx is objecting to a society in which 'he who can buy bravery is brave, though a coward' (Ibid.: 130). It is interesting that Marx expresses this in terms of 'exchange', since he often sees the power and mediation of money as essentially distorting our human relationships.

Later he attempts to theorise this in terms of exchange values, organising a particular mode of production and distribution. As Marx attempts to set this in more formalistic terms as a tension between exchange values and use values, our individual qualities and needs become much less significant. Our relations with others somehow fall out of focus as attention is moved away towards considerations of different forms of value of goods, namely exchange values as opposed to use values. This does not mean that relationships can easily be other than they are, given the relationships of class, racial and sexual power we live in. We have to learn how to become 'consciously aware' as Gramsci has it, in order to be able to *work* to transform them.[6] If we talk of 'distortions', we are not assuming that these relationships have strayed from a pre-given norm, but we are saying something about their contradictory character and the terms in which we can critique them, and something about the sources of frustration and unease we can come to feel about them.

Marx focused upon the role of money, which 'serves to exchange every property for every other', in distorting our relationships. When he said that 'every one of your relations to man and to nature must be a *specific expression*, corresponding to the object of your will, of your *real individual* life', he was trying to say something about what could make our relationship with the world 'a human one'. He was saying something about the conditions for our growth and development as human beings. The point is that in a money-dominated society we cannot 'exchange love only for love, trust for trust'. These are not simply feelings, they are grounded in and expressions of particular forms of human relationships. Such ideas can be helpful in setting the terms for a relationship between politics and therapy.[7]

But Marx tended to focus too exclusively on the role of money, as he later did in the question of exchange values. A concern with the ubiquity of exchange values found a more generalised expression in Lukács'development of Marx's discussion of commodity fetishism, in his explorations of reification.[8] Lukács is enormously penetrating, while he also very much limits the terms of discussion:

> The specialised 'virtuoso', the vendor of his objectified and reified faculties, does not just become the (passive) observer of society'; he also lapses into a contemplative attitude vis-à-vis the workings of his own objectified and reified faculties. This phenomenon can be seen at its most grotesque in journalism. Here it is precisely subjectivity itself, knowledge, temperament and powers of expression that are reduced to an abstract mechanism functioning autonomously and divorced both from the personality of their 'owner' and from the material and concrete nature of the subject matter in hand. The journalist's 'lack of convictions', the prostitution of his experiences and beliefs, is comprehensible only as the apogee of capitalist reification.
>
> The transformation of the commodity relation into a thing of 'ghostly objectivity' cannot therefore content itself with the reduction of all objects for the gratification of human needs to commodities. It stamps its imprint upon the whole consciousness

of man; his qualities and abilities are no longer an organic part of his personality, they are things which he can 'own' or 'dispose of' like the various objects of the external world. And there is no natural form in which human relations can be cast, no way in which man can bring his physical and psychic 'qualities' into play without their being subjected increasingly to this reifying process.

(Lukács 1971: 100)

The journalist has to be able to turn a situation into a 'good story' and has to find a way of getting a 'good angle'. This often involves knowing what the editor wants to receive, rather than communicating the truth of the situation. This is not something you have much choice about if you 'want to get on in journalism' since it is simply built into doing 'a good job'. Often you are hardly aware of the compromises you make with yourself, since you learn to focus your energies on 'getting on'. In this way you automatically learn to manipulate your own qualities in order to produce the story in an 'acceptable' form.

You learn to use the different 'qualities' you have, very much as you learn to manipulate and control the 'various objects of the external world'. If you want to be a journalist, you are unknowingly forced into these processes if you 'want to get on'. As Lukács says, there is 'no way in which man can bring his physical and psychic "qualities" into play without their being subjected increasingly to this reifying process'.

But even if 'there is no natural form in which human relations can be cast', there are also contradictions in the situations people find themselves in, even in journalism. Lukács recognises the need to do more than show that 'the transformation of the commodity relation into a thing' involves more than 'the reduction of all objects for the gratification of human needs to commodities'. But unfortunately he does not really have a language to *show* this. He can simply say that 'it stamps its imprint upon the whole consciousness of man; his qualities and abilities are no longer an organic part of his personality'. The image of stamping an imprint upon the whole consciousness of man retains the externality of empiricism. Lukács is also limited by Marx's own conceptions of 'consciousness', which are too easily cast in rationalist terms and separated from a grasp of our emotional, psychological and bodily experience.

POWER AND LOVE

The difficulties we have in exchanging 'love only for love, trust for trust' can be only partly expressed in the idea of love as a commodity that can be secured if you have the money. It is not simply that people are looking to fall in love with someone rich and do not want to know if you are poor. It is not simply that you have an unfair advantage if you are rich, since you can buy love without deserving it.

When we say that love has become a commodity, we are saying something about the quality of human relationships. We are also saying something about the formation of wants, needs, desires and expectations within a patriarchal and heterosexual society. Lukács quotes Kant's description of sexuality and marriage, which he says has 'the naively cynical frankness peculiar to great thinkers':

> 'Sexual community', he says, 'is the reciprocal use made by one person of the sexual organs and facilities of another . . . is the union of two people of different sexes with a view to the mutual possession of each other's sexual attributes for the duration of their lives.
>   (Quoted in Lukács 1971: 100)

Treating others as sexual objects can so easily be an aspect of the sexual relations of power. Heterosexual relationships do not simply involve a reciprocal arrangement between two people, but instead are relationships in which a woman is traditionally supposed to subordinate her individual wants and needs and find her fulfilment and happiness in serving her husband, in exchange for the money that he brings into the home. If Marx was very aware of exchange relations, he did not understand enough about the sexual relations of power and subordination.

Marx tended to view power somewhat externally. It was through money that people maintained their power, especially in Marx's early writings. He never developed a full enough understanding of the sexual and racial relations of power, dominance and subordination. The ways in which sexuality is a commodity can hardly be separated within heterosexual relationships from the ways women are often seen by men as sexual objects. Nor can this be separated from the social relations of power.[9]

So, for instance, Pete might simply become aware that he often feels disappointed and let down when he gets into a relationship with a woman. The initial excitement seems to dissolve as soon as the relationship has been established. He might not understand why this happens, feeling that it must be due to the woman he is having a relationship with. He assumes that his satisfactions must come from 'the other', so that his disappointment comes because somehow 'she isn't good enough'.

For a long time Pete feels that things will be different if he gets off with the 'right woman', only to discover that this pattern just seems to repeat itself in his different relationships. He cannot really help feeling that all the excitement comes with the pursuit and the conquest. All his energy seems to be going into whether he can 'win' and 'succeed' in getting off with the woman on whom he has set his sights. This is where his excitement inevitably seemed to rest.

It took Pete time to realise that his relationships seemed to fall into a 'pattern', and that he seemed almost trapped by it. He did not consciously want to see women as sexual objects, but he recognised that this was the way he related to them. He did not really know how else to be. He thought that it was simply a matter of attraction, and he did not think that there was also an issue of power. On the whole it has been feminism and gay and lesbian policies that has forced Pete to think seriously about his sexuality and desire. He has felt very uneasy and uncomfortable with others as well as himself. He had always been one to prove himself in relationships with women. It made him feel good about himself in the past.

If Pete did not want to relate to women as sexual objects anymore, he did not really know *how* to treat them differently, nor did he know how to relate to his own sexuality differently.[10] He did not feel that he could simply choose to relate differently. He no longer experienced himself as the autonomous individual of liberal theory, able to relate to others in any way he wanted. Nor did he feel that sexuality could be other than performance. He knew that this made it hard for him to feel loving tenderness, and for him to be open and vulnerable enough to receive the love that someone was ready to give him. He always felt he had to prove himself and felt that he was not really deserving, or good enough, to receive love from someone else. Often he kept these doubts and feelings to himself.

In a relationship of heterosexual power and inequality in which sexuality is deeply marked as performance, it is difficult to 'exchange love for love, trust for trust'. Relationships are also deeply affected by the sexual relations of power in the larger society, which mark our individual relations. The qualities we develop are sanctioned in society. So, for instance, a dominant heterosexual masculinity is culturally identified with strength and rationality. In Cartesian terms, this separates us, as heterosexual men, from our bodily experience, which we so easily relate to as a machine under our control. It also separates us from a vulnerability and emotionality that is too easily identified with weakness and fears of homosexuality. It is often easier for us, as men, to be angry than it is to be sad. Often when part of us would want to express sadness, we find ourselves getting angry and hitting out at people, sometimes those we love most dearly.[11] We live out patterns in our relations, be they heterosexual or gay, we are barely conscious of. Our individuality can feel deeply flawed. We do not have the kind of control over our lives that liberal social theory would have us believe. This is the enormous issue Freud opened up.

AUTONOMY AND SUBORDINATION

The norms and values of liberal society very much assume an autonomy for the individual that is often impossible to realise in the prevailing social relations of dominance and subordination. The liberal notions of freedom and autonomy cannot simply be assumed, since they are often compromised in the realities and differences of our everyday experience. There is no way, as Kant wanted to suppose in his Enlightenment vision, that this 'autonomy' could somehow be guaranteed to us through our rationality.[12] If it is something that we have a capacity for, like the capacity for responding morally to situations, it is also, as Simone Weil came to appreciate, something that can be *undermined* and negated in the social relations of our lives.

It was Freud who recognised that the 'freedom' which liberal society promises us cannot be realised unless we are also prepared to work with our emotional lives. He was aware that so much of our experience, both psychic and emotional, is influenced by patterns of feeling and response, largely set in our childhood relationships. Marx discusses a different form of necessity, created by the social relations of class power that subject our everyday lives to the necessities of wage-labour. Marx establishes another context in which we are not 'free' in the way liberal self-conceptions would have us assume.

If we are to learn from both Marx and Freud, our freedom and autonomy is something that has to be struggled for, not simply about social relations of class, racial, ethnic and sexual power, but *also* in the inner structure of our psychic, emotional and bodily experience. Freud maintains a strong sense of the ways we are unconsciously influenced in living out our histories. The super-ego, strongly rooted in parental authority and early education, continues to influence us in the present, often without our awareness.

Freud thought that materialistic conceptions of history had underestimated the importance of our personal histories and unconscious lives and therefore the difficulties of changing:

It seems likely that what are known as materialist views of history sin in underestimating this factor. They brush it aside with the remark that human 'ideologies' are nothing other than the product and superstructure of their contemporary economic conditions. This is true, but very probably not the whole truth. Mankind never lives entirely in the present. The past ... lives on in the ideologies of the super-ego and yields only slowly to the influences of the present and to new changes; and so long as it operated through the super-ego it plays a powerful part in human life, independently of economic conditions.

(Freud 1973: 67)

Such sentiments warn us both about ahistorical tendencies of structuralist interpretations of Freud's work, but also about the psychological reductionism of much of socialist theory, tied as it is to rationalistic visions of personal and collective change. Such rationalism is especially important in illuminating the disappointments of collective experiences in the early 1970s, when it was assumed, for example, in the libertarian Left that feelings of jealousy, possessiveness and envy would easily dissolve if people lived in more equal and collective situations. If we are not simply to reproduce the idea that 'individuality' is inherently possessive and constantly acquisitive, we need to imagine in our notions of identity and difference the possibility of individual needs, nourishment and fulfilment.

Weber can help us grasp the damage and limitation of a competitive individualism that assumes individuals are eternally unfulfilled rather than recognising how we are constantly striving *against* feelings of inadequacy because we have rarely learnt how to identify what gives us fulfilment. This is important if we are not to reproduce unwittingly ideas that people can change through acts of will alone. Social theories need more sense of the possibilities and difficulties of personal change and social transformation. An awareness of reductionism helps us to abandon once and for all orthodox Marxist assumptions that the socialisation of production will somehow automatically bring about the creation of a more egalitarian and human society. History has all too painfully helped us realise that if we are still to appreciate the importance of Marx's work rather than abandon it as yet another grand narrative of modernity, we have to learn how to engage more critically with his intellectual and political inheritance.

FRAGMENTATION AND FREEDOM

The Frankfurt School recognised how important Freud was in transforming the very terms of theoretical discussion. They recognised that the writings of Adler and others, who wanted to socialise Freud's theories, were introducing talk of the values, norms and morality that Freud himself had challenged:

> While they [the revisionists] unceasingly talk of the influence of society on the individual, they forget that not only the individual, but the category of individuality is a product of society. Instead of first extracting the individual from the social process so as then to describe the influence which forms it, an analytic social psychology is to reveal in the innermost mechanism of the individual the decisive social forces.
>
> (Adorno, cited in Jacoby 1975: 30)

Russell Jacoby's impressive book *Social Amnesia*, has explored what is at issue here by giving an important account of the debates. He helps us focus our attention on what is a central issue, even if his own account moves towards a frustrating objectivism that cannot appreciate the significance of sexual politics:

> Exactly what has been called the contribution of Adler and the neo-Freudians, the discovery of self or personality, is the loss of the critique of the individual. The Freudian concepts exposed the fraud of the existence of the 'individual'. To be absolutely clear here: the Freudian concepts exposed the fraud, not so as to penetrate it, but undo it. That is, unlike mechanical behaviourists, the point was not to prove that the individual was an illusion; rather it was to show to what extent the individual did not yet exist. To critical theory, psychoanalysis demonstrates the degree to which the individual is de-individualised by society. It uncovers the compulsions and regressions that maim and mutilate the individual . . .
>
> . . . Freud undermines, wrote Marcuse, 'one of the strongest ideological fortifications of modern culture – namely, the notion of the autonomous individual.' 'His psychology does not focus on the concrete and complete personality as it exists in its private and public environment, because this existence conceals rather than reveals the essence and nature of the personality.' Rather he dissolves the personality and 'bares the sub-individual and pre-individual factors which (largely unconscious to the ego) actually *make* the individual: it reveals the power of the universal in and over the individuals'.
>
> (Jacoby 1975: 30)

So Freud shows how the notion of the 'autonomous individual' can serve to mystify the everyday lived reality of our experience. We can still recognise the validity and sense of dignity and self-worth people can achieve through the individual rights they share as citizens. At the same time we have to be fully aware of the diverse Black and ethnic, working-class, feminist and gay and lesbian struggles that have established these rights. They were not easily conceded as liberalism often tempts us to suppose. Although a language of rights allows people to feel that they are 'as good as the next person', this feeling can easily be 'manipulated by the institutions of social forces of the social process' (Adorno, cited in Jacoby 1975: 64).

We need to explore the ways in which insights into post-modernism also reflect fundamental changes in the labour process as we move towards post-Fordist production methods. These processes affect the experience of people in work and out of work as well as affect their behaviour in other areas of their lives.[13] So, for instance, we gain a sense of how traditional relationships between 'work', 'identity' and 'masculinity' have been challenged with changes brought about with the de-skilling of work. If the Frankfurt School did not give enough thought to changes in the social organisation of production, they left us with critical insights into some of the crucial mediations. They gave us hints of some of the determinants of personal experience which social theory has hardly begun to identify:

> The actual weakness of the father within society, which indicates the shrinkage of competition and free enterprise, extends into the innermost cells of the psychic household; the child can no longer identify with the father, can no longer accomplish the internalization of the familial demands, which with all their repressive moments still contributed decisively to the formation of the autonomous individual. Therefore there is today actually no longer the conflict between the powerful family and the no less powerful ego; instead the two, equally weak, are split apart.
>
> (Adorno and Horkheimer 1974: 141–2)

EXPERIENCE AND EMPOWERMENT

These determinants have to be related to the different realities of class, racial, ethnic and sexual identities and experiences within post-modern societies. If Jacoby is right that 'before the individual can exist, before it can become an individual, it must recognise to what extent it does not yet exist' (Jacoby 1975: 81), he does not understand the ways these issues, crucial to empowerment, have been focused within, say, the experience of the women's movement, the gay and lesbian movements and in various forms of the Black consciousness and post-colonial theories.

The vision of 'the disintegration of the ego under the impact of the massified society' can be too stark, unless it *also* recognises the living contradictions within people's identities and experience. We also need to appreciate the pain and fears associated with a loss of self and the ways people have learnt to use various forms of psychotherapy to heal this abiding sense of unreality and fragmentation. If feminisms have helped women identify how they are oppressed and denied the possibilities of living as people in their own right, it has also been forced to appreciate differences between women and so helped create different collective identities or race, ethnicity and sexuality which promise to be both 'individual' *and* 'social'.

In various forms of feminist psychotherapy there have also been attempts to integrate the experiences of consciousness-raising with a critical appreciation of therapeutic methods.[14]

Similarly for men. The more sense I have of power differences between men and the fact that my experience is not simply my private and 'unique' individual experience, but is also shared with other men who have grown up under different pressures and expectations into diverse masculinities, the greater my grasp of the social and historical formation of 'self'. This does not dissolve or reduce my individuality into an objective investigation of class, racial and sexual identities, however important these continue to be in 'who I am', but it *can* help me come to terms with an abiding sense of unreality and displacement and the different ways in which I do not exist as an 'autonomous' individual.

Given the social relations of power and dominance within which I am obliged to live in a capitalist and patriarchal society, it can be helpful to be realistic about what kinds of personal and collective changes are possible. This was an issue which divided Marcuse and Fromm in an earlier generation.[15] Marcuse thought it quite wrong to hope for 'happiness' within a society that so often takes advantage of such liberal language and aspirations for its own ends of capital accumulation. Fromm took a different path, wanting to learn from whatever traditions – both Eastern and Western – were available to guide people to greater development and self-fulfilment.[16] With the impact of feminism and ecological politics we would set this discussion in different terms from those of the 1950s. In his later years, Marcuse learnt significantly from feminism, and he would probably have stated his position differently under its influence.[17] The discussion about the possibilities of change is still very much with us. Threats to the planet have hopefully made us more aware of the profound consequences of individual action.

Through sharpening our understanding of the ways we systematically deny an individual expression we can sense how *easily* we compromise our integrity and inner knowledge. Through recognising how we continue to be trapped by forms of competitive and possessive individuality we learn *how* we also subvert a sense of identity and difference and collude in a denial of our humanity. As our dignity and self-worth is undermined we fail to express ourselves, out of fear of others or a sense of inadequacy which has been part, as I have argued, of a secularised Protestant inheritance. This makes it easier to grasp the continuing relevance of Marx's saying that 'in bourgeois society capital is independent and has individuality, while the living person is dependent and has no individuality'. This thought, expressed in the *Communist Manifesto* (1848), was echoed in the *Grundrisse,* where he says, 'It is not individuals who are set free by competition; it is, rather, capital which is set free' (Marx 1973: 650).

Resisting a dash into post-modernism we still need to develop a much fuller understanding of how the insights of Marx and Freud can still help us grasp the everyday realities of our experience despite the limitations and contradictions of their thought, which remains tied to an Enlightenment modernity and its vision of science and progress. Recognising 'difference' involves coming to terms with class, gender, sexual and racial identification and experience. This involves a historical and psychological understanding of the denial of human needs through exploitation and oppression. Identities can only be shaped if people have the time and space, both individually and collectively, to challenge prevailing relations in the process of empowering themselves. If needs and desires are historically conditioned, this does *not* mean that they are not denied, displaced and repressed, as are aspects of our individuality. Nor do notions of creative individuality which recognise our need to respect our integrity and self-esteem as well as our need for equal relations with others, deny the class, ethnic and sexual reality of our experience.

If we want to avoid an abstract utopianism that sets up an ideal we have to be ready to sacrifice for, we need to insist on learning from historical experiences rather than making them conform to our pre-existing conceptions. We need also to be fully aware of the contradictions in people's everyday experience as these help sharpen people's sense of what they want for themselves and what they need from others to live more full, decent and equal lives. Such notions of 'identity' and 'difference' do not pose an abstract conception of humanity, but recognise that a socialist vision, if it to be renewed, has to rekindle the idea that social justice also involves the creation of a free society in which differences are respected, human needs satisfied and fulfilment gained, not sacrificed.

The discourses of socialism have generally remained discourses of modernity and so have often implicitly taken for granted its Protestant sources. This has fostered a hidden culture of self-denial which devalues the body and emotional life. It has made it difficult to think creatively about the conditions of fulfilment and empowerment since individuals were fundamentally conceived of as rational selves. Within modernity the categorical distinction between reason and nature reflected the dominance and power of white Western men, who were able to make 'civilisation' in their own image. This led to the denigration of nature as it was reduced to matter, and to the subordination of women who were deemed to be closer to it. It also served as a crucial argument in the legitimation of slavery and colonial oppression.

With feminism, ecology and post-colonial theory we have learnt to rethink modernity in different terms. Not only have emotions and feelings been acknowledged more freely as sources of knowledge, but we have learnt to hear the sufferings of animals and nature. We have slowly learnt to think of ourselves *as part of* nature rather than to assume a superiority that allows progress to be conceived of as the control and domination of nature. We can now call for a renewal of traditions of the social theory that for too long has identified progress with control and domination of both inner and outer nature. We are learning to ask new questions as we recognise ourselves as emotional, somatic and spiritual beings, rather than simply the rational selves that we have grown to identify with in the dominant terms of modernity. As we learn to respect these different aspects of our being we grow in our own authority as individuals. We forsake traditions of self-denial as we learn to think about freedom, justice and equality in different terms. This is part of a process of individual and collective empowerment.

Chapter 10

Conclusion
Modernity, morality and social theory

With the revolutions in Eastern Europe in 1989 and the events that followed with the break-up of the Soviet Union there is a widespread sense that we are living in 'new times'. As the early hopes of change have given way to the agonies of 'ethnic cleansing' we have witnessed in Bosnia, there is a growing sense that our inherited traditions of social, moral and political thought have somehow failed to illuminate the realities that we live. In part it can feel that we are paying the price of never having come to terms in our intellectual culture with the relationship of the Holocaust to modernity.

It has been too easy to sidestep the horrors of Auschwitz and Hiroshima as moments of aberration and madness that have little to teach us about the processes of 'normal' life. But the language of 'eradication' is too deeply embedded in the moral texture of modernity, for it is invoked in the ways we are traditionally taught, within a Protestant culture, to treat our emotional lives. As we learn to *deny* devalued aspects of the self, so we also learn to discount aspects of our histories which confront us with difficult and unsettling questions.

The ground upon which we have built our sense of politics as having to do with freedom, equality and justice within the public realm has shifted, so much so that we are left wondering about the meaning of politics itself. The questioning of feminism about the relationship of 'the personal to the political' has helped to question the autonomy of different spheres that has been a defining feature of modernity. We have learnt to recognise suffering, power and injustice within the realm of personal relationships and so have been forced to rethink the relationship between the 'private' and the 'public'. This has encouraged an awareness of the extent to which prevailing traditions of social theory, drawing from Marx, Weber and Durkheim, have only been able to recognise injustice and oppression as 'real' and 'objective' when it has taken place within the public realm of 'politics'.

Ecological awareness has helped us question the distinction between nature and culture that has been such a guiding factor within structuralist traditions, as if we can so neatly separate the 'biological' from the social and historical. It is only because the Scientific Revolution reduced living nature to dead matter that could be explained in mechanistic terms that we learnt to treat nature as 'given'. We learnt to take for granted within an Enlightenment vision of modernity that progress involved the control and domination of nature.

This was equally significant in our relationship to our inner emotional lives, which we learnt with Kant to treat as forms of determination and unfreedom, as it was in our relationship with nature more generally. We learnt to *disdain* any sense of the 'natural' and it became unavailable to us. Within modernity we learnt to identify our 'humanity' with reason alone and so as embodying an implicit relationship of hierarchy and superiority. We devalued our emotions and feelings as sources of knowledge. It was only through reason that we could guide our lives and find freedom and autonomy as rational selves.

I have explored the relationship of modernity to a particular masculinist form of rationalism that is built around a categorical distinction between reason and nature. With the identification of a dominant masculinity with reason we learn that, particularly as white, heterosexual men brought up within a Protestant tradition, our relationships with our bodies and emotional lives are relationships of control. We fear contact with our emotions and feelings for they threaten a control that has become crucial to sustaining the dominant notions of heterosexual male identity. It is this vision of estrangement from our bodies and emotional lives that has been central to a Cartesian vision of modernity.

We are left as rational selves with a thin and attenuated sense of self, for we learn to denigrate our emotions and feelings as sources of knowledge. As rational selves we are able to make choices through reason alone. Often this is an 'unreasonable' form of reason for it is separated from emotional and somatic aspects of the self. As we learn to treat our bodies as machines we can no longer hear what they have to say. The body has no voice, as the natural and animal world has no voice. We have become deaf to its sufferings and often we only heed its messages when it has broken down in illness. Often, even then, we carry on regardless, so affirming our masculine will and determination.

Since the French Revolution the framework of political discourse has been provided by a distinction between Left and Right, between socialism and capitalism. Somehow we seem to have lost our bearings politically and it has been easy to interpret the events in Eastern Europe and the former Soviet Union as a vindication of capitalism and of the market as the primary legislator of value. But if the market fails to deliver it seems as if someone has to be blamed, and we see the emergence of racist anti-Semitic movements in different parts of Europe. When Western Europe is suffering an economic crisis of its own, it has been easy to disappoint the expectations of those who were looking for help.

But with the failure of the market values so dominant in the 1980s, there seems to be a crisis of culture and values that touches both sides of Europe. In part, the pervasive discussions around the evaluation of modernity have helped to shift the traditional political terms. At some level it has helped us to ask different questions, but too often discussions around postmodernity have led to a generalised rejection of the 'grand narratives' of modernity, including Marxism. We have been left bereft of a *moral* language when values and moralities have been treated as yet one more discourse amongst others. It has been difficult to escape a pervasive form of moral relativism.[1]

MORALITY AND MODERNITY

Learning to think about the relationship of modernity to morality we are forced to evaluate the identification of morality with reason. Somehow the thinness of inherited conceptions of personal identity and the self connects to the inadequacies in moral vision and understanding. This is as true in philosophy as it is in social and political theory. As we learn to think of ourselves as rational selves, so we learn to think of moral issues as individual concerns which can be settled through reason alone.

After all, as Kant has it, it is reason that gives us access to the moral law. We learn to subordinate our 'inclinations' so that we can do what is required of us by the moral law. As reason is superior to nature for Kant, so society is superior to the 'individual' for Durkheim.[2] Social rules provide us with a means of escape from the 'egoistic self' so that we can live out a higher vision of ourselves. We cannot trust our own knowledge of ourselves but have to defer to a superior authority which can legislate 'what is best for others'. So it is that 'society' takes the place of the moral law.

I have argued that modernity provides us with a secularised form of Protestantism but that we have learnt to take its structures so much for granted that they have become largely invisible to us. Weber teaches us something important about capitalism and modernity for, as I have tried to show, traditions which have sought to challenge the moral culture of capitalism have often unwittingly reproduced its assumptions. As we have learnt to think of oppression and injustice in distributive terms alone, we have been blind to the diversity of hurts and sufferings people are forced to endure.

Within a Protestant culture people often learn to suffer in silence as they learn to deny their needs and desires. We inherit a weak sense of entitlement that often makes people take pride in 'doing without'. This is tied to a particular vision of heterosexual masculinity, for we often learn that, as men, we do not have emotional needs. If, as men, we learn to treat needs as a sign of weakness, it will be difficult to share our vulnerability. We will shut others out as we learn to manage on our own. Those who have reached out will often feel rejected and silently resentful. And, as heterosexual men, we will never grow in our wholeness, for we will never have learnt from the experience that, if we reach out, others can be there to support and love us. We will continue to treat our love as a scarce commodity.

Weber's *The Protestant Ethic and the Spirit of Capitalism* can help us think about the complex issues of entitlement. For there is a way that men can feel entitled to the services of others. In heterosexual relationships we can easily feel that, if we work for the family, then it is only right for women to look after the home and care for the children. In part this reflects a moral culture of self-denial, for if men have to sacrifice themselves at work so women, in the traditional picture, are supposed to sacrifice themselves for men and children. This helps explain women's weaker sense of entitlement, for women often grow up feeling that they can only find happiness through providing happiness for others. Otherwise they are being selfish.

So, as Carol Gilligan has helped illuminate, it can be difficult for women to learn to include themselves in the moral situation. But this is also because their moral experience as women is rendered invisible within the dominant rationalist conception of morality.[3] It is hard to validate an ethic of care and concern if morality is about proving our moral worth as individuals. For one thing, as Foucault came to realise towards the end of his life, it is hard to care for others if we have never learnt how to care for ourselves. He had to look outside the terms of modernity and its visions of the rational self to begin to explore *how* we can learn to care for the self.[4]

Within modernity we learn that caring for the self is a form of self-indulgence. We learn, as men, to disdain emotional life as a sign of weakness. It has little place within an intellectual culture that is defined in terms of reason alone. As male identities remain established largely within the public sphere of work and the achievements that go with it, it is easy to take personal and sexual relationships for granted. It is hard to acknowledge the emotional work that goes into sustaining an emotional relationship, for this has little connection with affirming our male identities. Rather, emotions are experienced as a sign of weakness, so that we have to be careful to control how we can be in the private realm, lest there be a leakage and we find ourselves unable to be 'in control' at work. If there is a particular relationship between masculinity and reason, women also grow up in the shadow of this ethic. It sets the terms by which they have to prove themselves. They often learn to be independent in their own ways and can also find it hard to care for themselves emotionally. They learn to go without, sharing a cultural fear of pleasure and nourishment.

We learn about the Enlightenment vision of modernity as a movement towards reason, science, freedom and progress. The social world is to be made into a rational order as it becomes organised according to the dictates of reason and science. This was to be an 'objective' process that individuals were to subordinate themselves to if they did not want to stand in the way of progress. This dream of a rational social order became part of the dream of modernity. But we also became blind to the relationship between modernity and slavery and the ways people of colour were denigrated and enslaved as part of nature.[5] The West was to create modernity in its own image and so to set the terms by which different nations were to move from 'backwardness' to 'civilisation'. As Simone Weil noted, it allowed any working-class man to feel inherently superior to the 'natives' he met in Polynesia, for he was the 'possessor of science', culture and civilisation, which 'they' obviously lacked.[6]

We also became blind to the witchburnings that were part of the reorganisation of power according to gender, as men appropriated knowledge as their own. Science was to become a masculine possession, for what women were left with was 'personal' and 'subjective'. Crucial to this was the notion that if women refused to subordinate themselves to the new 'masculinist philosophy' they proved themselves to be beyond the pale of reason, so that they had to be saved from themselves.[7] Emotions, dreams, intuitions, fantasies were all devalued as forms of unreason, as Foucault explored the construction of reason in *Madness and Civilisation*. They were no part of our identities as rational selves. Rather we had to learn to devalue and denigrate these aspects of our experience lest they 'interfere' with the pure light of reason.

Women came to be identified with a sexuality which could tempt men away from their true vocation in reason. So, as men, we absorbed a deep fear of female sexuality, which had to be silenced and controlled if it was not to threaten our existence as rational selves. The fear of the flesh carried a long history within Christianity, for there was an abiding connection between the body and sin. The body was a prison which had trapped the pure soul which was struggling to free itself. So it is hardly surprising that we inherit deeply ambivalent feelings about our bodies and emotional lives. Sexuality becomes a curse we would rather be free of, and so within a patriachal culture it is something that men learn to blame women for. It is as if heterosexual men would often prefer not to deal with sexual feelings at all.

ANTI-SEMITISM, RACISM AND MODERNITY

Disdain for nature was integral to our inherited visions of modernity. If women were deemed to be closer to nature then they could only discover freedom through relating to the reason of men. But if African men and women were suited by nature to slavery, then there was nothing that could redeem them. Similarly, for Voltaire Jews could no more be accepted within the pale of culture than the Romans could be expected to include slaves when they talked about the rights of citizens in civilised society. Voltaire looked back to pagan, Greco-Roman antiquity as the golden age that had been ruined by the advent of Christianity. As Arthur Hertzberg has described it in *The French Enlightenment and the Jews*, 'In his own mind Voltaire was a Cicero redivivus who had come to recreate the world. The glory of the new age of Enlightenment would be that Europe would restored to its true foundations (Hertzberg 1968: 299).

Voltaire had abandoned the religious attack on the Jews as ex-Christians, only to redirect his hatred to their innate character. The quarrel was no longer between Christians and Jews but between the bearers of Western culture and those who had infected it with Oriental ideas. He praised Cicero for his anti-Semitic oration, *Pro Flacco*, saying, 'I would not be in the least bit surprised if these people would not some day become deadly to the human race' (cited in Hertzberg 1968: 300).

Voltaire's vision of Enlightenment mirrors the exclusions of ancient Rome, which was a civilisation that fostered slavery. His discussions reveal the ways reasonableness and honesty become tools of exclusion. As far as he was concerned, the Hebrews 'had no idea of that which we call taste, delicacy, or proportion' (Ibid.: 301). In *Il faut prendre une partie* he says to the Jews, 'You seem to me to be the maddest of the lot. The Kaffirs, the Hottentots, and the Negroes of Guinea are much more reasonable and more honest people than your ancestors, the Jews. You have surpassed all nations in impertinent fables, in bad conduct, and in barbarism. You deserve to be punished, for this is your destiny' (Ibid.: 301).

The voice of Enlightenment established its own exclusions that were to feed its own anti-Semitism. It add its own weight to the traditions of Christian anti-Semitism. As Sartre realised, modernity was very much a mixed blessing for the Jews, for they were only to be accepted as citizens to the extent that they were ready to deny their Jewishness, regarding it simply as an issue of personal belief.[8] Like others caught in the same historical traps, Jews had to work to become acceptable through becoming 'other' than they were. As Jews, we were often to become invisible. Within modernity it was only individual differences of taste that were to be acknowledged, as forms of collective identity were treated as forms of unreason that we had to 'rise above' in a movement towards freedom and autonomy.

As we have already seen, Kant prepared the crucial ground for freedom to be identified with an inner faculty of reason, while we supposedly had an external and determined relationship with both nature – the empirical realm of emotions, feelings and desires designated as 'inclinations' – and with culture and history. Both these spheres were part of an 'empirical' realm that was set against the 'intelligible' realm of reason. So just as we learnt to separate ourselves from our emotional lives, seeing them as no part of our identities as rational moral selves, so we still also learn to disconnect or 'rise above' our collective class, ethnic, gender and sexual histories and cultures. Not only were these forms of unfreedom but they proved a weakness of the will, for they proved that we could not exist as free and equal individuals in our own right. So, for instance, to be influenced by one's class background or ethnic community reflected a form of 'unreason' for it supposedly showed that we were not yet ready or prepared to guide our lives by reason alone.

If we are to think about Auschwitz helpfully, we have to be ready to situate it within the contradictory terms of modernity. We cannot treat it simply as a moment of madness that exists outside the rational reaches of history and culture. We have to ask difficult questions as Simone Weil was prepared to, about the ways Hitler was also living out the dreams of Roman power and greatness that he had learnt in his history books and which we are still teaching to our children. It seems as if the claims of the West are so intimately tied up with Rome that it is difficult to think critically about our inheritance. This becomes more complex because of Rome's relationship to Christianity, so that a rhetoric of poverty, humility and powerlessness was tied to the realities of imperial power.

Christianity learnt to accommodate itself to the rule of Caesar's power and to place its concern with spirituality in a different realm. We were to be less concerned with redeeming this world, than with preparing ourselves for the world to come. The universalism of Rome was to find expression in the claims of the universal church. If Jews refused to accept the truth of this new revelation, then they condemned themselves to be punished. They only had themselves to blame for their stubborn refusal to see the truth.[9] But Jews saw their covenant with God in different terms and they sought to redeem this world as a partnership with God.

The universalism of Rome took a different form within modernity. It was science that was to become the legislator of truth. If healers and herbalists refused to accept the authority of science, they only had themselves to blame. So, the familiar story goes, they brought punishment on themselves. If they were prepared to see reason, they would accept the authority of science. If they persisted in their stubborn ways, then they put themselves beyond the pale of rational discourse. It was the split between science and morality that has been structured into the universalism of modernity, which had learnt to identify science with 'progress' and 'civilisation'. It was the 'impartiality' and 'objectivity' of science that was to be set against the 'irrationality' of ritual, customs and traditional practices. These had to be able to prove themselves before the tribunal of science if they were to be accepted. So it was that science allowed the West to redefine the terms of modernity.

NATURE, SCIENCE AND EMOTIONAL LIFE

Simone Weil explores the split between 'humanism' and 'science' which has characterised the modern world. With the death of nature we live in an empirical world that can be explained according to the laws of nature. Within the dualism of a Cartesian tradition our selves are identifed with reason and mind, while we are left with an *externalised* relationship to our bodies and emotional lives which are deemed to be part of the empirical world of nature. So it is that the split between reason and nature reflects the distinction between the humanities and the sciences. We are left with a fragmented conception of self as reason and estranged from somatic and emotional life. There is no place for the heart and for feelings within this dualistic conception. Unlike Plato's conception of the tripartite divisions within the soul, we are left with the notion that it is reason alone which has to control the body and emotional life. Since reason alone, in Kant's ethical theory, is the source of freedom and morality, we learn to disdain our 'inclinations', for they distract us from the path of pure reason.

The 'disenchantment' of nature means that reason becomes the source of meanings and values. A modern conception of humanism is defined, as human reason alone can assign meanings and values to a world that has become bereft of value and meaning. There are few limits that are built into our *uses* of nature, for the earth is no longer considered as the sacred mother. Mining remains an example of this historical transformation from an 'organic' towards a 'mechanistic' conception of nature. Mining was no longer perceived as a violation of the mother's body requiring respect and spiritual preparation. Rather the earth became a means of production and rights over the

land became an issue of ownership and private property. With progress defined in terms of the control and domination of nature there
was little regard for our relationships with nature and the animal
world. These are understood in mechanical terms, so that the only
value they have is the value which humans assign to them through
the uses made of them.

The Cartesian vision of modernity also helped transform our relationship with ourselves. The self became identified with reason alone
and became separated from somatic and emotional life. We learnt to
treat emotions as 'subjective' and 'irrational' so that they formed no
part of our personal identities. Discussions around post-modernity
have focused too quickly upon the coherence of the Cartesian self,
setting this against the 'fragmentations' of identities that we know
from the post-modern. But this is to reproduce significant masculine
assumptions, for it perpetuates in its own way that abiding distinction between reason and nature and equally works to disdain somatic
and emotional life. If we are to recover the self we have to explore
the terms of its fragmentation and the ways it becomes undermined
through the invalidation of inner emotional life. It is in this sense that
we inherit a one-dimensional self within modernity as we become
estranged and fearful of other aspects of our being.

It is this fragmentation into different 'spheres' of life, each of which
can be grasped in its own terms, that has characterised modernity.
So it is that modernity is underpinned by a separation between science
and morality which allows social theorists to talk of a distinction
between 'structures' and 'values'. With Kant, we learn to talk about
science, ethics and politics in quite different terms, since they supposedly refer to different terrains of human experience. Once morality
is organised around the Kantian question of 'what ought I to do?',
it is established in individual terms and so separated from the collective terms of politics and social theory. Politics becomes an issue of
the use of power for political ends and it has nothing to do with 'truth'
and 'honesty', for in the 'real world' of politics we supposedly cannot
be concerned with such 'subjective' and 'value-laden' considerations.
As we so often hear, 'morality is all very well, but in the real world
we have to be concerned with interests'.

SOCIALISM, MARKETS AND MORALITY

Gramsci and Simone Weil are crucial voices in reclaiming the moral
terms of Marx's writings. They are concerned in different ways with
the relationship of morality to politics and they help to question the
ways in which Marxism has so often been conceived in scientistic
terms. Somehow the disdain for moral concerns goes hand in hand

with an impoverished conception of the self and so with a blindness to the injuries and sufferings of power and oppression. I have tried to show how this does an injustice to Marx's concern and how it reflects one sense in which Marx's writings go against the grain of modernity. On the other hand, in important respects Marx remains a child of the Enlightenment dreams and shares in its disdain towards morality and values.

Marx was trapped by the hopes of science, even though he may have wanted to challenge the terms of political economy and had learnt from Hegel about the weakness of segregating different spheres of life. For Hegel had appreciated the abstractness of the Kantian moral self and had sought a more substantial conception of self. But Hegel's tradition placed too much hope in historical transformation and in the idea that the community can somehow provide individuals with a 'higher' conception of the self. He did not help people trust themselves, but in crucial respects sustained the self-denial that was integral to a Protestant ethic. He prepared the way for the subordination of individuals to the state as the embodiment of a higher morality.[10]

We have been forced to ask how socialism has remained part of the project of modernity as a means of grasping its difficulties in appreciating feminist and ecological challenges. Socialism has remained largely a rationalistic project which has sustained an instrumental attitude towards people. It has presented itself as 'more rational' than pure capitalism and has been prepared to legislate 'what is best for people' in the name of reason, for reason alone is supposedly able to discern a 'just ordering of society'. Again, it is people's selfish and egoistic natures that stand in the way of recognising the 'truth' of the socialist project, however we might think of this in a post-communist world. The crucial point here is that reason can supposedly legislate 'what is best for people', for people themselves are trapped in their own selfish concerns.

Through reason we can discern what it is that people need and through a 'rational organisation' of society we can at least see that peoples' basic needs are catered for. This treats reason as a source knowledge that should be given a sovereign place, for it can legislate in a 'fair' and 'just' way without having to consider people's own expression of their needs and desires. Supposedly it is the 'impartiality' and 'universality' of reason that makes it both 'independent' and 'objective'.

The libertarian Right was able to challenge this socialist vision of planning in the 1980s partly because the welfare state had generated its own bureaucratic forms of administration, for example in the health service, which left many people feeling angry and powerless. It was supposedly a service organised in 'their own interest', but people often felt hurt and offended by its instrumental ways. The market was deemed a source of freedom for it supposedly promised to express people's own choices through the market decisions they made for themselves. This vision of market freedom appropriated a language of freedom and empowerment, for by introducing markets in different spheres of life it promised to 'set people free' to make their own choices. If they did not like the way they were treated in one hospital they could choose to take their custom elsewhere. But some of these early hopes were dashed as people were forced to recognise that they did not enjoy the same power in the market, so that, for instance, they might be able to buy their council house but they could not afford to keep up with the payments.

But the popularity of the libertarian Right in the 1980s did touch an important chord, for people wanted to have more power and control over their lives. They wanted to believe a new rhetoric of freedom because they rejected the ways their lives had been administered. The appeal of the Right reflected a pervasive disquiet with rationalist forms of political administration which often adopted an instrumental and patronising attitude towards people. The Left was slow to consider issues of consumerism and the market as it struggled to find different ways of listening and empowering people. Too often trapped in its own rationalism, it could not understand the appeal of Green politics and its more fundamental questioning. As the Greens questioned issues of science and progress they dared to set them in the context of people's fundamental relationship with nature. They could also talk of 'balance' and 'harmony' in the ways people learn to relate to their own inner natures. This allowed people to relate ethics and politics in new ways for it was empowering to learn that individuals *could* make a difference through the ways they individually chose to live. In its links with feminism and sexual politics, ecological politics was able to rethink the relation between the personal and the political, between emotions and power.[11]

The distinction between reason and nature has to be challenged if we are to begin to rework the relation between science and morality. With Kant's identification of morality with reason we separate it from emotional life and prepare the ground which Durkheim, and to some extent Marx, occupy in which moral development is made a feature of social development. We discern an identification between reason, morality and knowledge, since it is through reason that we can supposedly discern the duties and obligations that are set by the 'moral law'. Somehow people's own experience comes to be denied and denigrated as 'subjective' and 'personal' when it is set against the authority of reason. People learn to *discount* their experience and their struggles to live a decent life in often difficult conditions. Within a structuralist tradition, experience falls on the side of nature. It too easily becomes associated and identified with the generalised categories of 'humanism' and 'essentialism' so that experience becomes difficult to validate within dominant forms of social theory.

As language has taken the place of reason, so we learn, within a post-structuralist tradition, that experience is an effect of language. We lose any sense of the tension between language and experience for experience itself is taken to be discursive. Not only does this grow out of a misreading of Freud and Wittgenstein, but it reinforces a rationalist tradition that can only understand the body and emotional life in symbolic terms. We have little sense of the lived experience of the body and the expressive character of sexualities because these are reduced and silenced as they also fall on the side of nature. Reason alone has a voice, one which carries the power to silence 'others' within modernity.

MODERNITY, RATIONALISM AND EXPERIENCE

Enlightenment visions of modernity have been cast within the terms of a rationalist tradition. The self exists as the rational self, able to guide through reason alone. This makes it difficult to illuminate the tensions and contradictions within lived experience, which was equally true of an orthodox Marxist tradition that treated people's experience as a 'backward' sign of false consciousness when compared with the rational insights of 'scientific Marxism'. People were trapped within an experience they supposedly could not come to understand themselves.

Freud also gradually came to disdain the experience of his patients, for what mattered was the 'truth' of the analytic insight. Sometimes people would resist this truth about themselves even when it was offered to them. For Marx people's experience was shaped by social forces that they could not grasp, while for Freud it was shaped by unconscious forces over which they had equally little control. In this regard both Marx and Freud remain within the rationalist terms of modernity, though in very significant respects they both make breaks with it.

Modernity in the West forged an identification between science, progress and the domination of nature. It set the terms which 'others' supposedly 'lacked' and the conditions they were supposedly to meet in their movement from 'underdevelopment' to 'modernity'. This fostered its own forms of denial as it encouraged colonial peoples to feel diminished in their own eyes. They learnt to devalue their own customs and traditions as 'unscientific' and 'backward', a trend that has continued into the post-colonial world when people, for instance in São Paulo or Bogota are still trained to look towards New York, Paris and London for 'where it is at'.

It is an unending process of catching up with 'elsewhere', which makes it so much more difficult to foster indigenous cultural, political and intellectual traditions. Through the media and mass communications the West to a large extent sustains its authority. In part this has to do with the locus of economic and political power and the workings of cultural imperialism. Theories of post-modernity and post-colonialism have helped to challenge the Western eye of reason, but often, as I shall argue, very much in the West's own terms.

With theories of post-modernity there has been a growing scepticism about the notion of the rational self as a focus for a fixed and determined identity. There is more recognition of the complexities of identities as they have fragmented within a post-modern society. This has also fostered an unease about notions of class, race, gender and sexuality as providing the sources of a fixed identity that moves from 'unconsciousness' towards conscious awareness of itself as the subject of a grand historical narrative focused for example, around the exploitations of capitalist society or women's subordination and oppression within patriarchy. Lyotard has helped focus a growing unease with the grand historical narrative, the notion that there can be a single explanation for the sufferings that people endure in society.[12]

There is growing recognition of the shifting character of 'identities' that are constantly being reformed and rearticulated. This connects to an awareness of the centrality of media and communication in late capitalist societies and the place these have in forming and deconstructing different identities. But rather than seeing people as the victims of manipulation and control, there is a widespread desire to see this as an 'active' process in which people are making and remaking their identities out of whatever is culturally available to them. There are supposedly no fixed patterns or established frameworks, but people can enjoy the freedom of being able to create themselves through whatever images and consumer goods they find available.[13]

Discussions around post-modernity set issues connected with recovering the self in quite different terms. There might be a general scepticism about notions of the self if they suggest in humanist terms that the self is fixed, somehow waiting to be 'discovered' underneath the variety of identities that people inhabit in their everyday lives. But again this is a false opposition which reworks in a different language the Althusserian opposition which would see identities as either fixed and given, so as a form of 'humanism' or 'essentialism', or else as 'socially and historically constructed'. Post-structuralism also fosters a disdain for both nature and biology, which are placed outside the limits of reason and history. It helps produce its own forms of voluntarism, as if people are 'free' to take on whatever identities they happen to favour. It often seems to turn social life into a game that is not far removed from the presentations of self that we learnt from Erving Goffman.[14]

IDENTITIES, FREEDOM AND POST-MODERNITY

The creation of identities is supposedly an exercise in freedom and self-determination. But paradoxically it remains within a Kantian framework which separates a 'realm of necessity', the notion of identities as fixed and given, from a 'realm of freedom' in which people can 'create' their own identities. It looks to the present and the future but it leaves behind a past world of fixed identities that were supposedly bequeathed within modernity. But it can be misleading to contrast the notion of identities waiting to be discovered with the idea that people can create their own identities out of images that are culturally available.

So often Baudrillard locks us into the appearance of the present and so into a more superficial contact with ourselves.[15] We are left with a celebration of the present and of a realm of appearances that supposedly provides us with the only 'reality' we can still trust. But what we gain in our sense of freedom we so often *lose* in our sense of history. It is misleading to contrast in general terms an appreciation of 'appearances' with an exploration of underlying necessities that supposedly explain forms of social life. The idea that we could discover underlying laws that would explain social relationships was part of the dream of positivism. Too often, however, it discounted people's own experience as 'subjective' and 'anecdotal' when faced with the 'objectivity' of scientific laws. But this is not the only way that we can seek understanding.

The celebration of American-style consumerism and the information revolution can create its own forms of blindness. So often it can leave people drifting in a sea of unfulfilled expectations. Trapped by false oppositions we lose a sense of the different *levels* of our experience, the different depths of contract we can have with ourselves. Talk of 'depth' is easily dismissed by Baudrillard for it tempts people into failing to appreciate how much *is* available to them. But we *can* appreciate the diversity of opportunities which cultural changes have made available, without losing the possibilities of critique. We need to resist the drift in post-modern writing that too easily dispenses with a moral language, assuming that it ties us to a fixed conception of 'human nature' and identities. Often it is felt that to sustain a moral language has somehow to mean that we inevitably support a particular authority, position or judgement from which we can 'judge' others. If we want to be free from the burden of judging others according to our own implicit standards, then we supposedly have to be ready to dispense with morality and recognise that individuals have to be 'free' to make whatever identities they want for themselves.

Nietzsche reminds us constantly to consider our own lives before we begin to judge others. He recognises the ease with which we learn to pass judgement on others *before* we have really learnt how to take responsibility for ourselves. This is part of the hidden resentment that is structured into the Protestant moral culture we learn to take so much for granted within modernity. We need to challenge the easy self-righteousness that tempts people into judging others for not living up to prevailing social customs. Rather we have to learn how to take responsibility for the quality of our own experience, for the truth and honesty of our own lives. This is not, however, to dispense with morality, but rather to question the notion of morality as a fixed, pre-given set of principles and standards through which we learn to judge others.

This is part of Nietzsche's challenge to a Christian ethics that thinks that it can separate, once and for all, what is 'good' from what is 'evil'. It is also a challenge to a Kantian rationalism that assumes that reason can make this decision for us and that we can know ourselves through reason alone. So it is that Nietzsche helps us identify the Protestant voice in Kant and the Christian dualism that underpins Kantian philosophy. But this does not leave us with a relativism about values, though post-modern writers have often wanted to draw this conclusion from Kant. As Katherine Parsons has noticed, there is a paradoxical resonance, given the pervasive misogyny of his writings, with feminist insights into the 'affirmation' of experience.[16] He encouraged radicals like Emma Goldman to stand up for what they believed in their hearts to be true, regardless of the opposition they met.[17] Somehow there is a sense of the importance of truth and honesty with ourselves so that we do not betray or compromise an inner truth. This is the way we can grow in our own authority as individuals.

Modernity had reflected a split between morality and politics. As morality comes to be conceived of as an individual concern so it is marginalised and excluded from the dominant terms of social and political theory. As different traditions of social theory aspired to be 'scientific' they sought to exclude moral concerns for they feared that the 'objectivity' would thereby be compromised. Operating within a framework that treated values as 'subjective' it became difficult to think about dignity and oppression when morality could only be conceived of, in Durkheim's terms, as social rules or in Weber's terms of assigning meanings. Kant set the terms for an externalised vision of morality by treating individuals as 'egoistic' and 'selfish', therefore in need of an external intervention of reason and the moral law. Within social theory we tended to loose Kant's sense of inner life, for within his framework we could only have an inner relationship with reason that was given a social form in the prevailing rules of society. This meant that people had to be prepared to adapt to prevailing social rules if they were not to be treated as 'deviant' or 'pathological'.

Within the positivist terms of social theory this worked to foreclose any tension or contradiction between what individuals wanted or needed for themselves and the prevailing organisation of social institutions and practices. If social theory was to resist becoming a form of social engineering it had to sustain a fuller conception of self. This tension was also lost within an orthodox Marxist tradition that could assume that with the socialisation of the means of production the sources of exploitation and oppression had been removed. In the Soviet Union and Eastern Europe this meant that workers had no grounds to be dissatisfied, so that if they were it only proved that they were 'troublemakers' and 'enemies of the people'. As Simone Weil had recognised, there was no longer any understanding of *how* work gives dignity to human life since the Soviet Union was prepared to introduce assembly-line production. The degradation of work had been rendered invisible. This convinced Weil to do something immediately about the dignity of work, rather than to wait for the transformation of the capitalist mode of production. But this involved exploring the moral relations of dignity and oppression.[18]

The fluidity of post-modern discussion of identity also makes it difficult to appreciate Marx's sense of the creative need for labour. Yet this was integral to Marx's break with an Enlightenment rationalism. Marx recognised that people needed to express themselves through creative work as a way of affirming their identities. More recently feminism has also appreciated the need for women to discover the sources of their own expression through work, since housework and childcare would often not meet these needs. Women could so easily feel undermined in their sense of worth if they could not discover meaningful work.

But there is often a contradiction between capitalist relations at work and the alienation these produce, and what people need to sustain their sense of dignity and self-worth. It is a contradiction that people are forced to live with, but it makes a significant difference if people are conscious of it. But this means conceiving identities not in psychological terms but in their connection with social and political relations of power and subordination. It means coming to terms with the power of institutions and relationships to *undermine* people in their sense of self.

if we think for a moment again of how our identities have been shaped by our school experience we can develop a sense of some of the difficulties we were often up against. It might be that people are free to reject the identities prepared for them by school, but at the same time it takes time and effort to sustain oppositional identities. We often learn to live with a contradiction between a love of learning and the fear of 'getting things wrong' and being humiliated and made to feel small. Often we learn to hide our inner feelings so that we are less vulnerable to hurt and humiliation. We conceal our true feelings because we do not want to be exposed.

We learn to provide what the teacher wants from us as we learn to discount our own experience as 'subjective' and 'personal' and so as largely irrelevant to the knowledge that seems to be firmly and safely held in books. So it is, as Freire grasps it, that knowledge becomes estranged as a commodity that we learn to store in our notebooks.[19] Since this is the way things were, it is easy to think this is the way they have to be. Only years later might we be able to identify some of the unexpressed anger and fear that we carry in our bodies from these days. Often we prefer not to talk about these experiences, especially if they bring back painful memories.

Of course there is a plurality of identities and we do not all follow the same strategies of survival. But within similar regimes of schooling we had to come to terms with particular hierarchies and competitive relations. We might well have learnt to deal with our fears and anxieties in different ways, and these will be related, as Freud understood, to early childhood relationships. It can be difficult to work out *how* we were marked by our schooling in the diverse ways we think and feel. We might learn to put these experiences aside to get on with the rest of life, until they catch up with us and we recognise we need to 'work on them'. For example, a child who was sent away to boarding school at age eight might feel a deep sense of abandonment which makes it hard to trust that others can be there for him in intimate relationships. It might only be through getting together with other boys who have suffered similar experiences that he discovers an emotional language with which to begin to talk about what happened. This is to break a silence of years as he *recognises* the hurt and pain he has carried for so long. Of course many feel little need for this kind of emotional exploration, but if we are to believe Freud, they have learnt to carry their sufferings in different ways. The fact that people do not talk about it does not mean that it does not exist, as theories of discourse often have it, or that it does not block people from being able to establish a deeper connection with themselves.

At the same time we can cherish a teacher who had confidence in us long after our years of formal teaching are over. We can still be nourished and supported by the trust that they showed, even if we did not fully appreciate it at the time. This can make an enormous material difference to the ways we still feel about ourselves, giving us hope in difficult times. As Primo Levi understood, giving hope to others is a gift that we can pass on to our neighbours.[20] It is all the more striking given how judgemental teachers so often are, expecting the worst from us and somehow finding it hard to trust what we are capable of. Again this has to do with dignity and self-esteem and can help us connect morality to power, emotions to structures, as we rethink the terms of social theory that have made it so difficult to appreciate the impact of institutions on the sustaining of selves.

IDENTITIES AND MORALITY

Gramsci's sense of 'moral individuality' attempts to express the interrelation between 'individuality' and 'social and historical relations' in moral and political terms. For Gramsci, we come to know ourselves by coming to appreciate where we come from and the different traditions which are somehow expressed within our taken-for-granted 'common sense'.[21] But Gramsci's attempt to rethink a relation between morality and politics through his notion of 'moral individuality' so easily gets lost within a structuralist reading of his work. Unless we are prepared to think of individuality as articulated through the prevailing discourses, we are open to the accusation of 'essentialism'. The somewhat belated recognition that a structuralist theory failed to create a space for an adequate theory of the subject should have led to a questioning of its theoretical framework. Too often it led commentators to look to Foucault's work to fill a 'gap' in a revitalised post-structuralist framework.

This fails to illuminate the significance of Gramsci's writings in helping us to recover the self. Through his recognition of 'experience' and 'moral individuality' he is partly breaking with an Enlightenment rationalism and so with a dominant tradition on the Left. He refuses, for instance, to dismiss religion as a form of 'superstition' or 'irrationality' to be replaced by a 'scientific Marxism' that proves the 'backwardness' of traditional beliefs. For Gramsci it was important to engage critically with Catholicism as part of a popular culture which helped to constitute and order people's sense of themselves.

Thus, Gramsci is more sympathetic to different forms of local, traditional and religious beliefs, in wanting to engage with the meanings they had come to have in people's lives. Through acknowledging the real needs they responded to, you could begin to think about other ways in which these needs could be met. This fostered a respect for people's beliefs and a sense of the dignity people struggled to sustain in conditions of adversity. People on the Left had to learn to listen, which was difficult to do if you had learnt to assume that you already possessed 'the truth' that others were struggling for. This made Gramsci increasingly sceptical about the tone of a Leninist tradition, though his writings have so often been used to sustain such a tradition that it is difficult to appreciate how his work changed through his long reflections in prison.

Gramsci also breaks with both a tradition of Enlightenment rationalism and a tendency within post-modern writing when he questions the idea that identities can be freely created out of discourses that are culturally available. He refuses the structuralist opposition which says they are either 'given' or they must be 'socially and historically created'. So it is that identities are not given by nature, nor are they created through language. As I have argued, Gramsci recognises the contradictory character of 'common sense', but unlike a phenomenological tradition he insists that it carries different historical resonances. So it is that he learns from Hegel without following Hegel's identification of history with reason.

With Gramsci, we need to explore our experience with others so that we can become 'critically conscious' that it is not 'personal' and 'psychological' but is sustained through particular relations of power and subordination. A recognition of 'moral individuality' helps explain a resonance between Gramsci and feminist theory, when the latter is not theorised in structuralist terms. There is shared sense that the 'present' holds the relationships of the past in creative tension, so that in coming to terms with 'who we are' we have to acknowldge at a felt and experiential level 'where we have come from'.

It is in this way that Black, women's, Jewish, gay and lesbian politics do not reinstate fixed identities. This is a misreading because of difficulties of appreciating the complex relations between 'identity', 'power' and 'emotional life'. Coming to terms with one's experience involves coming to terms with a particular history, even one that a rationalist tradition has taught us to put aside because it can only weaken and disturb us. As Blacks have to come to terms with the terrors of slavery, so women have to explore a relationship with the witchburnings in Europe and North America. Similarly, Jews have to come to terms with the Shoah.

These histories have a weight which makes them unavoidable. It does not mean that we have to remain restricted and trapped by them, but it gives identities a moral *weight* that post-modern discussions of identities as 'free floating' can rarely appreciate. Within the terms of a consumerist culture it might be tempting to forget history and to live in the opportunities and fantasies offered by the present. All too often we feel happier to leave the history behind, especially if it is a history of pain and suffering. But then the West has always been ready to forsake history, for it has wanted to present modernity in its own image. In this regard Little changes with the post-modern.

Peoples who have been rendered invisible within the dominant narratives of modernity and who have endured the marginalisation and devaluation of their histories and cultures, stand in a different relationship to the promises of post-modernity. They might be less prepared to think about identities in such free-floating terms, since this becomes yet another way in which they are marginalised. For example, Blacks and Jews might find some common ground in a discussion of 'rootedness' and 'belonging' because they have lived so long with an ambivalent sense of roots. For within modernity they were encouraged to believe that they could only find 'freedom' and 'equality' if they were prepared to forsake their inherited traditions and cultures to join the 'common culture' of modernity. Often this was implicitly a white Christian culture that was set within the dominant masculine terms. They were forced to separate from a past that was systematically devalued in their own eyes as 'traditional' and 'backward'.

It might well be that the post-modern challenges to modernity have brought to light these diverse non-Western traditions for the first time. Post-modern awareness of difference and marginality has helped many people stand in the light of their own history and culture, rather than feel that they have to judge themselves lacking according to the universal standards of modernity. This is to open new ground that has to be carefully treasured. But at the same time we have to reinstate the moral and political relations of identities so that we do *not lose* a sense of historical meaning. For what has been gained can so easily be lost unless we learn to respect and illuminate the sufferings and oppressions that people have endured. It is too easy to wipe this out with the degradation of discourses of 'history' and 'truth' that is so often an aspect of post-modern discussions.

In recovering the self we have to honour the history that we carry rather than succumbing to the notion of a false polarity that either history remains a construction of the present or else 'truth' untouched by history is waiting to be revealed. This relativism has fostered in its own way a denial of the Holocaust and the destruction of European Jewry. If people do not learn to take responsibility for the past, they want to deny it. Often they assuage their guilt by being prepared to repeat the past, rather than feel genuine remorse. Within a Protestant moral culture we learn to deny more easily. We learn to eradicate uncomfortable feelings to sustain identities which do not disturb the peace of our consciences.

IDENTITIES, FRAGMENTATION AND EMPOWERMENT

Post-modern discussions of identity help us recognise issues of fragmentation and displacement but they are often bereft of a moral language which can also illuminate issues of honesty, dignity and integrity. Within Kantian ethics these terms were given a rationalist form, for it was supposedly only through acting on a sense of moral duty that we could accrue dignity and moral worth. We were supposedly autonomous moral agents, free to make our lives in the present as long as we showed the strength of will to 'rise above' the temptations of nature and the determinations of history and culture.

So it was that Kant's vision of modernity expressed a vision of radical freedom, for it was always possible for us to be free and autonomous as long as we separated ourselves from the determinations of nature and history. As I have argued, this largely depended upon reproducing a basic modernist distinction between reason and nature. Paradoxically we find echoes of this vision of radical freedom in the articulation of identities within many post-modern discourses. At some level it carries forward, rather than breaks with, a disdain for nature and history that characterised at least the Kantian vision of modernity.

The strength of post-modern visions is in their assertion that people can remake their own identities, rather than assume that we inherit fixed identities waiting to be rediscovered. This puts a welcome emphasis on freedom, which can often foster a tolerance or differences. Post-modernism can help to break with the moralism that characterised so much of the sexual politics of the 1970s, as if there were a single movement towards liberation that, for instance, women had to follow. The strength, love and support that women could draw from a notion of 'sisterhood' could so easily become constraining unless it could also recognise the very real differences in power that could distinguish the experiences of women because of their class, race, ethnicity or sexual orientation. It was easy to fall back into unwittingly reproducing the modernist notion that these differences were 'unreal' and 'distractions that served to blind us to the 'underlying' uniformities in women's experience.

Within an Enlightenment vision of freedom we were encouraged to accept that differences of class, race, general and sexual orientation were themselves 'superficial' and that we had to learn to 'rise above' these differences so that we could recognise a 'common' humanity. Through the process of separating from these 'artificial' differences we learnt to assert ourselves as free and autonomous individuals able to guide our lives through reason alone. Without diminishing notions of a 'common humanity' it might be that we have to rethink the liberal humanist terms in which these have been taught within modernity.

In reclaiming the significance of our ethnic, class, gender or sexual identities we are not being subsumed under some pre-given categories. Rather we are in the process of *recovering* the self through learning about its shared histories and cultures. Rather than learning, for instance, to feel ashamed of my Jewishness as something that needs to be tolerated by others, I learn to be proud of it. This is a process which Black and Asian students recognise as part of an experience of immigration when you learn to 'give up' what stands out as a difference so that you can assimilate and be accepted within the dominant Protestant culture. Within a liberal moral culture you learn to forsake the particularities of class, 'race', sexual orientation and ethnicities because you want to take your place as 'free and equal' citizens within a universal culture of modernity.

Children from miniority communities often learn to pay a price for acceptance. They learn to 'adapt' to the dominant culture, but at some level often carry a sense of guilt for betraying aspects of their own history and culture. This involves a compromise of dignity and integrity, for these notions have both individual and collective aspects. Of course coming to terms with the sense of displacement and the silences that often characterise family life is part of coming to terms with a contradictory and often painful history. This does not have to involve a return to traditional beliefs and values, though for some this might remain an important source of dignity and self-idenity. There might be many different creative ways in which we learn to relate to past histories and cultures and learn to live them within the present. This is not a static process and it is quite misleading when post-structuralist work presents collective histories and identities in fixed and static terms. Rather they are part of a complex individual and collective journey.

There are blind spots in post-modern discussions of the fragmentation of identities that need to be carefully considered. Sometimes they identify history with the belief in grand narratives of class or nation so that the notion of a historical consciousness inevitably tied to notions of progress is dispensed with. Post-modern theory easily overemphasises the ways in which identities can be created in the present out of what is culturally available, for it finds it difficult to recognise the consequences of a more superficial relationship to self when we dispense with any living sense of 'where we come from'. This does not prevent, as I have stressed, an open and creative response to history, culture and tradition, but it does mean *valuing* an inheritance enough to learn about it so that it is not replaced by an easy relativism that refuses to make judgements at all. As Herder initially saw it, the fact that it is a culture and tradition we have grown up in gives it a specific meaning for us, for in some ways it remains tied to our expression of identity. As he recognised, this does not involve notions of cultural exclusivity but makes it more important than a Kantian liberalism supposes, to learn about the truths and forms of expression of different cultures.[22]

Modernity in its Kantian Enlightenment form was always suspicious of collective identities. It could only see them as a sign of weakness of will, as a failure on the part of individuals to think for themselves and so to escape from the habits of traditional values. In this regard, sexual, class and ethnic politics represented a challenge to the terms of modernity for they recognised, in their very different ways, the *integrity* of difference. They appreciated that as people reclaimed their identities, say as women, Blacks, Jews, lesbians or gay men, they were also coming to terms with hidden histories that had been marginalised within malestream cultures. This was a break with the liberal individualism that characterised a liberal moral culture and which argued that we show our respect to others as human beings by choosing to 'ignore' or 'overlook' any potential differences so that we can relate to them as individuals in their own right. Though this was a welcome challenge to practices of discrimination, it fostered its own forms of invisibility and undermined people's sense of dignity and self-respect.

IDENTITY AND POLITICS

The politics of identity came to be recognised as a significant source of a renewed pluralism. It set quite different terms of respect and self-worth. Children were to be encouraged to take pride in their own histories and cultures within a multi-cultural education. But there was also a way in which identity politics could become fixed and moralistic if it suggested that there was a single form of Black identity or a single lesbian identity that people had to conform to. The language of deconstruction helped to show that there were many different forms of identity and that these clustered in different ways so that, for instance, a white Jewish middle-class male brought together a particular assembly of identities. More personally they involved for me coming to terms with particular histories and experiences, say of a family of refugees from Hitler in the late 1930s, losing most of the family in the Shoa and growing up in the emotionally frozen spaces of Anglo-Jewry in the 1950s.

We are all marked by our owncontradictory histories and collective identities. Often we cannot make sense of them easily, and even if we do, we often cannot change the impact they have had on the ways we feel and relate. They form part of a post-modern condition, since we would no longer want to relate to them within the repressive terms of modernity. We would not choose to treat these different aspects as 'superficial' or as forms of unfreedom, though it might be hard to say which feels most significant at a particular time.

The moralism of sexual politics often suggested that a particular identity, say, for example, as a lesbian woman or gay man, had to be given priority. There might have been a temptation to think that because this aspect of identity had been most 'oppressed' so it carried the most truth about a person. It is this centralising of identity that Foucault helped people to question, for he resisted the notion that sexuality revealed the 'truth' about a person, wanting to recognise it as one aspect amongst many. This is a difficult issue, for it often failed to appreciate the importance of 'coming out' for many gay men and lesbians and the ways this was linked to integrity and self-worth. But this was a time when Foucault's post-structuralist work sought to dispense with moral language. It was only much later that he became more sympathetic to connecting issues of identity with concerns of morality and power. In his earlier work he was more concerned with stripping the play of power of its moral pretensions.[23]

Discussions of post-modernity often share an ambivalence towards feminism and emotional life. Somewhat paradoxically post-modernity shares with modernity an unease about the collective identities of class, race, gender and sexual orientation, thinking they have to assume fixed and given identities. Often post-modern theories prefer to think of the diversity of identities that form particular clusters, feeling uncomfortable with talk about relations of power and subordination. This is to inherit some of the difficulties of Foucault's pervasive and amoral conception of power, which makes it difficult for post-modernity to draw upon the insights of feminism and sexual politics. Certainly women of colour have challenged many of the terms of white feminism, leaving us with a renewed sense of issues of 'race' and power. But if they remind us of the importance of different feminisms, challenging the notion that 'underneath the skin women are all sisters' they have helped to form new terms through which women can begin both to acknowledge the integrities of difference as well as to talk to each other. It is through exploration that a sense of difference *and* the possibilities of shared experience begin to develop. If the arrogance of universalist theories has been a significant aspect of Western notions of modernity, we must also be careful not to lose the ability to communicate across difference.

Having suffered from exploitation and oppression, people often also recognise the value of liberal notions of freedom, equality and human rights. They know the value of these sources of dignity and self-respect, for they know how much they have suffered without them. But a socialist tradition has found it hard to renew itself, partly because it has found it difficult to come to terms with differences of history and culture. But different traditions of resistance can learn from each other about how they have sustained a sense of human decency and dignity in conditions that would seek to undermine and destroy these very qualities.

If we can no longer appeal to traditional loyalties and communities with the notion that 'identities' are somehow fixed within them, we still need to recognise challenges to capitalist values, to the notion that exchange value exists as the exclusive source of value. Different movements of resistance have challenged the modernist notions that we must forsake histories of class, 'race', gender, sexuality and ethnicities, in order to exist as abstract individuals in our own right. They have appreciated the value of connectedness and belonging as a form of resistance in the face of capitalist ideologies.

If we are to rethink the relationship between 'individual' and 'community' we must carefully reassess the nature of fragmentation within post-modern societies. Rather than simply celebrating the pleasures of the present, we also have to be aware of the ways identities can be disorganised and disintegrated. It is too easy to be fooled by appearances. If we lose a sense of how, for instance, a Black woman might have come to terms with herself partly through coming to terms with the history of slavery and emancipation, we lose a sense of the relationship between history, culture and individual and collective empowerment. If we are tempted to devalue the past, we can hardly be surprised if we feel weakened and disorientated in the present.

It is easy to dispense with history if you are part of a dominant culture and so are in a position to take it more for granted. It becomes much *easier* to think of history as a construction which carries no truths of its own. It is a different matter if a people have suffered oppression, for then it becomes important in a new way to tell the stories to our children so that they do not forget, as Jews remember on Passover, 'We too were slaves in Egypt.' It is incumbent on each new generation to remember this experience as something that they themselves have gone through, not simply their ancestors in a distant past.

Again we need to conceive of the post-modern in terms which can illuminate the loss of a historical consciousness as something to be struggled against. If we lose a sense of our history we lose a sense of ourselves, and so recovering the self involves recovering a sense of history. Too often post-modern theories have continued modernity's antagonism towards history, in a new form which fails to appreciate the link between a sense of history and an *experience* of empowerment. Rather it tends to be antagonistic to the notion of empowerment, for this sustains a link between the 'personal' and the 'political'. So it fails to appreciate that we can ground and root ourselves in the particularities of history – women's, Black, Jewish, gay and lesbian – without thereby being fixed by an identity that is prepared and determined for us by history. Since this involves recognitions that are emotional and cognitive, it cannot be grasped in the rationalist language of much post-modern theory. A sensitivity to different 'senses' does not itself break with the notion of identities as cognitive construction.[24]

DIGNITY, EMPOWERMENT AND EMOTIONAL LIFE

The growth of the libertarian Right during the 1980s ushered in a long period in which, in A.H. Halsey's terms, 'the economic individual has been exalted, and the social community desecrated'. The glorification of the market as the legislator of value went hand in hand with a conception of individual freedom set aginst the encroachments of the state. There was widespread disillusionment with the forms of dependency that seemed to accompany welfare provisions which the government was able to tap by promising that people would be able to maintain more of 'their own money' to spend as they chose. In Britain this was given clearest expression through the Thatcherite sale of council houses, which allowed numbers of working-class people to own their homes for the first time. This promise struck a popular chord and it proved difficult for the Left to deny this right if people were enjoying this right themselves. This was part of a reordering of class relations that helped to sustain Conservative rule. The individual seemed to be sovereign, at least in market terms.

It proved difficult for a socialist tradition to rethink the relation between 'individual' and 'community' without falling into a defence of capitalist values and relations. It seemed as if the Left had been trapped into a defence of state provision. Socialism has its own traditions of paternalism. Within a Fabian tradition the utopian dream was essentially one of benevolent, well-bred Keynesians 'sorting things out' for the masses. Their admirable dedication to public service, as Zoë Heller has recently written, 'was actually predicated upon some fairly condescending attitudes towards those they served. It was Douglas Jay, after all, who famously advised: "In the case of nutrition and health, just as in the case of education, the gentleman in Whitehall really does know better what is good for people than the people know themselves"' (*The Independent on Sunday*, 22 November 1992: p. 3).

I have tried to explore some of the connections between such condescending paternalism and particular dominant forms of masculinity. Zoë Heller illustrates some of these issues in her interview with Peter Jay, who remains a great admirer of his father and who seems to inherit 'a tendency to similar patrician postures' (Ibid.: 3), so combining liberal sentiments with an imperious manner. This seems to be linked to an intellectual rationalism that is much prized in the conceptual analysis of Oxford philosophy. As Jay says, 'It's a question of demonstrable logical necessity. And anyone who does not agree is simply making a mistake, like saying twice two is five' (Ibid.: 3).

This belief in logic as the source of clarity and control fosters a particular form of male self-confidence which allows men to put others down if they are being emotional and in their 'subjectivity' are somehow proving that they lack reason and rationality. This is part of the power than men often share in relation to women within a modernity that identified masculinity with a particular form of reason. At least in public, it allows men to feel that they are *in control* of their lives. Men often pay a price for this in their private lives, because often we have not learnt other ways of relating.

In an earlier generation John Stewart Mill wrote of the pain of being brought up to believe in reason alone, for it hid the ways he remained emotionally less developed. Within a rationalist moral culture we have few ways of validating the significance of emotional and spiritual development. Often we learn to despise these aspects of our being as 'subjective' and 'irrational'. It goes against the grain of the moral culture to give time and attention to emotions and feelings, without feeling that this is a sign of weakness and self-indulgence.

Boys who have been sent away to public schools at an early age learn to survive on their own without needing the care and love of others. This can create a false sense of independence, but one which still pervades British cultural life. Often boys learn to live with a feeling of abandonment and rejection that makes it hard for them to trust themselves in more intimate relationships. It is easy for boys to feel, as Peter Jay describes it, 'a sense that life was an assault course created by someone else – that you were a rat put at the beginning of a maze and the purpose was to get to the other side' (Ibid.: 4). This bleak vision is recognisable to many men even if they did not come from the same class background.

As men, we often learn our masculinities from our fathers, but in subtle and unrecognised ways. Jay talks about a time, though he cannot actually remember it, 'when I was upset by things that were said about my father, and in consequence of that I developed, very early on, this extra membrane, this habit of simply not noticing and not being upset' (Ibid.: 4). This is part of an education into insensitivity that becomes part of the self-protection that boys often need to survive in the cold and hostile atmosphere of many schools. It creates habits that we are so used to that they become invisible to us, so much so that we often do not understand when others are trying to point out how it makes them feel. We do not often appreciate how these habits can weaken the forms of communication that are accessible to us as men, especially if we learn that communication is a matter of reason, language and logic. But often this means that, as men, we can feel isolated and lonely. Jay talks about how, when he got a job working for Robert Maxwell, 'I surrounded myself with an invisible but as it were impenetrable glass wall. So from day one, nothing he could say or do was ever going to get under my skin' (Ibid.: 4). This glass wall can serve as an indispensable form of self-defence, but it becomes a point of difficulty if we cannot let this wall down even if we want too.

Men often learn not to show their feelings even if they are upset, since this can reflect badly on the image they have of themselves. Not only are emotions a sign of weakness, sometimes reflecting a fear of homosexuality, but they reflect a lack of self-control. Often heterosexual men learn to parody and put down others who might readily show more feeling. This is part of a display of power played out between men that has a long tradition in the British imperial past. The boarding school produced its own imperial elite who could remain unaffected by what they experienced around them. It created a way of learning how to 'cut out' and 'shut down' so that men are not affected emotionally, or at least learn not to show it. There is a process of transformation that goes on and which dies hard. It is an experience it is easy for middle-class men to identify with as a form of self-defence. As Zoë Heller has it, Peter Jay repeatedly transforms 'sentiments or anything smacking of soft-bellied emotions into cerebral, invulnerable ideas. Kick as hard as you can, his glass wall really is impenetrable' (Ibid.: 5).

Within an Enlightenment vision of modernity it becomes difficult to recognise the dignity and moral worth of emotional life and the meaning it can give to individual and collective experience. Rather, we learn that emotions are a sign of weakness that can only distract from the moral worth of our actions. For men who have been brought up to identify with their rationality, it becomes difficult *not* to feel that our emotions betray us in the eyes of others. If we have internalised a fear of rejection it becomes hard to trust others or to feel that they can be there for us. This language comes to seem empty and rhetorical for we have so little in our experience that could give it meaning. We have learnt to disdain the body and emotional life, so it is hard to imagine that giving our emotions and feelings an appropriate space in our lives can be part of a process of empowerment.

We can be equally dishonest about our feelings as we can be about our ideas and thoughts, but somehow within modernity it has been made difficult to recognise the integrity of our emotional lives. This is something that Freud can help us grasp through the practice of analysis, for we can become aware of the *gap* that so often exists between what we think and how we feel. But within the dominant intellectual culture Freud is insistently interpreted within the rationalist terms of Lacan in which the unconscious is conceived of as a language.[25]

As long as reason is secure in its conviction that it alone can deliver impartial and objective knowledge, then it can always condescend and patronise inner emotional life. This reflects the ways that both 'inner' and 'outer' nature are experienced as a *threat* to the rule of reason and goes some way to explaining a language of eradication that has for so long been part of the West's relationship to the rest of the world. The aboriginal peoples of Tasmania were almost completely liquidated since they were deemed a threat to 'civilisation'. They served as a reminder that nature had not been 'conquered' and so were a challenge to the potency of reason. Since these are not 'humans' but 'animals', any feelings of outrage are supposedly misplaced. To protest is somehow to stand against reason, progress and civilisation. In Germany more recently, Germans who went out of their way to befriend and support Jews threatened by the Nazi racial laws were considered a threat to to well-being of the German *Volk* because Jews were deemed to be 'vermin' who undermined the health of the nation.

SCIENCE, MORALITY AND MODERNITY

It is crucial to understand the ways science was appropriated to legitimate the genocide of the Tasmanian peoples and later used by the Nazis. Science has not been the neutral instrument it often supposes itself to be. When we think of Auschwitz we are forced to rethink the relation of modernity to both slavery and science. Memories of the slave trade and the inhuman treatment of Africans are echoed in the use of Jews, political prisoners, gays and gypsies as slave labour. Treated as 'less than human' they could be used and abused by the Nazi officers before being exterminated 'as a service to humanity'. Exclusion and confinement had eventually led to the scientific practice of extermination. Scientists were to carefully study the lessons that had been drawn from the euthanasia programme against those who were mentally ill or suffered from learning difficulties. There are films which record how young doctors were trained to participate in these programmes by learning that if someone was 'useless' then you were doing them a service by putting them out of their misery. The medical oath to care for others was carefully subverted and provided with new meanings.

Science was used by the Nazis quite systematically to organise the 'Final Solution'. The gas vans that were used in the early years had been carefully constructed so that when the people were gassed to death the shift in weight that would fall on to the axle was carefully taken into account. The fact that it was suffering human beings who made up this 'critical mass' could be safely ignored for it did not have to 'interfere' with the technical problems that needed to be solved. As far as science was concerned, it could just have been sacks of potatoes that fell backwards at a critical moment. We have paid dearly for the split between 'science' and 'morality' that has been structured into modernity. It is the ease with which scientists could be recruited that remains so disturbing. Benno Müller-Hill has built up a detailed history of how the academic study of anthropology and psychiatry 'revealed itself, step by step, as a mass murder of nonconformists'. The split between facts and values, beween the realm of science and the realm of morality, needs to be carefully rethought if we are to reaffirm some of the promises of modernity.[26] It has been much easier to deny the past then to face the hard questions it leaves us with.

It was Freud's student, Wilhelm Reich, who attempted to apply Freud's insights into the repression of sexuality as part of developing a 'mass psychology'. He reflected upon the displacement of repressed emotions and feelings on to 'others' who were made to carry emotions that people were often unable to acknowledge in themselves. Freud had drawn an understanding of transference and projection from his clinical work with individuals, but he was also sensitive to the human miseries created by the denial of sexuality within Western culture. Freud grasped how emotions that were deemed unacceptable to the conscious mind worked to haunt our unconscious lives.

Freud attempted to question the autonomy of inner emotional life by grasping its connections to the cultural and historical repression of sexuality. Sometimes these insights were difficult to maintain, as Freud sought also to acknowledge the place of unconscious desires and fantasies. Some people argue that it was this very shift away from the 'seduction theory' that allowed for the development of a psychoanalytic method. I distrust this idea, recognising the difficulties it created for Freud in listening to and validating the experience of women who had been sexually abused.[27]

But what is significant here is Freud's awareness that emotions are not simply aspects of personal life and relationships. He recognised the human costs of the Western denial of the body and sexual life, even if he felt that the injuries could best be worked with as they showed themselves within individual lives. Reich was more interested in prevention, and for some time was more impressed by Marx's insights into class relations within capitalist societies. His attempts to deal with issues of contraception, abortion and space for sexual contact were part of acknowledging the human miseries created by their absence and the need to relate to everyday concerns of working people.

Reich was suspicious of notions of 'class consciousness' which were conceived in economistic terms alone. He challenged the terms of modernity in his recognition that we do not exist as rational selves alone, but as physical and emotional beings. He reinstated a language of the body and emotional life, even if he remained trapped by homophobic notions and a mechanistic belief in science and progress. But his work has been too readily dismissed as 'biologistic' and we have yet to come to terms with some difficult questions that he raises.[28]

Freud's insights into the fictions of the self carried radical implications that were often lost on Reich. He recognised that the notion of the autonomous self who was able to guide life through reason was a fiction of modernity. People did not have the freedom and autonomy a Kantian vision suggested because they shared a much more complex relationship to their emotional lives. As Susan Griffin's explorations of the denial of the body and emotional life within modernity show, it has been women, Blacks and Jews who have been made to carry unacknowledged emotions, for these cannot be controlled in the way that modernity promises. She attempts to connect issues of misogyny, racism and anti-Semitism to the workings of the 'pornographic mind', and even if she often leaves us with an over-generalised account, she raises difficult questions we have too often avoided. In her attempts to learn from both Freud and Reich, she attempts to rethink the relation between 'inner' and 'outer' life so that we do not fall back into assuming the autonomy of 'inner emotional life' but are ready to explore connections with power and projection.[29]

Social and political theory which organises itself around the rational choices of individuals often fails to appreciate that people are moved by unconscious desires they remain barely aware of. As Adorno acknowledged, Freud's insights into the fragmentation of selves, into the ways we exist in pieces, partly reflected the power of social institutions within late capitalist societies to disorientate and disorganise desires and needs. Freud understood that we needed to develop a relationship with our unconscious emotions and desires rather than judge them out of existence. Unless we were prepared to be more open and honest with ourselves we would not be able to temper the demands of the super-ego or listen to the stirrings of our desires.

Analysis was involved in a search for greater 'truth' and 'reality' within an experience that often felt 'unreal' and shut off behind a glass wall. For Freud refused to celebrate the injuries and hurts of fragmentation, as he refused to give up on a language of 'truth' and 'reality' which we find forsaken and devalued in so much post-modern writings. He sought for some sense of 'emotional integration', even if he had few illusions of how far this could go. He knew from his own marginality as a Jew in Viennese society not to hope for too much, but to seek some kind of balance between the different aspects of being.

Freud understood that if people were to deny their Jewishness in order to become accpetable to others, they would undermine the sources of their inner strength and dignity. However difficult it was, you had to accept 'who' you were rather than pretend to be different, to be acceptable to others. As Freud appreciated for himself, 'because I was a Jew I found myself free from many prejudices which restricted others in the use of their intellect; and as a Jew I was prepared to join the opposition and to do without agreement with the "compact majority"' ('Address to the Society of B'nai B'rith', cited in Freud: XX, 274).

As Marthe Roberts has explained it in *From Oedipus to Moses*, Freud thought he had inherited the courage of rebellion, for he saw the Jewish mind as 'essentially nonconformist, hence prophetic in the sense that its freedom from the intellectual tyrannies of the dominant society has always enabled it to innovate' (Roberts 1976: 4). This meant that, for Freud, dignity and inner strength could not be understood in emotional terms alone. The anti-Semitism that he experienced at university reminded him that he could not escape from his cultural experience as a Jew and that identities had to be conceived in historical and cultural terms. Again this is something psychoanalysis has often forgotten.

In contrast to Freud, Simone Weil had an ambivalent and hostile attitude towards her Jewishness. As far as she was concerned she was educated within the terms of French culture, which meant that she could go as far as to deny that the restrictions on Jews within the Vichy regime should be applied to her. But at the same time she understood a relation between uprootedness and disempowerment. In her later writing, *The Need for Roots* (1972), she appreciates how, for instance, the destruction of the Breton culture as it was integrated into the French state worked to disorganise individual lives. As people were robbed of a sense of their history and culture, so it *undermined* and hurt their individual lives. It went some way to explaining why so many of the prostitutes in Paris originally came from Britanny. People's sense of pride and self-worth had been attacked as their culture had been devalued in their own eyes. Franz Fanon (1970) made a similar point about the workings of French colonialism and the disintegrating effect this has had on the identities and emotional lives of Black people. It is a form of 'mental slavery', in Bob Marley's terms, that can continue long after the end of formal colonial rule.

Simone Weil remained hostile to the language of psychoanalysis, for it was often bereft of a moral and political vision, as it presented suffering in personal and emotional terms alone. From her experience of factory work, Weil had learnt the importance of sustaining people in their *own eyes* through enhancing their dignity and self-respect. This would not be effected through a change of ownership alone, but involved the control that people had over the everyday conditions of their work. She was concerned with developing a notion of science and technology that would not be focused upon maximising production alone, but would include the well-being of working people themselves. With Marx, she appreciated the importance of work as a source of human dignity, but she felt the need to transform the conditions and relations of work rather than to hope for some revolutionary change. She recognised how class relations had the effect of making people feel that they counted for very little, so that if the language of democracy was to be made into a reality, people had to learn to take more control of the conditions of their lives.

Weil helps us to question the legitimation of scientific knowledge that works to leave people without the authority to speak for themselves. A key moment in Enlightenment rationalism is the separation of knowledge as 'objective' and 'impartial' from people's own experience, which is taken to be 'subjective', 'partial' and 'unreliable'. As I have tried to show, this undermines people's trust in their own experience as a source of knowledge. It radically splits the conditions of knowledge from the everyday experience of people's lives. In their different ways, Gramsci and Simone Weil work to reinstate people's trust in their experience as a source of dignity and self-worth. They each recognise the necessity of creating a moral language that has been denied by scientistic and structuralist traditions which have treated experience and morality as part of nature. In this regard at least, they challenge the terms of modernity, for they recognise that the split between reason and nature has served to undermine the sources of dignity and empowerment. Although both Gramsci and Weil appreciate the kind of relation between forms of knowledge and forms of power which Foucault also explores, they think it has to be related to *moral* concerns if we are meaningfully to explore the sources of dignity and empowerment.

FEMINISM, ECOLOGY AND EMPOWERMENT

The women's movement in the early 1970s learnt both from the Black movement and from the anti-psychiatry movement in its recognition of the importance of listening to women share their experience of oppression and subordination. Women learnt to share experiences they had been taught to hide and feel ashamed of, as they had learnt to blame themselves for what they felt. The internalisation of guilt and responsibility slowly began to shift as women learnt to identify the sources of their oppression in the social relationships of gender power which diminished their experience and rendered them 'invisible'. As the new social movements encouraged people to rework their histories of denigration and marginalisation, so people began to find their *own voice* which allowed them to become more visible, at least to themselves. People learnt to talk for themselves as they insisted in speaking their own truths, rather than judging themselves according to the traditional patriarchal terms of Western modernity.

The notion of 'visibility' is somehow connected to the aspiration to 'find your own voice'. This is both an individual and collective practice, for it involves recovering personal and cultural aspects of the self. Again, this is to challenge a notion of the self conceived in personal and emotional terms alone. But at the same time it challenges the prevailing modernist distinction between reason and emotion, since it appreciates the need for emotional honesty and the courage to tell things as they are, rather than as you would have them be. In this sense different forms of consciousness-raising share with forms of psychotherapy insights into honesty and the integrity of emotional life.

As we share our emotions, rather than hide them, we enter a process of change which can take us into new ground. If you have learnt through long years of experience to be ashamed of your 'Blackness', 'Jewishness' or 'gayness', it can be difficult to reclaim these aspects of your experience. But we have learnt that you lose a lot more if you set your sights on proving yourself to others by denying significant aspects of your experience. But it is difficult to identify the ways you weaken and undermine yourself within the prevailing rationalist languages of social and political theory.

Reflecting on the example of the women's health movement raises significant issues about the relation of power, knowledge and emotional life. The authority of medical knowedge is reinforced at every visit to the doctor when we experience our bodies as an 'object' of this knowledge. It is as if our relationship to our own bodies is subtly discounted since we can only know them through our experience, which is 'subjective' and 'personal'. So it is that the doctor has 'knowledge' while we only have 'experience'. This reflects a split inherent within modernity and which characterises the authority of professional knowledge. As I have already argued, it also reflects the Cartesian dualism which leaves us with an 'externalised' and estranged relationship to our bodies which we perceive as no part of ourselves. I have argued that recovering the self involves an appreciation of the fact that we exist as embodied beings. For within the relations of traditional medicine we are assured that 'the doctor knows best' and that we have to trust in the doctor's authority.

Reason alone cannot heal the estrangement from our bodies, for we cannot decide through will and determination to live in a different relationship to our bodies. We might recognise that we have little connection with our bodies and little relationship with their different aspects, and this shift in awareness can be a significant start. Rather than treating our bodies as machines that need to be taken to the doctor whenever they break down, we can learn from the women's health movement, even as men, to develop a different *relation* to our bodies, as central aspects, in Foucault's terms, of 'caring for the self'.[30]

Foucault was concerned with subverting the ways modernity had taught us to prioritise 'knowing the self' as an epistemological quest over the classical notion of 'caring for the self'. As we learn to care for ourselves more, so we get to know ourselves in different ways. We begin to form a deeper connection with different aspects of our experience as we claim more of our histories and experiences. Rather than treating our symptoms in isolation, we begin to wonder what they can teach us about the ways we live our lives. This does not have to involve the guilt and responsibility that Susan Sontag usefully identifies, but can involve a more holistic conception of health and healing.[31] If doctors take to heart the injunction to 'heal thyself' they might learn to conceive of health in less mechanistic terms. This is by no means a rejection of science, but a call for its transformation and humility.

Ecology helps us rethink the relations of control that are built into medical modernity and which tempt us into thinking that we control our health through suppressing the symptoms of illness. As we begin to think more of illness in the holistic terms of 'imbalance', so we make connections with different aspects of our lives. We become more concerned with ways in which, for example, we may have weakened our immune system. Weber and Tawney have helped us appreciate how modernity has been shaped by the control of time so that time, as a scarce commodity, is not to be 'wasted'. So illness becomes a 'waste of time' that has to be endured until we get back to work. Often it means, especially as men, that we push ourselves beyond our *limits* for we recognise limits as a sign of weakness. Often we push ourselves into work, even when we are ill, to show that we can overcome the 'limits of nature'. This is a way of affirming our masculinity and is reflected in the fact that fewer men than women will visit the doctor. Even in the case of serious disease or illness, men are much more likely that women to visit the doctor at such a late stage there is little that can be done to help.

We begin to question the terms of modernity as we come to recognise time as a process. In this way ecology can reawaken a different relationship to both inner and outer nature. It can remind us of the humanity we have lost touch with as we have learnt to treat ourselves in mechanical terms. In this sense it can help in the recovering of the self, for it can help us to greater awareness of the fact that, like the rest of nature, we have our own limits. It is not a sin to be tired, but often we are slow to acknowledge tiredness because it can feel like admitting 'weakness' as a man.

The routines of modernity have left us with a way of disciplining and regulating the self, that Weber illuminates in its relation to the Protestant ethic. This fosters a culture of self-rejection and self-denial as we seek to shape our natures so that they accord with the dictates of reason. For instance, we discount such negative emotions as anger or fear and we refuse to recognise their reality in our lives, for they reflect badly on the image we seek to sustain of ourselves. As men, we are constantly attempting to squeeze our experience into patterns which we can defend rationally. We end up fearing pleasure and nourishment, for to admit needs becomes a sign of weakness for men. We become hard on ourselves as we are insensitive to the pain and hidden hurts we so often carry.

As men brought up within the terms of a Protestant moral culture, we are constantly testing ourselves against our limits. This is how we often learn to prove our masculinity, since it is never something that we can take for granted. So it is that we seek to control our lives against what we understand as the 'resistances' of nature. When we get ill we can feel that our bodies have let us down, rather than that we have been deaf to the signs we have been given. In its appreciation of different relationships to both the nature of 'inner' somatic and emotional life as well as to the 'outer' nature of the natural world, an ecological vision challenges the terms of modernity. It helps us think in terms of balance and harmony, rather than simply of control *as* domination. It helps us recognise ourselves as part of the natural world, rather than assuming that we assert our humanity through 'rising above' our 'animal natures', in Kant's terms. Recovering a more ecological vision of self does not have to blind us to the awkward and estranged relationship in which we have learnt to live with our bodies and emotional lives.

Too often an ecological vision has been blind to the workings of class, ethnic and gender relations of power and subordination. In its recognition of the need to question the self-rejections and denials of a liberal moral culture it can foster a belief that people can 'make their own reality'. While it is important to appreciate the ways that affirmations can help build a sense of self-esteem and self-worth, it can also be important to find an appropriate place for such 'negative' emotions as anger, fear and resentment. Otherwise it is too easy to create a new moralism, in which people fall into thinking that they can create more fulfilled lives by thinking more positively about themselves. A New Age consciousness has often dispensed with a sense of morality and politics that extend beyond the details of individual lives, as if we cannot be responsible for anything more than our own actions. While a renewed sense of individual responsibility which includes a sense of people learning *how* to take more responsibility for their emotional lives is desirable, it is crucial not to lose a sense of moral outrage at the realities of oppression and injustice. It has been easy to slip into thinking that if people are responsible for their own lives, then they only have themselves to blame for their sufferings and oppression.

FEMINISM, ECOLOGY AND MODERNITY

With these dangers in mind it can still be crucial to learn from Marx and so to explore, as I have tried to do, the complexities of Marx's relationship to modernity. Feminism can play a crucial role, for it grows out of an awareness of relationships of power and subordination. It recognises that it is not simply a matter of changing the ways that individuals relate to each other, however important this is, but of *also* transforming gender relations of power within the larger society. It also carries a sense of the miseries and sufferings of personal and emotional life, and refuses to discount them as matters of 'private' concern alone. But feminism has often shared a disdain for moral language, knowing how often women have been trapped by it, and it has taken time to explore the relation between feminism and moral theory.

A similar ambivalence towards 'nature' has characterised feminism, since gender differences were for so long legitimated as flowing from nature. This has tempted much feminist theory to cast itself within structuralist terms since this seemed a secure defence against arguments from nature and biology. But this has unwittingly drawn feminist work back into the terms of a modernity which it otherwise challenges in crucial ways. It has made it harder for an eco-feminism to develop as part of a significant challenge to dominant forms of social and political theory.

Ecology has been crucial in questioning the modernist conception of progress as involving the control and domination of nature. But concerns with the environment have often hidden the deeper challenges to the forms of life and relationships that characterise both the Protestant ethic and the spirit of capitalism. It helps if we question the notion of infinite individual appropriation as the source of happiness. This utilitarian conception, as I argued, drawing on Charles Taylor's work on Hegel, has underpinned notions of self that have characterised both Weberian and Durkheimian traditions within social theory. This vision of 'possessive individualism', as MacPherson (1962) so aptly named it, was given new life in the libertarian capitalist politics of the 1980s.[32] But as we become more aware of the ways industrialised societies have ravaged and wasted valuable natural resources and treated nature as a resource that can be exploited for human ends, we have learnt to respect cultures with a more respectful and holistic relation to nature.

For some ecological theory this fosters a wholesale rejection of industrial society and advocates a return to the traditional values and relationships that we see practised, for instance, in some North American Indian societies. But we can learn about the importance of reverance for nature and of reworking our relationship with nature, without thinking that we have to 'return' to some fictitious golden age when people lived in harmony and balance. There are important truths that we have lost and which a post-modern rejection of 'romantic solutions' fails to appreciate. But if we are not to be trapped by false oppositions we have to learn how to engage more critically with the terms of modernity, rather than to think that we have moved beyond into a different post-modern age, in which these questions are no longer relevant to us.

Post-modern theory helps us appreciate how, for instance, mass media, computers and new technologies have transformed the world that we live in. A sense of the globalisation of economic and social processes helps us to ask new questions that go beyond the traditional frameworks of social and political theory. But some of the old questions about liberty, equality and justice also take on new forms. The revolutions in Eastern Europe reminded us of the vitality of democratic language and aspirations, while we have also learnt how hopes can be dashed, as traditional and unresolved hatreds which remained checked by authoritarian rule can begin to surface in the nasty forms of racism and anti-Semitism.

Ecology has raised different kinds of issues about human needs and fulfilment that question both utilitarian and orthodox Marxist traditions. If people are hungry they need to eat, and we have been reminded of famine as a feature of a 'post-modern' world. We have been forced to rethink the relations between North and South and there is growing unease about debt and hunger as the destiny of so many people living in the South while there is enormous wastage of

food in the North. We have therefore been forced to think again about
the global relations of power and exploitation. If we are to refuse to
build a fence around these issues, we need a moral and political
language which can illuminate the inadequacies of our inherited traditions. Post-modern theory too easily dispenses with notions of 'truth'
and 'morality' as tying us back to a modernity we need to break with.
But, as I've tried to show, this grows out of partial engagement with
the terms of modernity.

The challenges which feminism and ecology have made to modernity have gone largely unrecognised in discussions around post-
modernity. Both movements challenge the ways we think, feel and
relate as men, not only to women and nature, but also to ourselves.
They offer different visions of what is involved in recovering the self.
They articulate different relations of authority and control, as they
recognise forms of control that come from developing *ongoing* relationships with our bodies and emotional and spiritual lives. They foster
different visions of health and healing as they encourage us to rethink
the ways we can grow and develop both in our individualities and
our collective identities. They tempt us into thinking that we have
to learn how to give more time to ourselves and to our relationships,
rather than subtly subordinating these aspects of our lives to the external goals of making money or proving ourselves within the public
realm. These ideas provide a particular challenge to traditional forms
of masculinity, since male identities have largely been sustained within
the public realm of work.

Different visions of authority and democratic rule are suggested
as people learn to take greater responsibility for their lives. They can
no longer rely on the authority of professional knowledge if they are
to grow in their own authority. This sets the dream of self-
determination and autonomy in new terms, for it is no longer defined
in rationalist terms alone. We have to learn to trust the integrity of
our emotions and feelings. This is part of the challenge of feminism
and psychotherapy, both of which recognise that reason cannot be
separated from emotions and feelings as if it falls into the realm of
'culture' while they belong to the realm of 'nature'.

Women have exposed the 'unreasonableness' of a masculine reason
that has been severed from emotion within modernity. As they have
learnt to trust their own experience they have questioned the notion
that men 'know best' because reason is their exclusive possession.
Through the process of consciousness-raising they have learnt different
ways of validating their experience, but also of learning that individuals
have to go through this process for themselves, making the particular
connections which illuminate their experience and relationships.
Others can share their experience with us, but we have to go through

this process ourselves. It is not a matter of 'sharing results', for such knowledge cannot be separated from the process through which it is gained.

Consciousness-raising involves a process that takes time and, though it is a very different experience for women and men, it is a process of learning that helps to reconnect to history and emotional life. It helps us recognise how our identities have been shaped by particular histories and experiences that we have learnt to discount and put aside within a liberal moral culture. It offers us ways of recovering the self. Women have learnt to use consciousness-raising as a way of identifying how they have been encouraged within the dominant rationalist culture, to devalue their experience and ways of knowing.

For within modernity women learnt that they could only be accepted within the magic circle of humanity *if* they proved themselves in terms of rationality. The women's movement helped to validate emotions and feelings as sources of knowledge and so strengthened women as they questioned the terms of modernity. It was not as if there was 'something wrong' with women, as they had learnt, but rather with the visions of 'humanity' that were set within the masculine terms of modernity.

Women learnt the healing power of listening to each other and being ready to share from the same level of experience. Men were more often trapped in intellectualising their experience and found that psychotherapy could sometimes help to crack the hold of a rationalism which argued that we could only share our feelings if we could first defend them rationally. It has been harder for men to use consciousness-raising for it has proved more difficult for us to *share* ourselves emotionally. At the same time, consciousness-raising can help broaden the personal terms of much psychotherapy which would seek to explain suffering and anguish in the context of early childhood relationships. It can be misleading to assume that we are constantly re-enacting early familial patterns, unless we are also ready to find space for the realities of class, race, ethnicity and sexual orientations. Often it can help to place some of our feelings in the broader context of the social relations of power and oppression which also helped to produce and sustain them. These then are all different ways in which we are rethinking the relation between 'inner' and 'outer' so that we can recognise the reality of different realms of experience. For a time it might help to explore a particular realm as if it were autonomous, as long as we also appreciate that this is a choice we have made.

MASCULINITY, MODERNITY AND SOCIAL THEORY

I have tried to show how a relationship between Protestantism and masculinity has worked to encourage women to blame themselves by making them turn their anger against themselves. Their suffering only proved their personal inadequacy. The internalisation of blame and responsibility as a feature of modernity was recognised by Nietzsche. He helps to question the secular and universal terms in which modernity was presented. Feminism has learnt in its own way the importance of affirming the experience of women, while recognising differences of power that separate them. Women of colour, lesbian women and Jewish women have at the same time helped to question a universalism that was often implicit within feminism and which could make it hard to recognise the particularities of culture and history.

Women found their different voices – often voices that break ranks and which dare to speak for themselves, rather than to conform to the 'accepted standards of reason'. It is a personal voice, but also a truthful voice, for it questions the modernist conception that truth can only be expressed in impersonal and universal terms. The fact that it is 'personal' does not make it less truthful or less 'rational' for not being 'universalised' or 'standardised'.

How we relate these different voices to each other is an issue which post-modernity recognises but hardly illuminates. Somehow we can understand these different voices in their honesty and directness, even if we cannot share their experience. We are beginning to appreciate that sharing an experience, say of women talking about violence on the streets, does make a difference to *how* women can talk to each other. Often there is also a voice of anger and outrage against racist oppression that can still touch us because it is a human voice, even if it is also a 'different' voice.

As people grow in their own authority they learn to speak for themselves rather than worry about what others might think. These are moral voices that would often be ignored by a post-modernity that would forsake the search for truth. We can recognise the integrity of these different voices without thinking we are left with relativism, for they are not presenting claims to a universalised vision of truth. But again, this does not make them less truthful. What is crucial is that women, Blacks, Jews, lesbians and gay men have all struggled to assert the particularities of their experience as they have broken with the universal claims of Western modernity. They have grown in their own authority as they have found their own voice.

There has been a hidden tension between modernity and democracy, for while modernity treasured the autonomy and independence of rational selves, its categorical distinction between reason and nature did not help people to trust in themselves. Rather, it encouraged people to discount their natures – their emotions, feelings and desires – and often to put their trust in external authorities who 'knew best' because they possessed professional knowledges. Supposedly it is our parents, teachers, doctors, managers who can legislate what is 'best for us' because we only have our personal experience, which has to be discounted in the face of their 'scientific' and 'objective' knowledge. Supposedly, it is through the different regimes of reason that the 'good' and the 'truth' is to be legislated for us, since it is through the impersonal and impartial voice of reason that the 'common good' and the 'general interest' is somehow to be discerned.

As people have learnt to question the terms of modernity they have discovered different ways of recovering the self. As women have questioned the ways they have grown up to see themselves and judge themselves lacking through the eyes of men, so they have struggled to see themselves through their own eyes. This does not mean rejecting all the values they have inherited, but of rethinking the terms of a tradition that has so often denigrated their experience and values and rendered them invisible within the public realm. This is a process that men and women of colour have had to go through as they challenged the terms of colonial rule and the relationships of modernity to colonialism. Similarly, Jews have had to question the terms of tolerance they have grown up to accept and the ways this has construed their own experience of Jewishness. The gay movement has uncovered structures of heterosexual power that have long diminished the experience, meanings and values of lesbians and gay men. This is a process of questioning the terms of modernity and finding the courage to ask different questions and form different meanings and values.

As we learn to rethink the relations between morality, truth and politics, we come to terms with the contradictory inheritance of modernity. We can appreciate the values of liberty, equality and social justice while questioning the terms in which these values were presented. If this involves reworking traditions of social and political theory, it also involves questioning the terms within modernity which so easily set science in opposition to morality and nature in opposition to culture.

If we are to learn from feminism and ecology in the remaking of social theory, we must learn to listen to others as well as ourselves. As we recover the self we must learn to respect the integrity of our emotional, somatic and spiritual lives. We must be careful not to legislate for others, but to listen and help them grow in their own authority. This is to recognise the place of truth and wisdom in our lives, before we rush on leaving important questions behind.

Notes

1 INTRODUCTION: MODERNITY, MORALITY AND POLITICS

1 A useful introduction to the writings of Antonio Gramsci is provided by Carl Boggs in *Gramsci's Marxism* (1976), though at times it falls into interpreting Gramsci's writings on power and hegemony within a Weberian framework which stresses the transmission of dominant values rather than the workings of relationships of power to produce consent. For work which helps trace Gramsci's intellectual and political development, see, for instance, Fiori 1980; Cammett 1977; Davidson 1977.

2 Introductions to Althusser are provided by *Althusser's Marxism* (Calinicoss 1976) and *Considerations of Western Marxism* (Anderson, P. 1975), which presents the development of Western Marxism very much within a framework of categories provided by Althusser. For a more general account of the development of Althusserian work and its influence on the Left, see Benton 1984; Clarke *et al.* 1980; Thompson, E.P. 1979.

3 Althusser's discussion of ideology can be found in his influential essays 'Marxism and Humanism', 'Contradictions and Overdetermination' and 'On the Materialist Dialectic' (Althusser 1970) and 'Ideology and Ideological State Apparatuses' (Althusser 1971). Althusser had challenged an orthodox Marxist tradition that saw ideology as a 'veil' that could somehow be removed to reveal underlying material relations. It also helped to question the framework of a sociology of knowledge that had opened up some of the cracks in a dominant Positivist tradition in the early 1960s. Stuart Hall's essay 'The Hinterland of Science: Ideology and the "Sociology of Knowledge"' (Hall *et al.* 1978 9–32) goes some way to explaining the appeal of learning to think in terms of ideology.

4 A useful introduction to Wittgenstein as a critique of formalism is given in Stanley Cavell's essay 'The Availability of the Later Wittgenstein' in Cavell 1969. An illuminating biography which places Wittgenstein in a cultural and philosophical context and which gives a sense of his intellectual development is provided by Monk 1986.

5 For a sense of the setting and development of Rudolf Bahro's work in the former East Germany as a dissident voice, see Bahro 1978. To understand his intellectual development as he moved to the West and became involved in both ecological and spiritual movements, see essays collected in Bahro 1982; 1984.

6 Illuminating introductions to the Frankfurt School and critical theory are given in Jay 1973, which tells the story centred on Max Horkheimer. For

a focus upon Theodor Adorno and Walter Benjamin, see Buck-Morss 1977. For useful collections of writings see Arato and Gebhart 1989 and Bronner and Kellner 1989.
7 The cultural relationship between dominant forms of masculinity, the Protestant ethic and traditions of self-denial is explored further in Ch. 4 'Self-denial' and Ch. 5 'Morality' in Seidler 1991a.

2 MORALITY

1 An introduction to the Marxism of the Second International is provided by 'Bernstein and the Marxism of the Second International' (Colletti 1971: 45–108). See also Salvadori 1979 and Ch. 1 'Conformist Marxism' in Jacoby (1981).
2 Austro-Marxism is usefully introduced in Kolakowski 1978, vol. 2. See also the collection of writings *Austro-Marxism* (Goode and Bottomore 1978).
3 Marcuse 1967 provides a helpful historical discussion of the emergence of positivism. See in particular 'The Foundations of Positivism and the Rise of Sociology' (1967: 323–88). For a useful contemporary collection of discussions, see Giddens 1974.
4 Althusser was generally dismissive of Lukács as a 'humanist' who relied upon what has come to be broadly known as an 'essentialist' conception of human nature. It was harder for Althusser to identify Lukács' rationalism as a weakness since this is something he generally shared. As far as the history of Marxism written with a structuralist tradition was concerned, Althusser made it difficult to appreciate the insights Lukács' *History and Class Consciousness* (1971) showed in crucially reworking Marx's relationship to Hegel.
5 Interesting discussions of Hegel's critique of Kant are found in Lukács 1975. See also Schmidt 1971.
6 Lenin's conception of morality and its relationship to a tradition of scientific Marxism are helpfully discussed in Besançon 1974. See also the discussion in Claudin-Urondo 1977.
7 Edward Thompson continued his reflections on the relationship of Marxism to morality in his essay 'The Poverty of Theory' (Thompson, E.P. 1971), where he is harsh on contributions to radical philosophy which helped to open up these concerns. See, for instance, Anthony Skillen 'Marxism and Morality', *Radical Philosophy*, 8, summer 1974. For a sense of how these discussions have developed, see, for instance, Skillen 1977; Lukes 1985; Miller, R.W. 1984; Nielsen and Patten 1981.
8 For some illuminating examples of this historical work, see Hill 1975; 1977; 1984; Hobsbawm 1962; 1977.
9 Gramsci talks about the importance of developing an oppositional philosophical culture which will contest the prevailing 'common sense' in 'The Philosophy of Praxis', 'The Study of Philosophy' (Gramsci 1971: 321–77).
10 This notion of Western Marxism has an important source in 'State and Civil Society' (Gramsci 1971: 206–76). He was seeking ways of recognising that the Bolshevik model, which might have suited conditions in Russia where there was a weak civil society and an absence of liberal democratic traditions, was most unsuitable within the conditions of Western Europe.
11 Gramsci's discussion on the fragmentation of Marxism in its orthodox form into a philosophy of materialism on the one hand and a science

of history and politics on the other is focused through a critical discussion of Bukharin in 'Problems of Marxism' (Gramsci 1971: 378–472).

12 An introduction to some early conceptualisations of ideology is provided by Lichtheim 1970; Larrain 1979; 1983; Plamenatz 1974; and the Centre for Contemporary Cultural Studies (1978).

13 A connection between the vitality of Marxism as a revolutionary theory whose concepts remain historically grounded, and the experience of working-class men and women exploited within the conditions of a capitalist mode of production, is sustained in Dunayevskaya 1971. Despite some of its rhetorical language it remains a significant introduction to a politically informed reading of Marx. It shows how development in Marx's intellectual concerns cannot be separated from the political and historical struggles he was engaging in.

14 Alvin Gouldner offers an insightful discussion of the relationship of utilitarianism to a taken-for-granted class culture in Chapter 3 of his *The Coming Crisis of Western Sociology* (1970).

15 The debate between Dewey and Trotsky remains helpful in illuminating some of the issues about the status of a 'proletarian morality' and the nature of the challenge it makes to dominant bourgeois forms of moral theory. Steven Lukes provides a helpful introduction to some of the issues that were raised in this debate in Lukes 1985.

16 For a helpful discussion about motivation in Chinese society in the period after the 1948 Revolution, when Mao was still the dominant voice, see Schurmann 1966.

17 The subordination of our natures so that we can act out of reason alone is given an ethical form in Kant's notion that we have to subordinate our 'inclinations' so that we can act out of a sense of duty. The need to reinstate our emotions and feelings as part of a discourse of morality appears as an important theme in Blum 1980; Seidler 1986; Williams, B. 1985.

18 The relationship of dominant forms of masculinity within modernity to reason and self-denial is a central theme in the early chapters of Seidler 1991a.

19 The idea that we have a possessive relationship with our qualities, including our bodies as the source of labour, and that freedom lies in being able to use whatever property is in our possession, is often attributed to Locke. Whether it is right to claim, as conservative libertarians have tended to, that my freedom to dispose of my property is no different to the slave holder's relationship to slaves, it has become an important notion to contest. See, for instance, discussion in Nozick 1974. Somewhat paradoxically it is also a claim that is crucial to the analytical reading of Marx in Cohen 1978. This vision of freedom could be one more reason to be suspicious of this influential reading of Marx.

20 Simone Weil helps to clarify the ways Western culture since the Greeks has held work and human labour in low esteem, as some kind of necessary evil. Though Weil was concerned with reinstating the dignity of human labour, she was more suspicious of Marx's notions which treat labour as a form of human fulfilment and self-realisation. This links to Weil's hostility to a Hegelian reading of Marx. See the discussion in Ch. 6 'Work' in Blum and Seidler 1989: 143–93.

3 MODERNITY

1 For a useful discussion on the ways the Scientific Revolution of the seventeenth century conceived of itself explicitly in gender terms, as the development of a new masculinist philosophy, see Farringdon 1969; Ch. 3 in Easlea 1981. See also the illuminating and disturbing passages brought together by Griffin 1982b.

2 Useful introductions to Descartes and the growth of Cartesian rationalism are provided by Kenny 1968; Rée 1974; Williams, B. 1978.

3 Thoughts about the way Kant develops particular notions in Descartes' rationalism can be found in Rorty 1979. See also the introductory essay 'Introduction: Pragmatism and Philosophy' in Rorty 1982.

4 Interesting ideas on the relationship of gender to taken-for-granted traditions of rationalism are explored in Lloyd 1984. See also the landmark collection Harding and Hintikka 1983, which sets out to 'root out sexist distortions ... in the "hard core" of abstract reasoning thought most immune to infiltration by social values'. More recently a feminist attempt to maintain notions of reason and objectivity, arguing for a different relationship between feminism and traditional philosophy, has been set out in Antony and Witt 1993.

5 Reflections on the relationship between the mechanistic conception of nature in the Scientific Revolutions and the witchburnings in Europe and North America have been offered in Merchant 1980; Daly 1984; Griffin 1982b; Easlea 1981.

6 Simone Weil reflects upon difficulties with a conception of equality that is grounded in a language of rights in her essay 'Human Personality' in Weil 1962. This theme is also explored in Ch. 8 'Respect, Rights and Injustice' in Seidler 1991b: 124–42.

7 For some helpful discussion of Hegel's conception of equality and citizenshp, see Taylor, C. 1979; Avineri 1972.

8 Useful reflections upon the relationship of morality to politics in Kant's writings are given in Murphy 1970; Williams, 19xx. See also the lectures in Arendt 1982.

9 A thoughtful introduction to Feuerbach that helps to place him in historical and cultural context is Wartofsky 1977. See also McLellan 1970 and the discussion in Taylor, C. 1978.

10 Difficult questions about Marx's relationship to his Jewishness are raised by Isaiah Berlin in 'Benjamin Disraeli, Karl Marx and the Search for Identity' (Berlin 1981: 252–86). See also the discussion in Carlebach 1978. In a different historical context similar issues are raised in Friedlander 1990 about Jewish identities in post-1968 France.

11 Useful discussion of the relationship between Marxism and religion is found in McLellan 1990. It is an issue for the writings in Kolakowski 1969 and 1978.

12 For some helpful introductions to Durkheim's conception of the relationship between individual and society see Thompson, K. 1982; Lukes 1983; Giddens 1978. Giddens has also edited a useful selection of Durkheim's writings.

13 An interesting discussion of individual liberties and rights in relation to freedom is provided by Raz 1986. See also the discussions collected in Waldron 1985. For discussion of the struggles for collective rights, see Ch. 9 'Morality, Subordination and Oppression' in Seidler 1991b: 143–67.

14 Adorno and Horkheimer 1973 is a difficult if illuminating text about some

of the contradictions of an Enlightenment inheritance. Its silence in relation to questions of gender is, I try to argue, partly explained by its failure
to think through the implications of an Enlightenment identification of
masculinity with reason.

15 Interesting discussions of Freud's relationship with religion are provided
by Roberts 1976; Rieff 1965; Gay 1988.

16 A useful discussion of Owenite socialism is provided by Harrison 1969.
See also the insightful discussion of the Owenite relationship to feminism
in Taylor, B. 1983.

17 An exploration of the ways conceptions of 'negative' and 'positive' reason
have served to underpin conflicting traditions of social theory is a central
theme in Marcuse 1967, which is principally concerned with Hegel's
writings. See also the essay 'Philosophy and Critical Theory' in (Marcuse
1968: 134–58); and Marcuse 1972, in particular 'A Study on Authority'
written in 1936 (1972: 49–156).

18 A brief and insightful history of the relationship of positivism to social
theory is presented by Kolokowski 1972. There is also interesting discussion in Gouldner 1970, Part 3. For a sense of how this discussion
developed in post-war Germany in relation to Critical Theory, see Adey
and Frisby 1976.

4 AUTHORITY

1 For some interesting reflections on the relationship of Weber to Marx
see, for instance, Lowith 1991; 1993. See also Mommsen 1974; Hennis
1987; Lash and Whimster 1987.

2 The extent to which Mill actually learnt this lesson is still an open issue,
especially as it concerns issues of democracy. I am drawing upon a
particular emphasis in Mill 1964 which some argue is far from
characteristic of his work as a whole. But nevertheless it indicates a crucial
tension in Mill's writings and we can sense him being pulled in different
directions. To reflect upon these issues further, see Ryan 1974; 'John
Stuart Mill and the Ends of Life' in Berlin 1969: 173–206; Gray and Smith
1991; Skorupski 1991.

3 The possibilities of treating a person justly within an unjust society are
a central concern in the concluding chapter 'Liberalism and the Autonomy
of Morality' in Seidler 1986: 118–223. For some useful reflections upon
Plato, see Murdoch 1990; Gouldner (1967); Wolin 196.

4 Some implications of Plato's division of the human soul are discussed
in Murdoch 1992; Tillich 1954.

5 Durkheim's vision of society as a moral reality which presents individuals
with a higher vision of themselves to which they are obliged to conform
through external regulation and constraint, is presented in Durkheim
1961 and 1974, while its early formulations can be followed in Durkheim
1964. For some helpful discussion on these themes, see Lukes 1983;
Giddens 1977.

6 To understand the Frankfurt School's relation to different forms of reason,
see Horkheimer 1974, which shows an intent to reinstate a more substantial conception of reason against ways it had been subjectivised and for-
malised within a Cartesian tradition. See also interesting discussion in
Dews 1987.

7 For a sense of Marcuse's work in relation to tolerance see 'The Struggle

against Liberalism in the Totalitarian View of the State' in Marcuse 1968: 1–42, and 'Repressive Tolerance', his contribution to Wolff et al. 1969: 81–123. To help place some of these ideas in the context of the development of Marcuse's work, see Kellner 1984.

8 Simone Weil appreciated that it was difficult for workers to exercise their freedom of expression at work, for if they said what they really felt it could easily lose them their jobs. These themes are explored in the context of Weil's thought and politics in Ch. 6 'Work' in Blum and Seidler 1989: 143–193.

9 For some useful discussions of democracy in relation to traditions of socialism, see Levine 1984; Graham 1986; 1972; Held 1986; 1993.

10 A discussion of different forms of individualism is helped if we recognise its possessive character within classical liberal theory. See, for instance, MacPherson 1962; 1973. For some recent more general reflections see Heller et al. 1986. See also Keat and Abercrombie 1990 for a sense of how possessive notions of individualism emerge in new forms around an enterprise culture.

11 The relationship of dominant forms of masculinity to particular notions of self-control is explored in Ch. 'Control' in Seidler 1989.

12 The relationship of the Scientific Revolution of the seventeenth century to notions of progress as the control and domination of nature is explored in Merchant 1980; Griffin 1982b. It has become a central concern for ecological and eco-feminist movements.

5 NEEDS AND DESIRES

1 I have explored some of the hidden assumptions in relation to moralism and personal and political change in the sexual politics of the 1970s in Seidler 1991a.

2 Connections between will, reason and sexuality, particularly in relation to the experience of men, are further explored in Ch. 3 in Seidler 1989. See also the discussions in Brittan 1989; Connell 1987; Weeks 1984.

3 For a discussion of the Frankfurt School's recognition of the formal and instrumental conception of reason that accompanied a modernity largely shaped within the terms of a Cartesian rationalism, see Horkheimer 1974. See also an illuminating discussion of these themes in Bucks-Morss 1977.

4 Useful historical accounts of sexuality are provided by Brown, P. 1989; Bremmer 1989. For some sense of the development of Foucault's thinking about sexuality we can compare the influential first volume of A History of Sexuality (1979) with The Uses of Pleasure (1984) and the different emphasis we discover in the later The Care of the Self (1990). A sense of how Foucault came to abandon some of the assumptions of his earlier work can be drawn from his writing in Martin et al. 1988.

5 Herbert Marcuse discusses the impact of Husserl in 'The Concept of Essence' (Marcuse 1968: 43–87) and so helps to illuminate the relationship of critical theory to phenomenology. For a more general introduction, see the discussion in Smart 1983; Baumann 1978.

6 Kellerman 1975 and 1980 both help to open up consideration of the emotional life of the body. See also the work of Boadella in Boadella 1987 and 1988. In their different ways they engaged with Reich's pioneering work on the body and somatic experience and the ways this was developed in Lowen 1963 and 1976. This work has yet to connect to the

reconsideration of the place of the body and somatic experience with traditions of philosophy and social theory. These have largely shaped the mind–body split, set within the terms of a Cartesian rationalism. For a different approach to issues of the body in relation to social theory, see Turner, B. 1984 and 1992a.

7 Recent work by Alice Miller traces some of these problems of invalidation through childhood. She reveals some of the ways we learn to identify with our oppressors. She emphasises not only the cruelty but the more harmful negation of the child's reaction. The slap is bad, she says, but the stifling of the scream is worse. In Miller, A. 1990, she argues that what is terrible about Buster Keaton, who was knocked about on stage in his parents vaudeville act while never allowed to react facially, is that he was forced to repress the trauma, so that years later he could say: 'My parents were my first bit of great luck.' Her point is that the 'poisonous pedagogy' we have inherited – which punishes and ultimately undermines a child's true emotional responses – creates people who are predisposed to collude in lies, and who are 'psychically dead'.

8 The revival of an orthodox interpretation of Marxism within analytical Marxism which seeks to defend a form of technological determinism is evident in Cohen 1978. There are similar tendences at work in Wood 1981. Sometimes they link the development of productive forces and human well-being by saying that productive forces develop 'human productive powers'. Against this, Simone Weil argues in essays collected as *Oppression and Liberty* that material well-being does not necessarily bring greater dignity or moral well-being.

9 For some sense of the development of phenomenology within sociology in the early 1970s and the hopes that it carried, see Filmer *et al.* 1972; O'Neil 1970; Young, M. 1971.

10 Some interesting discussions of Weber's conception of rationalisation are found in Turner, B. 1992b; Brubaker 1984; Bologh 1990.

6 IDEOLOGY

1 Useful introductions to Marx's conception of ideology are provided by Larrain 1979; Plamenatz 1974; Eagleton 1991.

2 A discussion of the place of self-denial within modernity is provided in the early chapters of Seidler 1991a. It has been a theme in different ways in the writings of Nietzsche, Scheler and the Frankfurt School, though it has remained very much in the shadows of contemporary social theory. Somehow the emphasis upon discourse has worked to consolidate its own forms of rationalism.

3 Helpful discussions of liberal conceptions of freedom and equality, though often coming from quite different positions, are given in Guttman 1980; Sandel 1983; Seidler 1986; Walzer 1983.

4 Insights into the development of Marx's relationship to morality are provided by Lukes 1985; Skillen 1977; Weil 1958; Miller, R.W. 1984; Thompson, E.P. 1979.

5 A useful discussion of Thatcherism is provided by Hall and Jaques 1983.

6 Reflections upon the processes of schooling have often been too easily dismissed on the Left with the empty label of 'progressivism' on the assumption that the Left libertarian critiques were blind to the issues of class, race and gender. Sadly this left a space for the discussion on

education to move firmly to the Right. There is still a great deal to learn from Holt 1969; Dennison 1971; Freire 1974; Kohl 1988. A useful review of the strengths and weaknesses of this literature is provided by Graubard 1972.

7   The relationship of dominant forms of masculinity to notions of self-control is further discussed in Ch. 4 'Control' in Seidler 1989.

8   Weber's ideas of value are discussed further in Gouldner 1972; Winch 1990; Hennis 1987; Velody *et al.* 1992; Turner, C. 1992.

9   To grasp Althusser's conception of ideology see 'Ideology and Ideological State Apparatuses' (Althusser 1971: 121–73). This aspect of Althusserian work has been critically assessed in 'The Poverty of Theory' (Thompson, E.P. 1979); Larrain 1983; Clarke *et al.* 1980.

10 Søren Kierkegaard reflects upon the idea of freedom and choice in friendships. See *Either/Or* (1971), where some of these liberal assumptions are laid bare. He shows how significant can be the attitudes we take towards life in the ways that we regard our friendships. This aspect of Kierkegaard's writings is explored in Chs 3 and 4 in Seidler 1991b.

11 For some brief reflections on Erich Fromm's relationship with Reich, see Jacoby 1975; Jay 1973. See also the intellectual biography of Fromm, *Erich Fromm: The Courage to be Human* (Funk 1982), and the biography of Reich, *Fury on Earth: A Biography of Wilhelm Reich* (Sharaf 1985).

12 Some of these processes of denial and invalidation are illuminated in the writings of Alice Miller. See, for instance, *The Drama of the Gifted Child* (1981) and her more recent *Breaking Down the Wall of Silence* (1992), which gives insight into her changing relationship with a psychoanalytic tradition.

13 Kafka's relationship with his father, which cast a long shadow over his whole life, is written about in his *Letter to my Father* (1954). The Kafka biography by Ronald Hayman (1981), brings this out. See also the essays Franz Kafka' and 'Max Brod's Book on Kafka' (Benjamin, W. 1973: 111–40; 141–8).

14 For a discussion of Lukács conception of totality, see Arato and Breines 1979. See also Martin Jay's attempts to investigate conceptions of totality within Western Marxism in *Marxism and Totality* (1984).

15 A challenge to the identification of justice with distributive conceptions of justice alone is a theme in Seidler 1986. Simone Weil has an appreciation of the significance of non-distributive conceptions of justice. It is also a theme in Murdoch 1992.

7   IDENTITIES

1   Gramsci set out a crucial discussion of some of the implications of assembly-line production as a new stage in the capitalist labour process in 'Americanism and Fordism' in *The Prison Notebooks* (1971: 277–318). See also Braverman 1974, which proved a crucial text in awakening interest in the labour process as the core of Marx's analysis of the workings of the capitalist mode of production. For some sense of the widespread discussion it provoked, see, for instance, Nicols 1980; Brown, R. 1992.

2   A useful discussion of the conception of needs in Marx's writings is given in Heller 1974. From within a largely structuralist framework there is interesting discussion in Soper 1981. For a different response, see my

essay 'Trusting Ourselves: Marxism, Human Needs and Sexual Politics' in Clarke *et al*. 1980: 103–56. See also the stimulating discussion of human needs in Ignatieff 1984.

3 For some attempts to make use of Marx's insights to develop a politically sensitive framework for psychoanalytic theory, see, for instance, Sève 1978; Lichtman 1982; Schneider 1975; Fromm 1973; Kovel 1989.

4 There have been different attempts to assimilate Marx's discussions of alienation into a reformulated sociology of work, one of the most influential of which was Blauner 1964. These are important for at least opening up issues of the freedom and control which particular labour processes give to groups of workers. Simone Weil insists upon the possibilities of transforming relations within industrial organisations rather than waiting for capitalist property relations to be challenged. This theme is explored in Ch. 6 'Work' in Blum and Seidler 1989: 143–93.

5 These issues of freedom are discussed by Simone Weil in *Seventy Letters*. I have explored the ways these insights into freedom and power unsettle prevailing forms of liberal moral and political theory in Ch. 8 'Liberalism and the Autonomy of Morality' in *Kant, Respect and Injustice* (Seidler 1986 118–223).

6 For some reflections on the relationship of citizenship to the economy see Marshall and Bottomore (1991); Keane 1988a; 1988b; Held 1989.

7 We also have to consider changes in the mining communities, especially in the light of the pit closures that took place in the wake of the 1984 miners' strike. This closure programme was accelerated with the closures announced in 1992, which have served to devastate the industry in different parts of the country.

8 Simone Weil has some interesting remarks on how others 'read' us and how we 'read' others in our relationships with them. Some of these remarks are collected in *Gravity and Grace* (1952). There is some illuminating discussion which relates to these themes in Winch 1989.

9 For some reflections on the ways Sartre attempts to reconcile certain existentialist insights with what he learnt from Marx during the Resistance, see, for instance, *Search for a Method* (1963) which is the first part of his major work *Critique of Dialectical Reason* (1976). See also *Between Existentialism and Marxism* (1974), in particular 'The Itinerary of a Thought' (1974: 33–64).

10 A useful account of the historical experience of women's oppression and the struggles against it is provided by Rowbotham 1971; 1973.

11 For some interesting early reflections on marriage as an institution see Mary Wollstonecraft's *Vindication of the Rights of Women* (1992).

12 I have discussed conceptions of personal change and the place of reason and emotion in our inherited notions of personal and political change in *Recreating Sexual Politics* (1991a). See also the discussion of these themes in Rowbotham 1983; Segal 1987; Connell 1987; Ruddick 1990; Benjamin, J. 1990.

8 CONTRADICTIONS

1 The relationship between liberal conceptions of morality and Protestant conceptions of self-denial is further discussed in Chs 4, 5 and 6 in *Recreating Sexual Politics* (Seidler 1991a). For an illuminating historical discussion, see Hirschman 1977.

2 For some useful discussion of how questions of power emerge within the context of education, see, for instance, Apple 1985; Young and Whitty (1977).

3 For an exploration of men's different responses to feminism, see Seidler 1991c; Porter, M. 1993; Jardine and Smith 1987.

4 Men are beginning to explore their different masculinities, which have for so long been taken for granted, at least within the public realm. See, for instance, *Rediscovering Masculinity* (Seidler 1989) and *Recreating Sexual Politics* (Seidler 1991a). See also Connell 1987; Hearn 1987; Segal 1990.

5 For a discussion of some of the implications of Weber's conceptions of human action in terms of gender, see, for instance, Bologh 1990; Sydie 1987; Seidler 1994.

6 Insights into the ways ecological theory works to challenge notions of progress as involving the control and domination of nature are provided by Griffin 1982b; Merchant 1980.

7 A stimulating introduction to Herder's social and political theory is 'Herder and the Enlightenment' (Berlin 1976: 143–216).

8 A useful introduction to different forms of feminist theory is provided by Jagger 1983; Eisenstein 1984; Ramazanoglu 1989.

9 Simone Weil's changing conceptions of revolution are discussed in Ch. 3 in Blum and Seidler 1989.

10 For some useful reflections on the politics of teaching, see, for instance, McLaren and Leonard 1992; Giroux 1992; Carlson 1992.

11 Discussions of the relationship between education and class are provided by Apple 1985; and Wexler 1991.

12 Explorations of the Marxism of the Second International are developed in *Marxism and Philosophy* (Korsch 1970) 'What is Orthodox Marxism?' in *History and Class Consciousness* (Lukács 1971; 1–26). See also Salvadori 1979.

13 Marx's conception of justice as the extent to which Marx accepts that capitalist society can only be judged in terms of its own criteria of justice has been discussed in, for instance, Allen Wood's *Karl Marx* (1981). See also Buchanan 1982; Cohen *et al.* 1980.

9 EMPOWERMENT

1 The relationship of labour to the overcoming of necessity is crucial to Simone Weil's grasp of the dignity of labour. She separates herself from Marx's view of labour as a form of self-realisation. This is discussed in Ch. 6 'Work' in Blum and Seidler 1989: 143–93.

2 Reflections on Reich's relationship to Freud are provided in *Reich Speaks of Freud* (Reich 1967). See also Boadella 1988, Sharaf 1985.

3 The Frankfurt School is most usefully discussed in *The Origin of Negative Dialectics* (Buck-Morss 1977), which helps to bring out some of the unresolved tensions in their work. For an exploration of some of the tensions between the Frankfurt School and traditions of post-structuralist work, see Dews 1987. For a sense of Habermas' relationship to an earlier generation see Dews 1992.

4 A useful introduction to theories of post-modernity is given in Bauman 1991b. See also Foster 1985; Smart 1993; Featherstone 1988.

5 Questions of the relationship between identities and community are

raised in a helpful way by Anderson, B. 1991. See also Chapman and Rutherford 1988; Squires 1993.

6 Gramsci talks about becoming 'critically conscious' in our relationships in *The Prison Notebooks* (1971: 324, note 1). I think there are important resonances with the awareness of consciousness-raising in the women's movement. Sheila Rowbotham makes explicit reference to Gramsci in the introduction to her *Women's Consciousness, Man's World* (1973).

7 For some helpful reflections on the relationship between therapy and politics, see Ernst and Goodison 1981; Wyckoff 1976.

8 A useful introduction to the writings of Georg Lukács which helps to situate them culturally and politically is Michael Löwy's *Georg Lukács: From Romanticism to Bolshevism* (1979).

9 For some useful discussion of the relationship of sexuality to power, see Foucault 1979, vol. 1. See also Foucault 1980. For a sense of how Foucault's thinking about these issues changed over time, see Kritzman 1990. For some critical discussions of Foucault's work, see, for instance, Hoy 1986.

10 For some interesting discussions of heterosexual and gay men's relationships to sexuality, see, for instance. Seidler 1992; Porter and Weeks 1990.

11 Reflections on the relationship of masculinities to violence are given in Ch. 5 'Male Violence' in *Men, Sex and Relationships* (Seidler 1992: 127–80). See also the useful discussion in Segal 1990.

12 Liberal conceptions of autonomy are discussed in a helpful way in Sandel 1983; Raz 1986; Seidler 1986.

13 For reflections on changes in the labour process partly stimulated by Harry Braverman's *Labour and Monopoly Capital* (1974), see Bob Young's 'Labour and Monopoly Capital', in *Radical Science Journal*, no. 4 1976: 81–93; and Russell Jacoby's, 'Essay Review of Braverman', in *Telos*, Fall 1976: 199–206 and the collection *The Labour Process and Class Struggle*, CSE Pamphlets No. 1 (1979), which explores some of the resonances and tensions with labour process theories developed within the context of Italian analyses. For more recent discussions of post-Fordism as a break with the dominance of assembly-line production, see, for instance, Robin Murray's 'Fordism and Post-Fordism' (Hall and Jacques 1990: 38–53) and Mike Rustin's 'The Trouble with New Times' (Ibid.: 303–20).

14 For some understanding of the history and development of feminist psychotherapy, see Eichenbaum and Orbach 1983. See also Benjamin, J. 1990; Chodorow 1992.

15 For a brief discussion of this disagreement beween Marcuse and Fromm, see Jay 1973, Ch. 3.

16 A sense of Fromm's intellectual and spiritual development in his later writings is given in his *To Have or To Be?* (1992). See also the intellectual biography *Erich Fromm: The Courage to be Human* (Funk 1982).

17 For a sense of Marcuse's intellectual development and the impact of feminism upon his later thinking, see, for instance, Kellner 1984.

10 CONCLUSION: MODERNITY, MORALITY AND SOCIAL THEORY

1 Useful introductions to the notion of post-modernity are provided by Bauman 1991a; 1991b. See also Foster 1985; Featherstone 1988; Smart 1993.

2 Durkheim's conception of morality in its relation to Kantian ethics is discussed in his *Sociology and Philosophy* (1974) and in Lukes 1983. Related issues of gender are examined in Seidler 1994.

3 Carol Gilligan explores the difficulties women sometimes have in including theselves in their moral deliberations in her *In a Different Voice* (1982). These themes are also illuminated in Ruddick 1990; Kittay and Meyers 1987.

4 Foucault's later thoughts on caring for the self are schematically presented in Martin *et al.* 1988: 16–49. See also Foucault 1990, which in significant respects marks a break with Foucault's original conception of a history of sexuality.

5 For some useful reflections which help us think about the relationship of modernity to slavery see, for instance, Davis 1989; Williams, E. 1964.

6 Simone Weil discusses how science becomes grounds within modernity for working-class people in the West to be able to feel superior, when she talks about the split between humanities and science in *The Need for Roots* (1972).

7 The impact of the Scientific Revolution and the 'masculinist' philosophy it helped to generate on the relationships between women and nature is explored in Griffin 1982b and Merchant 1980.

8 Sartre explores the relationship between Enlightenment, citizenship and Jewishness as a central theme in *Anti-Semite and Jew* (1960). It is a discussion that influenced Franz Fanon in his rethinking of Black consciousness and identities in *Black Skin/White Mask* (1970). Sartre returned to this theme at the end of his life, more able to acknowledge a more positive vision of Jewish cultures and identities, rather than treating them as the effects of anti-Semitism.

9 Discussions of the role of Christian anti-Semitism in helping to provide a background which allowed the Holocaust to take place are provided by Franklin Littell in *The Crucifixion of the Jews* (1973). See also Libowitz 1987.

10 Interesting reflections on the ways that Hegel provided grounds for the subordination of individuals to the State are provided in Taylor, C. 1979; Marcuse 1967; Avineri 1972; Plant 1984.

11 The relationship of feminism to ecology is explored in Griffin 1982a and 1982b.

12 A useful introduction to Lyotard's writings on post-modernity are provided in his *The Post-Modern Condition: A Report* (1985).

13 Post-modern conceptions of identities are explored in Foster 1985; Featherstone 1988; Rutherford 1990.

14 A discussion of Erving Goffman's influential notions of the self is provided in Goffman 1959.

15 A useful introduction to the writings of Baudrillard which helps to place him in cultural and historical context is provided by Gane 1991. See also Kellner 1989 and Gane 1993.

16 For some reflections upon the difficult relationship between Nietzsche and traditions of feminist work, see, for instance, Patton 1993.

17 Emma Goldman (1984) writes about the influence of Nietzsche on her generation of radical activists.

18 Simone Weil talks about the dignity of work and the attempts she makes to suggest certain reforms to factory life in *Seventy Letters* (1965). This is also a theme discussed in Blum and Seidler 1989: 143–93.

19 See Paulo Freire's discussion in *The Pedagogy of the Oppressed* (1974) and the interesting engagement with his work in McLaren and Leonard 1992.

20 Primo Levi's important reflections on the Holocaust are to be found in *If This is a Man* (1992) and the much later writing in *The Drowned and the Saved* (1989).

21 Gramsci's discussion of 'moral individuality' is to be found in the *Prison Notebooks*, Part III, 'The Philosophy of Praxis'. For a sense of the temptations and dangers in a structuralist reading of Gramsci, see for instance Mouffe (1979).

22 A helpful introduction to Herder and questions of identity is provided by Isaiah Berlin, 'Herder and the Enlightenment in Berlin 1976: 143–216.

23 Some sense of the shifts in Foucault's later thinking about identity, morality and politics are provided in Kritzman 1990.

24 The echoes of the Exodus story in movements for social justice in different historical periods is explored by Michael Walzer (1985).

25 A helpful introduction to Lacan's work is provided in Benevenoto and Kennedy 1987.

26 Insights into the workings of Nazi science can be gained from R.J. Lifton's *Nazi Doctors: Medical Killing and the Psychology of Genocide* (1986) and Benno Müller-Hill's *Murderous Science* (1988).

27 For a sense of the evaluations that Masson makes of Freud's work with women see, for instance, Ch. 3, 'Dora and Freud' in Masson 1990.

28 Reich's discussion of class consciousness and his critiques of economistic notions of Marxism are provided in Reich 1972. See also Reich 1974a and b and Theweleit's interesting engagement with some of the ideas in *Male Fantasies* (1987; 1989).

29 Susan Griffin's invocation of the 'pornographic mind' is found in her *Pornography and Silence* (1980). Whatever the limits of this notion it helps her make some crucial connections about the relationship of sexism, racism and anti-Semitism within modernity.

30 A useful introductio to the women's health movement is provided in *Our Bodies Our Selves* (Phillips and Rakusen 1989).

31 Susan Sontag (1991) questions the place of guilt and responsibility in changing conceptions of health and illness in *Illness as a Metaphor*. More recently she has explored the discourses that have surrounded AIDS in *AIDS as a Metaphor*.

32 For a sense of how C.B. MacPherson introduces the ideas of possessive individualism and helps to place them historically see his *The Political Theory of Possessive Individualism* (1962) and *Democratic Theory: Essays in Retrieval* (1973).

Bibliography

Adey, G. and Frisby, D. (1976) *The Positivist Dispute in German Sociology*, London: Heinemann.

Adorno, Th. (1967) *Prisms*, London: Neville Spearman.

Adorno, Th. and Horkheimer, M. (1973) *Dialectic of Enlightenment* (trans. J. Cumming), London: Allen Lane.

—— (1974) *Aspects of Sociology*, London: Heinemann.

Althusser, L. (1970) *For Marx* (trans. B. Brewster), London: Verso.

—— (1971) *Lenin and Philosophy and Other Essays*, London: Verso.

—— (1972) *Reading Capital*, London: Verso.

Anderson, B. (1991) *Imagined Communities*, London: Verso.

Anderson, P. (1975) *Considerations of Western Marxism*, London: New Left Books.

Antony, L. and Witt, C. (ed.) (1993) *A Mind of One's Own: Feminist Essays in Reason and Objectivity*, Boulder, CO: Westview Press.

Apple, M. (1985) *Education and Power*, London: Routledge.

Arato, A. and Breines, P. (1979) *The Young Lukács and the Origins of Western Marxism*, London: Pluto Books.

Arato, A. and Gebhardt, E. (eds) (1989) *The Essential Frankfurt School Reader*, Oxford: Blackwell.

Arendt, H. (1982) *Kant's Political Thought*; Lectures on Kant's Political Philosophy, ed. R. Beiner, Brighton: Harvester

Avineri, S. (1972) *Hegel's Theory of the Modern State*, Cambridge: Cambridge University Press.

Bahro, R. (1978) *The Alternative in Eastern Europe*, London: New Left Books.

—— (1982) *Socialism and Survival*, London: Heretic Books.

—— (1984) *From Red to Green*, London: Verso Books.

Balbus, I. (1982) *Marxism and Domination*, Princeton: Princeton University Press.

Bauman, Z. (1978) *Hermeneutics and the Social Sciences*, London: Hutchinson.

—— (1990) *Modernity and the Holocaust*, Cambridge: Polity Press.

—— (1991a) *Modernity and Ambivalence*, Cambridge: Polity Press.

—— (1991b) *Intimations of Postmodernity*, London: Routledge.

Benevenoto, B. and Kennedy, R. (1987) *The World of Jaques Lacan: An Introduction*, London: London Free Associates.

Benjamin, J. (1990) *Bonds of Love*, London: Virago.

Benjamin, W. (1973) *Illuminations* (trans. H. Zohn), London: Collins/Fontana.

Benton, T. (1984) *The Rise and Fall of Althusserian Marxism*, London: Routledge.

—— (1993) *Natural Relations*, London: Verso.

Berlin, I. (1969) *Four Essays on Liberty*, Oxford: Oxford University Press.

—— (1976) *Vico and Herder: Two Studies in the History of Ideas*, New York: Random House.

—— (1981) *Against the Current*, Oxford: Oxford University Press.

Bernstein, R. (1985) *Habermas and Modernity*, Cambridge: Polity Press.

Besançon, S. (1974) *The Intellectual Origins of Leninism*, Oxford: Blackwell.

Blauner, R. (1964) *Alienation and Freedom*, Chicago: Chicago University Press.

Blum, L. (1980) *Friendship, Altruism and Morality*, London: Routledge.

Blum, L. and Seidler, V.J. (1989) *A Truer Liberty: Simone Weil and Marxism*, London: Routledge.

Blume, J. (1979) *Then Again Maybe I Won't*, London: Pan.

Boadella, D. (ed.) (1976) *In the Wake of Reich*, London: Coventure.

—— (1987) *Lifestreams*, London: Routledge.

—— (1988) *Wilhelm Reich: The Evolution of his Work*, London: Routledge.

Boggs, C. (1976) *Gramsci's Marxism*, London: Pluto Press.

Bologh, R.W. (1990) *Love or Greatness: Max Weber and Masculine Thinking*, London: Routledge.

Bordo, S. (1987) *The Flight to Objectivity: Essays in Cartesianism and Culture*, New York: SUNY Press.

Braverman, H. (1974) *Labour and Monopoly Capital*, New York: Monthly Review Press.

Bremmer, J. (ed.) (1989) *From Sappho to De Sade: Moments in the History of Sexuality*, London: Routledge.

Brittan, A. (1989) *Masculinity and Power*, Oxford: Blackwell.

Brittan, A. and Maynard, M. (1984) *Sexism, Racism and Oppression*, Oxford: Blackwell.

Bronner, S. and Kellner, D. (eds) (1989) *Critical Theory and Society*, New York: Routledge.

Brown, P. (1989) *The Body and Society: Men, Women and Sexual Renunciation in Early Christianity*, London: Faber.

Brown, R. (1992) *Understanding Industrial Organisations*, London: Routledge.

Brubaker, R. (1984) *The Limits of Rationality*, London: Allen & Unwin.

Buchanan, A. (1982) *Marx and Justice: A Radical Critique of Liberalism*, Totowa, NJ: Rowman & Allanheld.

Buck-Morss, S. (1977) *The Origin of Negative Dialectics*, Brighton: Harvester Press.

Burtt, E.A. (1932) *The Metaphysical Foundations of Modern Physical Science*, London: Routledge & Kegan Paul.

Calinicoss, A. (1976) *Althusser's Marxism*, London: Pluto Press.

Cammett, J.H. (1977) *Antonio Gramsci and the Origins of Italian Communism*, Stanford: Stanford University Press.

Caplan, P. (ed.) (1987) *The Cultural Construction of Sexuality*, London: Tavistock.

Capra, F. (1985) *The Turning Point*, London: Wildwood House.

Carlson, D. (1992) *Teachers and Crisis*, New York: Routledge.

Cavell, S. (1969) *Must we Mean What we Say?*, New York: Scribners.

Centre for Contemporary Cultural Studies (1978) *On Ideology*, London: Hutchinson.

Chapman, K. and Rutherford, J. (1988) *Male Order: Unwrapping Masculinity*, London: Lawrence & Wishart.

Chodorow, N. (1978) *The Reproduction of Mothering*, CA: University of

California Press.

—— (1992) *Feminism and Psychoanalysis*, Oxford: Polity Press.

Clarke, S., Lovell, T. McDonnell, K., Robins, K. and Seidler, V.J. (1980) *One Dimensional Marxism: Althusser and the Politics of Culture*, London: Allison & Busby.

Claudin-Urondo, C. (1977) *Lenin and the Cultural Revolution*, Brighton: Harvester Press.

Cohen, G. (1978) *Karl Marx's Theory of History: A Defence*, Oxford: Oxford University Press.

Cohen, M., Nagel, T. and Scanlon, T. (eds) (1980) *Marx, Justice and History*, Princeton: Princeton University Press.

Colletti, L. (1971) *From Rousseau to Marx*, London: New Left Books.

Connell, R.W. (1987) *Gender and Power*, Cambridge: Polity Press.

CSE (1979) *The Labour Process and Class Struggle*, London: CSE Pamphlets 1.

Daly, M. (1978) *Gyn/Ecology: The Meta-ethics of Radical Feminism*, London: Women's Press.

—— (1984) *Pure Lust*, London: Women's Press.

Davidson, A. (1977) *Antonio Gramsci: Towards an Intellectual Biography*, London: Merlin Books.

Davis, D.B. (1989) *The Problem of Slavery in Western Culture*, Oxford: Oxford University Press.

Dennison, G. (1971) *The Lives of Children*, Harmondsworth: Penguin.

Dews, P. (1987) *Logics of Disintegration*, London: Verso.

—— (ed.) (1992) *Autonomy and Solidarity: Interviews with Jurgen Habermas*, London: Verso.

Dreyfus, H. and Rabinow, P. (1982) *Michel Foucault: Beyond Structuralism and Hermeneutics*, Brighton: Harvester Press.

Dunayevskaya, R. (1971) *Marxism and Freedom*, London: Pluto Press.

Durkheim, E. (1950) *The Rules of Sociological Method*, New York: Free Press.

—— (1958) *Socialism and Saint-Simon*, Yellow Springs, OH: Antioch Press.

—— (1961) *Moral Education*, Glencoe, IL: Free Press.

—— (1964) *The Division of Labour in Society*, New York: Free Press.

—— (1974) *Sociology and Philosophy*, New York: Free Press.

Eagleton, T. (1986) *Against the Grain*, London: Verso.

—— (1991) *Ideology: An Introduction*, London: Verso.

Easlea, B. (1981) *Science and Sexual Oppression* London: Weidenfeld & Nicolson.

—— (1982) *Witch Hunting, Magic and the New Philosophy*, Brighton: Harvester.

Ehrenreich, B. and English, D. (1979) *For Her Own Good*, London: Pluto Books.

Eichenbaum, L. and Orbach, S. (1983) *Understanding Women*, Harmondsworth: Penguin.

—— (1984) *What Do Women Want?*, London: Fontana Books.

Eisenstein, H. (1984) *Contemporary Feminist Thought*, London: Allen & Unwin.

Elshtain, J.B. (1986) *Public Man, Private Woman*, Princeton, NJ: Princeton University Press.

Ernst, S. and Goodison, L. (1981) *In Our Own Hands*, London: Women's Press.

Ernst, S. and Maguire, M. (eds) (1987) *Living with the Sphinx*, London: Women's Press.

Ettorre, E.M. (1980) *Lesbians, Women and Society*, London: Routledge.

Faderman, L. (1976) *Surpassing the Love of Men*, London: Junction Books.

Fanon, F. (1970) *Black Skin, White Masks*, London: Paladin.

Farringdon, B. (1969) *The Philosophy of Francis Bacon*, Liverpool: Liverpool University Press.

Fay, B. (1978) *Social Theory and Political Practice*, London: Allen & Unwin.
Featherstone, M. (ed.) (1988) *Postmodernism*, London: Sage.
Fernbach, D. (1981) *The Spiral Path*, London: Gay Men's Press.
Filmer, P., Phillipson, M., Silverman, D. and Walsh, J. (1972) *New Directions in Sociological Theory*, London: Macmillan.
Fink, H. (1981) *Social Philosophy*, London: Methuen.
Fiori, G. (1980) *Antonio Gramsci: Life of a Revolutionary*, London: New Left Books.
Foot, P. (1978) *Virtues and Vices*, Oxford: Blackwell.
Foreman, A. (1977) *Femininity as Alienation*, London: Pluto Press.
Foster, H. (ed.) (1985) *Postmodern Culture*, London: Pluto Press.
Foucault, M. (1971) *Madness and Civilisation*, London: Tavistock.
—— (1976) *Birth of a Clinic*, London: Tavistock.
—— (1979) *A History of Sexuality*, London: Allen Lane.
—— (1980) *Power/Knowledge: Selected Interviews and Other Writings*, ed. Colin Gordon, Brighton: Harvester.
—— (1984) *The Uses of Pleasure*, London: Penguin.
—— (1990) *The Care of the Self*, Harmondsworth: Penguin.
Freire, P. (1974) *The Pedagogy of the Oppressed*, Harmondsworth: Penguin.
Freud, S. (1922) *Introductory Lectures on Psychoanalysis*, London: Allen & Unwin.
—— (1961) *Civilisation and its Discontents*, New York: Norton.
Freud (1973) *New Introductory Lectures*, Harmondsworth: Penguin.
Freud (1974) *The Standard Edition of the Complete Psychological Works of Sigmund Freud*, London: Hogarth Press.
Friedlander, J.H. (1990) *Vilna on the Sein*, New Haven: Yale University Press.
Frisby, D. (1986) *Fragments of Modernity*, Cambridge, MA: MIT Press.
—— (1992) *The Alienated Mind: The Sociology of Knowledge in Germany 1918–33* (2nd edn), London: Routledge.
Fromm, E. (1991) *The Fear of Freedom*, London: Routledge.
—— (1973) *The Crisis of Psychoanalysis*, Harmondsworth: Penguin.
—— (1992) *To Have Or To Be?*, London: Abacus.
Frosh, S. (1987) *The Politics of Psychoanalysis*, London: Macmillan.
Funk, R. (1982) *Erich Fromm: The Courage to be Human*, New York: Continuum.
Gane, M. (1991) *Baudrillard: Critical and Fatal Theory*, London: Routledge.
—— (1993) *Baudrillard Live: Selected Interviews*, London: Routledge.
Gay, P. (1988) *Freud: A Life in Our Time*, London: Dent.
Gerth, H. and Mills, C.W. (eds) (1946) *From Max Weber*, London: Routledge.
Giddens, A. (1971) *Capitalism and Modern Social Theory*, Cambridge: Cambridge University Press.
—— (ed.) (1974) *Positivism and Sociology*, London: Heinemann.
—— (1977) *Studies in Social and Political Theory*, London: Hutchinson.
—— (1978) *Durkheim*, London: Fontana.
—— (1990) *Consequences of Modernity*, Cambridge: Polity Press.
—— (1991) *Modernity and Self-identity*, Cambridge: Polity Press.
Gilligan, C. (1982) *In a Different Voice: Psychological Theory and Women's Development*, Cambridge, MA: Harvard Univesity Press.
Gilroy, P. (1987) *There Ain't No Black in the Union Jack*, London: Unwin Hyman.
Giroux, H. (1992) *Border Crossings*, London: Routledge.
Goffman, E. (1959) *The Presentation of Self in Everyday Life*, New York: Doubleday Anchor Books.
Goldman, E. (1984) *Living my Life*, London: Pluto Press.

Goldman, L. (1971) *Immanuel Kant*, London: New Left Books.
—— (1979) *Lukacs and Heidegger*, London: Routledge & Kegan Paul.
—— (1986) *The Human Sciences and Philosophy*, London: Jonathan Cape.
Gombin, R. (1978) *The Radical Tradition*, London: Methuen.
Good, P. and Bottomore, T. (eds) (1978) *Austro-Marxism*, Oxford: Oxford University Press.
Goode, P. (1979) *Karl Korsch: A Study in Western Marxism*, London: Macmillan.
Gorz, A. (1967) *Strategy for Labour*, Boston: Beacon Books.
—— (ed.) (1976) *The Division of Labour: The Labour Process and Class Struggle in Modern Capitalism*, Brighton: Harvester Press.
—— (1983) *Ecology as Politics*, London: Pluto Press.
Gouldner, A. (1971) *The Coming Crisis of Western Sociology*, London: Heinemann Educational Books.
—— (1967) *Enter Plato*, London: Routledge & Kegan Paul.
—— (1972) *For Sociology*, Harmondsworth: Penguin.
Graham, K. (1986) *The Battle of Democracy*, Brighton: Harvester University Press.
Gramsci, A. (1971) *The Prison Notebooks*, London: Lawrence & Wishart.
—— (1975) *Letters from Prison*, ed. L. Lawner, London: Jonathan Cape.
—— (1985) *Selections from the Cultural Writings*, London: Lawrence & Wishart.
Graubard, A. (1972) *Free the Children*, New York: Vintage.
Gray, J. and Smith, G.W. (1991) *Mill On Liberty: In Focus*, London: Routledge.
Griffin, S. (1980) *Pornography and Silence*, London: Women's Press.
—— (1982a) *Made from this Earth*, London: Women's Press.
—— (1982b) *Women and Nature*, London: Women's Press.
Grimshaw, J. (1986) *Feminist Philosophers*, Brighton: Harvester Press.
Gutmann, A. (1980) *Liberal Equality*, Cambridge: Cambridge University Press.
Haberman, J. (1971) *Towards a Rational Society*, London: Heinemann.
—— (1990a) *The Philosophical Discourse of Modernity*, Cambridge: Polity Press.
—— (1990b) *Moral Consciousness and Communicative Actions*, Cambridge: Polity Press.
—— (1992) *Post-Metaphysical Thinking*, Cambridge: Polity Press.
Hall, S. and Jacques, M. (eds) (1983) *The Politics of Thatcherism*, London: Lawrence & Wishart.
—— (eds) (1990) *New Times: The Changing Face of Politics in the 1990s*, London: Lawrence & Wishart.
Hampshire, S. (ed.) (1978) *Public and Private Morality*, Cambridge: Cambridge University Press.
Harding, S. and Hintikka, M. (1983) *Discovering Reality*, Dordrecht: D. Reidel.
Harrison, J.F.C. (1969) *Robert Owen and the Owenites in Britain and America: The Quest for the New Moral World*, London: Heinemann.
Harvey, D. (1990) *The Condition of Postmodernity*, Oxford: Blackwell.
Havel, V. (1987) *Living in Truth*, London: Faber.
Hawkes, T. (1977) *Structuralism and Semiotics*, London: Methuen.
Hawthorne, G. (1976) *Enlightenment and Despair*, Cambridge: Cambridge University Press.
Hayman, R. (1981) *Kafka*, London: Weidenfelt & Nicholson.
Hearn, J. (1987) *The Gender of Oppression: Men, Masculinity and the Critique of Marxism*, Brighton: Harvester Press.
Hearn, J. and Morgan, D. (eds) (1990) *Men, Masculinities and Social Theory*, London: Unwin Hyman.
Held, D. (1986) *Models of Democracy*, Cambridge: Polity Press.

—— (ed.) (1989) *Political Theory and the Modern State*, Cambridge: Polity Press.
—— (ed.) (1993) *Foundations of Democracy*, Cambridge: Polity Press.
Heller, A. (1974) *The Theory of Need in Marx*, London: Allison & Busby.
—— (1986) *Beyond Justice*, Oxford: Blackwell.
Heller, T., Sosna, M. and Wellbery, D. (1986) *Reconstructing Individualism: Autonomy, Individuality and the Self in Western Thought*, Cambridge: Cambridge University Press.
Hertzberg, A. (1968) *The French Enlightenment and the Jews*, New York: Schocken.
Hennis, W. (1987) *Max Weber: Essays in Reconstruction*, London: Routledge.
Hill, C. (1975) *The World Turned Upside Down*, Harmondsworth: Penguin.
—— (1977) *Milton and the English Revolution*, London: Faber.
—— (1984) *The Experience of Defeat: Milton and Some Contemporaries*, London: Faber.
Hirschman, A.O. (1977) *The Passions and the Interests*, Princeton, NJ: Princeton University Press.
Hobsbawm, E.J. (1962) *The Age of Revolution: Europe 1789–1848*, London: Abacus.
—— (1977) *The Age of Capital*, London: Abacus.
Holt, J. (1969) *How Children Fail*, Harmondsworth: Penguin.
Hooks, B. (1984) *Feminist Theory: From Margin to Centre*, Boston: South End Press.
Horkheimer, M, (1972) *Critical Theory: Selected Essays*, New York: Seabury Press.
—— (1974) *The Eclipse of Reason*, New York: Seabury Press.
Hoy, D. (ed.) (1986) *Foucault: A Critical Reader*, Oxford: Blackwell.
Hulme, P. and Jordanova, L. (eds) (1990) *The Enlightenment and its Shadows*, London: Routledge.
Huyssen, A. (1986) *After the Great Divide*, Bloomington, IN: Indiana University Press.
Hyppolite, J. (1969) *Studies on Marx and Hegel*, London: Heinemann.
—— (1974) *Genesis and Structure of Hegel's Phenomenology of Spirit*, Chicago: Northwestern University Press.
Ignatieff, M. (1984) *The Needs of Strangers*, London: Chatto & Windus.
Irigaray, L. (1983) *Speculum of the Other Woman*, Ithaca, NY: Cornell University Press.
—— (1985) *The Sex Which is Not One*, Ithaca, NY: Cornell University Press.
Jacoby, R. (1975) *Social Amnesia*, Boston: Beacon Press.
—— (1981) *Dialectic of Defeat: Contours of Western Marxism*, Cambridge: Cambridge University Press.
Jagger, A. (1983) *Feminist Politics and Human Nature*, Brighton: Harvester Press.
Jameson, F. (1972) *The Prison House of Language*, Princeton. NJ: Princeton University Press.
—— (1991) *Postmodernism or the Cultural Logic of Late Capitalism*, London: Verso.
Jardine, A. and Smith, P. (1987) *Men in Feminism*, New York: Routledge.
Jay, M. (1973) *The Dialectical Imagination: A History of the Frankfurt School and the Institute of Social Research 1923–50*, London: Heinemann.
—— (1984) *Marxism and Totality*, Cambridge: Polity Press.
Kafka, F. (1954) *Letter to my Father*, New York: Schocken.
Keane, J. (1988a) *Democracy and Civil Society*, London: Verso.
—— (1988b) *Civil Society and the State*, London: Verso.

Keat, R. and Abercrombie, N. (eds) (1990) *Enterprise Culture*, London: Routledge.

Kellerman, S. (1975) *Your Body Speaks its Mind*, New York: Simon & Shuster.

—— (1980) *Somatic Reality*, Berkeley, CA: Center Press.

Kellner, D. (1984) *Herbert Marcuse and the Crisis of Marxism*, London: Macmillan.

—— (1989) *Jean Baudrillard: From Marxism to Post-modernism and Beyond*, Cambridge, Polity.

Kennedy, E. and Mendus, S. (1987) *Women in Western Political Philosophy*, Brighton: Harvester Press.

Kenny, A. (1968) *Descartes: A Study of his Philosphy*, New York: Random House.

Kittay, E. and Meyers, D.T. (1987) *Women and Moral Theory*, Totowa, NJ: Rowman & Littleheld.

Kierkegaard, S. (1971) *Either/Or* (trans. D. and L. Swenson), Princeton, NJ: Princeton University Press.

Kohl, H. (1988) *36 Children*, Oxford: Oxford University Press.

Kolakowski, L. (1969) *Towards a Marxist Humanism*, New York: Grove Press.

—— (1972) *Positivist Philosophy: From Hume to the Vienna Circle*, Harmondsworth: Penguin.

—— (1978) *Main Currents in Western Marxism*, Oxford: Oxford University Press.

—— (1993) *Religion*, London: Fontana.

Korsch, K. (1938) *Karl Marx*, London: Chapman & Hall.

—— (1970) *Marxism and Philosophy*, London: New Left Books.

Kovel, J. (1981) *The Age of Desire*, New York: Pantheon Books.

—— (1989) *The Radical Spirit*, London: Free Association Books.

Kritzman, L. (1990) *Michel Foucault: Politics, Philosophy, Culture*, New York: Routledge.

Larrain, J. (1979) *The Concept of Ideology*, London: Hutchinson.

—— (1983) *Marxism and Ideology*, London: Macmillan.

Lash, S. and Whimster, S. (1987) *Max Weber, Rationality and Modernity*, London: Unwin Hyman.

Levi, P. (1989) *The Drowned and the Saved*, London: Abacus.

—— (1992) *If This is a Man/The Truce*, London: Abacus.

Levine, A. (1984) *Arguing for Socialism*, New York: Routledge.

Libowitz, R. (1987) *Faith and Freedom: A Tribute to Franklin Littell*, Oxford: Pergamon.

Lichtheim, G. (1970) *The Concept of Ideology and Other Essays*, New York: Vintage.

Lichtman, R. (1982) *The Production of Desire*, New York: Free Press.

Lifton, R.J. (1986) *Nazi Doctors: Medical Killing and the Psychology of Genocide*, London: Macmillan.

Littell, F. (1973) *The Crucifixion of the Jews*, New York: Harper & Row.

Lloyd, G. (1984) *The Man of Reason: 'Male' and 'Female' in Western Philosophy*, London: Methuen.

Lowen, A. (1963) *The Betrayal of the Body*, London: Collier Macmillan.

—— (1976) *Bioenergetics*, Harmondsworth: Penguin.

Lowith, K. (1991) *From Hegel to Nietzsche*, Columbia: Columbia University Press.

—— (1993) *Max Weber and Karl Marx*, London: Routledge.

Löwy, M. (1979) *Georg Lukács: From Romanticism to Bolshevism*, London: New Left Books.

Lukács, G. (1971) *History and Class Consciousness*, London: Merlin Press.
—— (1972) *Political Writings 1914–1929*, London: New Left Books.
—— (1975) *The Young Hegel*, London: Merlin Press.
Lukes, S. (1979) *Power*, London: Macmillan.
—— (1983) *Emile Durkheim: His Life and Work*, London: Allen Lane.
—— (1985) *Marxism and Morality*, Oxford: Oxford University Press.
Lyotard, J.-F. (1985) *The Postmodern Condition: A Report on Knowledge*, Manchester: Manchester University Press.
McCarthy, T. (1978) *The Critical Theory of Jürgen Habermas*, Boston: MIT Press.
MacIntyre, A. (1981) *After Virtue*, London: Duckworth.
—— (1984) *Whose Reason? Whose Justice?*, London: Duckworth.
McLaren, P. and Leonard, P. (eds) (1992) *Paulo Freire: A Critical Encounter*, London: Routledge.
McLellan, D. (1970) *The Young Hegelians*, London: Macmillan.
—— (1980) *The Thought of Karl Marx*, London: Macmillan.
—— (1990) *Marxism and Religion*, London: Macmillan.
MacPherson, C.B. (1962) *The Political Theory of Possessive Individualism*, Oxford: Oxford University Press.
—— (1972) *The Real World of Democracy*, Oxford: Oxford University Press.
—— (1973) *Democratic Theory: Essays in Retrieval*, Oxford: Oxford University Press.
Marcuse, H. (1967) *Reason and Revolution*, London: Routledge.
—— (1968) *Negations*, London: Allen Lane.
—— (1972) *Studies in Critical Philsophy*, London: New Left Books.
Marshall, T.H. and Bottomore, T. (1991) *Citizenship and Social Class*, London: Pluto Press.
Martin, L., Gutman, H. and Hutton, P. (1988) *Technologies of the Self*, London: Tavistock.
Marx, K. (1973) *Grundrisse*, Harmondsworth: Penguin
—— (1975) *Economic and Philosophical Manuscripts of 1844*, Harmondsworth: Penguin.
—— (1976) *Capital*, vol. 1 (trans. B. Fowkes), Harmondsworth: Penguin.
Marx, K. and Engels, F. (1976) *Collected Works*, London: Lawrence & Wishart.
Masson, J. (1990) *Against Therapy*, London: Fontana.
Merchant, C. (1980) *The Death of Nature: Women and the Scientific Revolution*, San Francisco: Harper &Row.
Mill, J.S. (1964) *On Liberty*, London: Dent.
—— (1971) *Autobiography*, ed. J. Sturinger, Oxford: Clarendon Press.
—— (1985) *The Principles of Political Economy*, Harmondsworth: Penguin.
Miller, A. (1981) *The Drama of the Gifted Child*, New York: Basic Books.
—— (1983) *For Your Own Good: Hidden Cruelty in Child-rearing and the Roots of Violence*, London: Faber.
—— (1990) *The Untouched Key*, London: Virago.
—— (1992) *Breaking Down the Wall of Silence*, London: Virago
Miller, J.B. (1976) *Towards a New Psychology of Women*, Harmondsworth: Penguin.
Miller, R.W. (1984) *Analyzing Marx: Morality, Power and History*, Princeton, NJ: Princeton University Press.
Millett, K. (1971) *Sexual Politics*, London: Virago.
Mitchell, J. (1971) *Women's Estate*, Harmondsworth: Penguin.
—— (1984) *Women: The Longest Revolution*, London: Virago.
Moller Okin, S. (1980) *Women in Western Political Thought*, London: Virago.

Mommsen, W. (1974) *The Age of Bureaucracy*, Oxford: Blackwell.
Monk, R. (1986) *Ludwig Wittgenstein*, London: Vintage.
Morgan, D. (1992) *Discovering Men*, London: Routledge.
Mouffe, C. (1979) *Gramsci and Marxist Theory*, London: Routledge.
Müller-Hill, B. (1988) *Murderous Science: Elimination by Scientific Selection of Jews, Gypsies and Others: Germany 1933–1945*, Oxford: Oxford University Press.
Murdoch, I. (1976) *The Fire and the Sun*, Oxford: Oxford University Press.
—— (1992) *Metaphysics as a Guide to Morals*, London: Chatto & Windus.
Murphy, J. (1970) *Kant: The Philosophy of Right*, London: Macmillan.
Nicholson, L. (1990) *Feminism/Postmodernism*, New York: Routledge.
Nicols, T. (ed.) (1980) *Capital and Labour*, London: Fontana.
Nielsen, K. and Patten, S. (1981) *Marxism and Morality, Canadian Journal of Philosophy*, special issue Vol. 7.
Nozick, R. (1974) *Anarchy, State and Utopia*, New York: Basic Books.
Ollman, B. (1979) *Social and Sexual Revolution*, London: Pluto Press.
O'Neil, J. (1970) *Sociology as Skin Trade*, London: Heinemann.
Pateman, C. (1988) *The Sexual Contract*, Oxford: Polity Press.
Patton, P. (1993) *Nietzsche, Feminism and Political Theory*, London: Routledge.
Phillips, A. and Rakusen, J. (1989) *The New Our Bodies, Ourselves: A Health Book for and by Women*, London: Penguin Books.
Plamenatz, J. (1974) *Ideology*, Oxford: Oxford University Press.
Plant, R. (1984) *Hegel: An Introduction*, Oxford: Blackwell.
Poliakov, L. (1974) *The Aryan Myth*, London: Heinemann.
Porter, K. and Weeks, J. (1990) *Between the Acts: Lives of Homosexual Men 1885–1967*, London: Routledge.
Porter, M. (ed.) (1993) *Men and Feminism*, London: Routledge.
Porter, R. (1981) *A History of Madness*, London: Routledge & Keegan Paul.
Poster, M. (1975) *Existential Marxism in Postwar France*, Princeton, NJ: Princeton University Press.
Ramazanoglu, C. (1989) *Feminism and the Contradictions of Oppression*, London: Routledge.
—— (1993) *Up Against Foucault*, London: Routledge.
Rawls, J. (1972) *A Theory of Justice*, Oxford: Oxford University Press.
Raz, J. (1986) *The Morality of Freedom*, Oxford: Oxford University Press.
Rée, J. (1974) *Descartes*, London: Allen Lane.
Reich, W. (1967) *Reich Speaks of Freud*, New York: Farar, Strauss & Giroux.
—— (1972) *Sex-Pol Essays: 1929–1934*, ed. Lee Baxendall, New York: Vintage.
—— (1974a) *The Sexual Revolution*, New York: Farrar, Strauss & Giroux.
—— (1974b) *The Function of the Orgasm*, Harmondsworth: Penguin.
Reiff, P. (1965) *Freud: The Mind of the Moralist*, London: Methuen.
Roberts, M. (1976) *From Oedipus to Moses*, London: Routledge.
Rorty, R. (1979) *Philosophy and the Mirror of Nature*, Princeton, NJ: Princeton University Press.
—— (1982) *Consquences of Pragmatism*, Brighton: Harvester Press.
—— (1988) *Contingency, Irony and Solidarity*, Cambridge: Cambridge University Press.
Rousseau, J.J. (1964) *The First and Second Discourses*, ed. Roger D. Masters, New York: St Martin's Press.
Rowbotham, S. (1971) *Hidden From History*, London: Pluto Books.
—— (1973a) *Women's Consciousness, Man's World*, Harmondsworth: Penguin.
—— (1973b) *Women, Resistance and Revolution*, Harmondsworth: Penguin.

—— (1983) *Dreams and Dilemmas*, London: Virago.
Ruddick, S. (1990) *Maternal Thinking: Towards a New Politics of Peace*, London: Women's Press.
Ryan, A. (1974) *J.S. Mill*, London: Routledge & Kegan Paul.
Salvadori, M. (1979) *Karl Kautsky and the Socialist Revolution 1880–1938*, London: New Left Books.
Said, E. (1991) *Orientalism,: Western Conditions of the Orient*, Harmondsworth: Penguin.
Sandel, M. (1983) *Liberalism and the Limits of Justice*, Cambridge: Cambridge University Press.
Sartre, J.-P. (1960) *Anti-Semite and Jew*, New York: Schocken.
—— (1963) *Search for a Method*, New York: Vintage.
—— (1974) *Between Existentialism and Marxism*, London: New Left Books.
—— (1976) *The Critique of Dialectical Reason*, London: New Left Books.
School of Barbiana (1970) *Letter to a Teacher*, Harmondsworth: Penguin.
Schmidt, A. (1971) *The Concept of Nature in Marx*, London: New Left Books.
Schurmann, F. (1966) *Ideology and Organisation in Communist China*, Berkeley, University of California Press.
Schneider, M. (1975) *Neurosis and Civilisation*, New York: Seabury Press.
Sedgewick, P. (1982) *Psycho-Politics*, London: Pluto Books.
Segal, L. (1987) *Is the Future Female?*, London: Virago.
—— (1990) *Slow Motion: Changing Masculinities, Changing Men*, London: Virago.
Seidler, V.J. (1986) *Kant, Respect and Injustice: The Limits of Liberal Moral Theory*, London: Routledge.
—— (1989) *Rediscovering Masculinity: Reason, Language and Sexuality*, London: Routledge.
—— (1991a) *Recreating Sexual Politics: Men, Feminism and Politics*, London: Routledge.
—— (1991b) *The Moral Limits of Modernity: Love, Inequality and Oppression*, London: Macmillan.
—— (ed.) (1991c) *The Achilles Heel Reader: Men, Sexual Politics and Socialism*, London: Routledge.
—— (ed.) (1992) *Men, Sex and Relationships: Writings from Achilles Heel*, London: Routledge.
—— (1994) *Unreasonable Men: Masculinity and Social Theory*, London: Routledge.
Sève, L. (1978) *Man in Marxist Theory*, Brighton: Harvester Press.
Sharaf, M. (1985) *Fury on Earth: A Biography of Wilhelm Reich*, London: Macmillan.
Skillen, A. (1974) 'Marxism and Morality', *Radical Philosophy*, 8.
—— (1977) *Ruling Illusions: Philosophy and the Social Order*, Brighton: Harvester Press.
Skorupski, J. (1991) *J.S. Mill*, London: Routledge.
Smart, B. (1983) *Sociology, Phenomenology and Marxian Analysis*, London: Routledge.
—— (1991) *Modern Conditions, Postmodern Controversies*, London: Routledge.
—— (1993) *Postmodernism*, London: Routledge.
Smith, D. (1992) *Texts, Facts and Femininity*, London: Routledge.
Sontag, S. (1991) *Illness as a Metaphor/Aids and its Metaphors*, London: Penguin.
Soper, K. (1981) *On Human Needs*, Brighton: Harvester Press.
Spender, D. (1980) *Man Made Language*, London: Routledge.
Squires, J. (ed.) (1993) *Principled Positions: Postmodernism and the Recovery of Value*, London: Lawrence & Wishart.

Sydie, K.A. (1987) *Natural Women, Cultured Men*, Milton Keynes: Open University Press.
Tawney, R. (1926) *Religion and the Rise of Capitalism*, Harmondsworth: Penguin.
Taylor, B. (1983) *Eve and the New Jerusalem*, London: Virago.
Taylor, C. (1978) *Hegel*, Cambridge: Cambridge University Press.
—— (1979) *Hegel and Modern Society*, Cambridge: Cambridge University Press.
—— (1985) *Philosophy and the Human Sciences*, Cambridge: Cambridge University Press.
—— (1990) *Sources of the Self*, Cambridge: Cambridge University Press.
Theweleit, K. (1987 and 1989) *Male Fantasies*, Vols 1 and 2, Cambridge: Polity.
Thompson, E.P. (1970) *The Making of the English Working Classes* Harmondsworth: Penguin.
—— (1979) *The Poverty of Theory and Other Essays*, London: Merlin Press.
Thompson, K. (1982) *Emile Durkheim*, London: Tavistock.
Tillich, P. (1954) *The Courage to Be*, London: Fontana.
Turner, B. (1984) *The Body and Society*, London: Routledge & Kegan Paul.
—— (1992a) *Regulating Bodies*, London: Routledge.
—— (1992b) *Max Weber: From History to Modernity*, London: Routledge.
Turner, C. (1992) *Modernity and Politics in the Work of Max Weber*, London: Routledge.
Velody, I., Lassman, P. and Martins, H. (eds) (1992) *Max Weber's 'Science as a Vocation'*, London: Routledge.
Waldron, J. (ed.) (1985) *Theories of Rights*, Oxford: Oxford University Press.
Walzer, M. (1983) *Spheres of Justice*, New York: Basic Books.
—— (1985) *Exodus and Revolution: A Political Mediation*, New York: Basic Books.
Wartofsky, M. (1977) *Feuerbach*, Cambridge: Cambridge University Press.
Weber, M. (1930) *The Protestant Ethic and the Spirit of Capitalism*, London: Allen & Unwin.
—— (1949) *The Methodology of the Social Sciences*, New York: Free Press.
—— (1964) *Theory of Social and Economic Organisations*, New York: Free Press.
Weeks, J. (1977) *Coming Out: Homosexual Politics in Britain*, London: Quartet.
—— (1984) *Sexuality*, London: Harwood/Tavistock.
—— (1985) *Sexuality and its Discontents*, London: Routledge.
Weil, S. (1952) *Gravity and Grace*, London: Routledge & Kegan Paul.
—— (1958) *Oppression and Liberty*, London: Routledge & Kegan Paul.
—— (1962) *Selected Essays 1934–43*, ed. R. Rees, Oxford: Oxford University Press.
—— (1964) *Seventy Letters*, London: Oxford University Press.
—— (1972) *The Need for Roots*, Routledge & Kegan Paul.
Wexler, P. (1991) *Social Analysis of Education*, New York: Routledge.
Williams, B. (1972) *Morality*, Cambridge: Cambridge University Press.
—— (1973) *Problems of the Self*, Cambridge: Cambridge University Press.
—— (1978) *Descartes: The Project of Pure Enquiry*, Harmondsworth: Penguin.
—— (1981) *Moral Luck*, Cambridge: Cambridge University Press.
—— (1985) *Ethics and the Limits of Philosophy*, London: Fontana.
Williams, E. (1964) *Capitalism and Slavery*, London: Deutsch.
Williams, H. (1986)*Kant's Political Philosophy*, New York: St Martin's Press.
Winch, P. (1989) *Simone Weil: 'The Just Balance'*, Cambridge: Cambridge University Press.
—— (1990) *The Idea of a Social Science*, 2nd edn, London: Routledge.
Wittgenstein, L. (1958) *Philosophical Investigations*, 2nd edn, Oxford: Blackwell.
—— (1975) *On Certainty*, Oxford; Blackwell.

—— (1980) *Culture and Value* P. Winch trans., Oxford: Blackwell.

Wolff, R.P., Moore, B. and Marcuse, H. (1969) *A Critique of Pure Tolerance*, Boston: Beacon Press.

Wolin, S. (1961) *Politics and Vision*, London: Allen & Unwin.

Wood, A. (1981) *Karl Marx*, London: Routledge.

Wollstonecraft, M. (1992) *A Vindication of the Rights of Women*, London: Penguin.

Wyckoff, H. (1976) *Love, Therapy and Politics*, New York: Grove Press.

Young, I. (1990) *Justice and the Politics of Difference*, Princeton, NJ: Princeton University Press.

Young, M. (ed.) (1972) *Knowledge and Control*, London: Macmillan.

Young, M. and Whitty, G. (ed.) (1977) *Society, State and Schooling*, Ringmar: The Falmer Press.

Zaretsky, R. (1976) *Capitalism, the Family and Personal Life*, London: Pluto Books.

Index

130–1; and morality 6–11, 51,
166–9, 172 (*see also* ideology);
related to epistemology 52, 75,
78; and theory 1–6, 158; *see also*
personal/political *and individual
emphases e.g.* sexual politics
Portugal 55
positivism 12–13, 33, 34, 37, 38,
40, 76, 79, 98, 111, 171, 173;
and authority 41, 42–5, 57, 58,
60, 67, 68
possessive individualism,
individuality 9, 57, 92, 155, 195
post-colonial theories, politics xv,
8, 10, 16, 145, 154, 157, 170
post-feminism xi
post-Fordism 210n13
post-modern theory xv, xvi, 14, 15,
34, 40, 69, 74, 90, 145, 153, 170,
176, 177, 178–80, 183, 189, 195,
196; *see also* fragmentation
post-modernity x, xi, xviii, 28, 77,
160, 166, 181, 182, 198;
identities and freedom 171–5
post-structuralism x, xi, xiv, xviii,
xx, 1, 2, 4, 10, 45, 80, 83, 169,
170–1, 175, 179, 181
power x, xv, 10, 75, 78, 85, 99,
167, 191, 199; aristocratic 20, 30,
39, 41; emotions and 168;
Foucault and 181; freedom and
53, 54, 94–7, 168; and love xix,
103, 148–50; *see also*
empowerment
power relations 49, 54, 59, 69,
73–4, 81, 92, 99, 130, 173, 181,
193, 197; global 196; Marxism
and 14–15, 18–19, 38–9, 84,
104–5, 109, 111, 128, 167; and
morality 14–15, 18–19, 64, 84,
123, 196; women and xiii, 127,
194 (*see also* women, oppression
and subordination of); *see also*
individual kinds e.g. schooling
experience; sexual relations
powerless 134; *see also* oppression;
subordination
private/public 7, 64, 117, 121, 158
production 24–6, 28, 57, 82,
111–17, 152; and power
structures and relations 14–15,
111–17, 142

progress 179; identified with
science and control of nature 7,
11, 25, 29, 39, 40, 51, 53, 63,
106, 136, 157, 159, 162, 165–6,
194, 205n12, 209n6
Protestant ethic 23, 25–7, 40, 42,
64, 81, 82, 92, 97, 158, 160, 172,
177, 193, 198; and capitalism 25,
26, 45, 82, 85, 195 (*see also under*
Weber, Max); and human
nature 25, 66, 88, 90, 103, 115;
individualism 43–4, 51, 122;
related to socialism 7, 9, 105,
114, 115, 116, 156
psychiatry 187; anti-psychiatry
movement 191
psychoanalysis 103, 153, 169, 186,
187–9, 190; *see also* Freud,
Freudianism
psychology 98
psychotherapy xvi, xx, 143, 154,
155, 196, 197; *see also*
consciousness-raising
public/private 7, 64, 117, 121,
158
purposive action 106, 125, 127

qualities, and contradictions 131–4
queer theory 69

race 7, 8, 20, 53, 74, 78, 117, 181,
197; relations of 10, 54, 58, 128,
130, 149, 178
racial identity 10, 55, 72, 73, 154,
155, 156, 170, 179, 181
racism, racial oppression ix, x, 18,
19, 98, 144, 145, 160, 163–5, 188,
195, 198
radicalism 52, 178
rational self x, xv, 3, 61, 159, 165–6
rationalisation, Weber's principle
of 46–8, 79
rationalism xii, xx, 73, 81, 97, 172,
178, 184, 191; and authority 41,
51, 52–5; and experience and
modernity 169–71; identified
with morality and masculinity
see under reason; and
instrumentalism 75, 79; and
Marxism and socialism 8, 29,
66–8, 69–70, 73, 105, 125–6, 148,
152; and religion 31–4, 48; and